Mass Media and Society

MASS MEDIA AND SOCIETY

Naval Prabhakar
Narendra Basu

Commonwealth

Mass Media and Society

Edition : 2019

ISBN 81-311-0020-0

Published by :
COMMONWEALTH PUBLISHERS PVT. LTD.
e-mail : commonwealthbooks@gmail.com

Distributed by :
CAMPUS BOOKS INTERNATIONAL
ARPAN PUBLICATIONS
4831/24, Prahlad Street,
Ansari Road, Darya Ganj,
New Delhi - 110002
Ph. : 23275511, 23257835
e-mail : arpanpublications@gmail.com
campusbooks@hotmail.com

Typesetting by :
Rishu Computers
Delhi

Printed at :
Divine Digital Press
Delhi

Preface

The communication media are the different technological processes that facilitate communication between the sender of a message and the receiver of that message. The mass media include newspapers, magazines, radio, and films, CDs, internet, etc. The media communicate information to a large, sometimes global, audience. Near-constant exposure to media is a fundamental part of contemporary life but it is TV that draws our attention the most as one of the primary socializing agent of today's society.

Media are very integral part of our lives and therefore they generate popular interest and debate about any social problem that we can think of. From a sociological perspective we can consider the role of media in our daily lives (the micro level) within the context of larger social forces such as the economy, politics, religion and technological development (the macro level).

Media often act as the bridge between our personal/ private lives and the public world. We see ourselves and our place in society through mass media. It is because of this connection that we need to pay special attention to mass media if we want to understand how society functions.

The mass media is a powerful socializing agent. For sociologists significance of the media is not limited to the content of media messages. Media affect how we learn about our world and interact with one another. Media literally mediate our relationship with social institutions. We base most of our knowledge on government news accounts, not experience. We are dependent on the media for what we know and how we relate to the world of politics because of the media-politics connection. We read or watch political debates followed by instant analysis and commentary by 'experts'. Politicians rely on media to communicate their message. Similar dynamics are present in other mediated events such as televised sports and televangelism.

Media is part of our routine relations with family and friends. They define our interaction with other people on a daily basis as a diversion, sources of conflict, or a unifying force. Media have an impact on society not only through the content of the message but also through the process.

This book explores the relationship between mass media and people. Topic such as role of media in democracy, the influence of internet, importance of media literacy and the place of media in society are also elaborately described.

Naval Prabhakar
Narendra Basu

Contents

1

Indian Society: Historical and Sociological Perspectives

Indian society is multifaceted to an extent perhaps unknown in any other of the world's great civilizations. Virtually no generalization made about Indian society is valid for all of the nation's multifarious groups. Comprehending the complexities of Indian social structure has challenged scholars and other observers over many decades. The ethnic and linguistic diversity of Indian civilization is more like the diversity of an area as variable as Europe than like that of any other single nation-state.

Living within the embrace of the Indian nation are vast numbers of different regional, social, and economic groups, each with different cultural practices. Particularly noteworthy are differences between social structures in the north and the south, especially in the realm of kinship systems. Throughout the country, religious differences can be significant, especially between the Hindu majority and the large Muslim minority; and other Indian groups—Buddhists, Christians, Jains, Jews, Parsis, Sikhs, and practitioners of tribal religions—all pride themselves on being unlike members of other faiths.

Access to wealth and power varies considerably, and vast differences in socioeconomic status are evident everywhere. The poor and the wealthy live side by side in urban and rural areas. It is common in city life to see a prosperous, well-fed man or woman chauffeured in a fine car pass gaunt street dwellers huddled beneath burlap shelters along the roadway. In many villages, solid cement houses of landowners rise not far from the flimsy thatched shacks of landless laborers. Even when not so obvious, distinctions of class are found in almost every settlement in India.

Urban-rural differences can be immense. Nearly 74 percent of India's population dwells in villages, with agriculture providing support for most of these rural residents. In villages, mud-plastered walls ornamented with traditional designs, dusty lanes, herds of grazing cattle, and the songs of birds at sunset provide typical settings for the social lives of most Indians. In India's great cities, however, millions of people live amidst cacophony—roaring vehicles, surging crowds, jammed apartment buildings, busy commercial establishments, loudspeakers blaring movie tunes--while breathing the poisons of industrial and automotive pollution.

Gender distinctions are pronounced. The behavior expected of men and women can be quite different, especially in villages, but also in urban centers. Prescribed ideal gender roles help shape the actions of both sexes as they move between family and the world outside the home. Crosscutting and pervading all of these differences of region, language, wealth, status, religion, urbanity, and gender is the special feature of Indian society that has received most attention from observers: caste.

The people of India belong to thousands of castes and castelike groups—hierarchically ordered, named groups into which members are born. Caste members are expected to marry within the group and follow caste rules pertaining to diet, avoidance of ritual pollution, and many other aspects of life. Given the vast diversity of Indian society, any observation must be tempered with the understanding that it cannot apply to all Indians. Still, certain themes or underlying principles of life are widely accepted in India.

Hierarchical Society

India is a hierarchical society. Within Indian culture, whether in the north or the south, Hindu or Muslim, urban or village, virtually all things, people, and groups of people are ranked according to various essential qualities. If one is attuned to the theme of hierarchy in India, one can discern it everywhere. Although India is a political democracy, in daily life there is little advocacy of or adherence to notions of equality. Castes and castelike groups—those quintessential groups with which almost all Indians are associated—are ranked. Within most villages or towns, everyone knows the relative rankings of each locally represented caste, and people's behavior toward one another is constantly shaped by this knowledge. Between the extremes of the very high and very low castes, however, there is sometimes disagreement on the exact relative ranking of castes clustered in the middle.

Castes are primarily associated with Hinduism but also exist among other Indian religious groups. Muslims sometimes expressly deny that they have castes--they state that all Muslims are brothers under God—but observation of Muslim life in various parts of India reveals the existence of castelike groups and clear concern with social hierarchy. Among Indian Christians, too, differences in caste are acknowledged and maintained. Throughout India, individuals are also ranked according to their wealth and power. For example, there are "big men" (bare admi , in Hindi) and "little men" (chhote admi) everywhere. "Big men" sit confidently on chairs, while "little men" come before them to make requests, either standing or crouching down on their haunches, certainly not presuming to sit beside a man of high status as an equal. Even men of nearly equal status who might share a string cot to sit on take their places carefully—the higher-ranking man at the head of the cot, the lower-ranking man at the foot.

Within families and kinship groupings, there are many distinctions of hierarchy. Men outrank women of the same or similar age, and senior relatives outrank junior relatives. Several other kinship relations involve formal respect. For example, in northern India, a daughter-in-law of a household shows deference to a daughter of a household. Even among young siblings in a household, there is constant acknowledgment of age differences: younger siblings never address an older sibling by name, but rather by respectful terms for elder brother or elder sister. However, an older sibling may address the younger by name.

Many status differences in Indian society are expressed in terms of ritual purity and pollution. Notions of purity and pollution are extremely complex and vary greatly among different castes, religious groups, and regions. However, broadly speaking, high status is associated with purity and low status with pollution. Some kinds of purity are inherent, or inborn; for example, gold is purer than copper by its very nature, and, similarly, a member of a high-ranking

Brahman, or priestly, caste is born with more inherent purity than a member of a low-ranking Sweeper (Mehtar, in Hindi) caste.

Unless the Brahman defiles himself in some extraordinary way, throughout his life he will always be purer than a Sweeper. Other kinds of purity are more transitory—a Brahman who has just taken a bath is more ritually pure than a Brahman who has not bathed for a day. This situation could easily reverse itself temporarily, depending on bath schedules, participation in polluting activities, or contact with temporarily polluting substances. Purity is associated with ritual cleanliness—daily bathing in flowing water, dressing in properly laundered clothes of approved materials, eating only the foods appropriate for one's caste, refraining from physical contact with people of lower rank, and avoiding involvement with ritually impure substances. The latter include body wastes and excretions, most especially those of another adult person. Contact with the products of death or violence are typically polluting and threatening to ritual purity.

Members of the highest priestly castes, the Brahmans, are generally vegetarians (although some Bengali and Maharashtrian Brahmans eat fish) and avoid eating meat, the product of violence and death. High-ranking Warrior castes (Kshatriyas), however, typically consume nonvegetarian diets, considered appropriate for their traditions of valor and physical strength. A Brahman born of proper Brahman parents retains his inherent purity if he bathes and dresses himself properly, adheres to a vegetarian diet, eats meals prepared only by persons of appropriate rank, and keeps his person away from the bodily exuviae of others (except for necessary contact with the secretions of family infants and small children).

If a Brahman happens to come into bodily contact with a polluting substance, he can remove this pollution by bathing and changing his clothing. However, if he were to eat meat or commit other transgressions of the rigid dietary codes of his particular caste, he would be considered more deeply polluted and would have to undergo various purifying rites and payment of fines imposed by his caste council in order to restore his inherent purity. In sharp contrast to the purity of a Brahman, a Sweeper born of Sweeper parents is considered to be born inherently polluted. The touch of his body is polluting to those higher on the caste hierarchy than he, and they will shrink from his touch, whether or not he has bathed recently.

Sweepers are associated with the traditional occupation of cleaning human feces from latrines and sweeping public lanes of all kinds of dirt. Traditionally, Sweepers remove these polluting materials in baskets carried atop the head and dumped out in a garbage pile at the edge of the village or neighborhood. The involvement of Sweepers with such filth accords with their low-status position at the bottom of the Hindu caste hierarchy, even as their services allow high-status people, such as Brahmans, to maintain their ritual purity.

Members of the Leatherworker (Chamar) caste are ascribed a very low status consonant with their association with the caste occupation of skinning dead animals and tanning the leather. Butchers (Khatiks, in Hindi), who kill and cut up the bodies of animals, also rank low on the caste hierarchy because of their association with violence and death. However, castes associated with ruling and warfare—and the killing and deaths of human beings—are typically accorded high rank on the caste hierarchy. In these instances, political power and wealth outrank association with violence as the key determinant of caste rank.

Maintenance of purity is associated with the intake of food and drink, not only in terms of the nature of the food itself, but also in terms of who has prepared it or touched it. This requirement is especially true for Hindus, but other religious groups hold to these principles to varying degrees. Generally, a person risks pollution--and lowering his own status--if he accepts beverages or cooked foods from the hands of people of lower caste status than his own. His status will remain intact if he accepts food or beverages from people of higher caste rank. Usually, for an observant Hindu of any but the very lowest castes to accept cooked food from a Muslim or Christian is regarded as highly polluting.

In a clear example of pollution associated with dining, a Brahman who consumed a drink of water and a meal of wheat bread with boiled vegetables from the hands of a Sweeper would immediately become polluted and could expect social rejection by his caste fellows. From that moment, fellow Brahmans following traditional pollution rules would refuse food touched by him and would abstain from the usual social interaction with him. He would not be welcome inside Brahman homes--most especially in the ritually pure kitchens—nor would he or his close relatives be considered eligible marriage partners for other Brahmans.

Generally, the acceptance of water and ordinary foods cooked in water from members of lower-ranking castes incurs the greatest pollution. In North India, such foods are known as kaccha khana , as contrasted with fine foods cooked in butter or oils, which are known as pakka khana . Fine foods can be accepted from members of a few castes slightly lower than one's own. Local hierarchies differ on the specific details of these rules.

Completely raw foods, such as uncooked grains, fresh unpeeled bananas, mangoes, and uncooked vegetables can be accepted by anyone from anyone else, regardless of relative status. Toasted or parched foods, such as roasted peanuts, can also be accepted from anyone without ritual or social repercussions. (Thus, a Brahman may accept gifts of grain from lower-caste patrons for eventual preparation by members of his own caste, or he may purchase and consume roasted peanuts or tangerines from street vendors of unknown caste without worry.)

Water served from an earthen pot may be accepted only from the hands of someone of higher or equal caste ranking, but water served from a brass pot may be accepted even from someone slightly lower on the caste scale. Exceptions to this rule are members of the Waterbearer (Bhoi, in Hindi) caste, who are employed to carry water from wells to the homes of the prosperous and from whose hands members of all castes may drink water without becoming polluted, even though Waterbearers are not ranked high on the caste scale.

These and a great many other traditional rules pertaining to purity and pollution constantly impinge upon interaction between people of different castes and ranks in India. Although to the non-Indian these rules may seem irrational and bizarre, to most of the people of India they are a ubiquitous and accepted part of life. Thinking about and following purity and pollution rules make it necessary for people to be constantly aware of differences in status. With every drink of water, with every meal, and with every contact with another person, people must ratify the social hierarchy of which they are a part and within which their every act is carried out. The fact that expressions of social status are intricately bound up with events that happen to everyone every day--eating, drinking, bathing, touching, talking—and that transgressions of these rules, whether deliberate or accidental, are seen as having immediately polluting effects on the person of the transgressor, means that every ordinary act of human life serves as a constant reminder of the importance of hierarchy in Indian society.

There are many Indians, particularly among the educated urban elite, who do not follow traditional purity and pollution practices. Dining in each others' homes and in restaurants is common among well-educated people of diverse backgrounds, particularly when they belong to the same economic class. For these people, guarding the family's earthen water pot from inadvertent touch by a low-ranking servant is not the concern it is for a more traditional villager. However, even among those people whose words and actions denigrate traditional purity rules, there is often a reluctance to completely abolish consciousness of purity and pollution from their thinking. It is surely rare for a Sweeper, however well-educated, to invite a Brahman to dinner in his home and have his invitation unself-consciously accepted. It is less rare, however, for educated urban colleagues of vastly different caste and religious heritage to enjoy a cup of tea together.

Some high-caste liberals pride themselves on being free of "casteism" and seek to accept food from the hands of very low-caste people, or even deliberately set out to marry someone from a significantly lower caste or a different religion. Thus, even as they deny it, these progressives affirm the continuing significance of traditional rules of purity, pollution, and hierarchy in Indian society.

Social Interdependence

One of the great themes pervading Indian life is social interdependence. People are born into groups—families, clans, subcastes, castes, and religious communities—and live with a constant sense of being part of and inseparable from these groups. A corollary is the notion that everything a person does properly involves interaction with other people. A person's greatest dread, perhaps, is the possibility of being left alone, without social support, to face the necessary challenges of life. This sense of interdependence is extended into the theological realm: the very shape of a person's life is seen as being greatly influenced by divine beings with whom an ongoing relationship must be maintained.

Social interaction is regarded as being of the highest priority, and social bonds are expected to be long lasting. Even economic activities that might in Western culture involve impersonal interactions are in India deeply imbedded in a social nexus. All social interaction involves constant attention to hierarchy, respect, honor, the feelings of others, rights and obligations, hospitality, and gifts of food, clothing, and other desirable items. Finely tuned rules of etiquette help facilitate each individual's many social relationships.

Western visitors to India are sometimes startled to find that important government and business officials have left their posts—often for many days at a time—to attend a cousin's wedding or participate in religious activities in a distant part of the country. "He is out of station and will be back in a week or two," the absent official's officemates blandly explain to the frustrated visitor. What is going on is not laziness or hedonistic recreation, but is the official's proper recognition of his need to continually maintain his social ties with relatives, caste fellows, other associates, and God. Without being enmeshed in such ties throughout life, a person cannot hope to maintain long-term efficacy in either economic or social endeavors.

Social bonds with relatives must be reinforced at family events or at rites crucial to the religious community. If this is not done, people who could offer vital support in many phases of life would be alienated. In every activity, there is an assumption that social ties can help a person and that their absence can bring failure. Seldom do people carry out even the simplest task on their own. From birth onward, a child learns that his "fate" has been "written" by divine forces and that his life will be shaped by a plan decided by more powerful beings. When a small child eats, his mother puts the mouthfuls of food into his mouth with her own hand. When a boy climbs a tree to pluck mangoes, another stands below with a basket to receive them. When a girl fetches water from the well in pots on her head, someone at her home helps her unload the pots. When a farmer stacks sheaves of grain onto his bullock cart, he stands atop the cart, catching the sheaves tossed up to him by his son.

A student applying to a college hopes that he has an influential relative or family friend who can put in a good word for him with the director of admissions. At the age of marriage, a young person expects that parents will take care of finding the appropriate bride or groom and arranging all the formalities. At the birth of a child, the new mother is assured that the child's kin will help her attend to the infant's needs. A businessman seeking to arrange a contract relies not only on his own abilities but also on the assistance of well-connected friends and relatives to help finalize the deal. And finally, when facing death, a person is confident that offspring and other relatives will carry out the appropriate funeral rites, including a commemorative feast when, through gifts of clothing and food, continuing social ties are reaffirmed by all in attendance.

Family Structure

In India, people learn the essential themes of cultural life within the bosom of a family. In most of the country, the basic units of society are the patrilineal family unit and wider kinship groupings. The most widely desired residential unit is the joint family, ideally consisting of three or four patrilineally related generations, all living under one roof, working, eating, worshiping, and cooperating together in mutually beneficial social and economic activities. Patrilineal joint families include men related through the male line, along with their wives and children. Most young women expect to live with their husband's relatives after marriage, but they retain important bonds with their natal families.

Despite the continuous and growing impact of urbanization, secularization, and Westernization, the traditional joint household, both in ideal and in practice, remains the primary social force in the lives of most Indians. Loyalty to family is a deeply held ideal for almost everyone. Large families tend to be flexible and well-suited to modern Indian life, especially for the 67 percent of Indians who are farmers or agricultural workers or work in related activities. As in most primarily agricultural societies, few individuals can hope to achieve economic security without being part of a cooperating group of kinsmen. The joint family is also common in cities, where kinship ties can be crucial to obtaining scarce jobs or financial assistance. Numerous prominent Indian families, such as the Tatas, Birlas, and Sarabhais, retain joint family arrangements even as they work together to control some of the country's largest financial empires.

The joint family is an ancient Indian institution, but it has undergone some change in the late twentieth century.

Although several generations living together is the ideal, actual living arrangements vary widely depending on region, social status, and economic circumstance. Many Indians live in joint families that deviate in various ways from the ideal, and many live in nuclear families—a couple with their unmarried children—as is the most common pattern in the West. However, even where the ideal joint family is seldom found (as, for example, in certain regions and among impoverished agricultural laborers and urban squatters), there are often strong networks of kinship ties through which economic assistance and other benefits are obtained.

Not infrequently, clusters of relatives live very near each other, easily available to respond to the give and take of kinship obligations. Even when relatives cannot actually live in close proximity, they typically maintain strong bonds of kinship and attempt to provide each other with economic help, emotional support, and other benefits. As joint families grow ever larger, they inevitably divide into smaller units, passing through a predictable cycle over time. The breakup of a joint family into smaller units does not necessarily represent the rejection of the joint family ideal. Rather, it is usually a response to a variety of conditions, including the need for some members to move from village to city, or from one city to another to take advantage of employment opportunities.

Splitting of the family is often blamed on quarrelling women--typically, the wives of coresident brothers. Although women's disputes may, in fact, lead to family division, men's disagreements do so as well. Despite cultural ideals of brotherly harmony, adult brothers frequently quarrel over land and other matters, leading them to decide to live under separate roofs and divide their property. Frequently, a large joint family divides after the demise of elderly parents, when there is no longer a single authority figure to hold the family factions together. After division, each new residential unit, in its turn, usually becomes joint when sons of the family marry and bring their wives to live in the family home.

Some family types bear special mention because of their unique qualities. In the sub-Himalayan region of Uttar Pradesh, polygyny is commonly practiced. There, among Hindus, a simple polygynous family is composed of a man, his two wives, and their unmarried children. Various other family types occur there, including the supplemented subpolygynous household—a woman whose husband lives elsewhere (perhaps with his other wife), her children, plus other adult relatives. Polygyny is also practiced in other parts of India by a tiny minority of the population, especially in families in which the first wife has not been able to bear children.

Among the Buddhist people of the mountainous Ladakh District of Jammu and Kashmir, who have cultural ties to Tibet, fraternal polyandry is practiced, and a household may include a set of brothers with their common wife or wives. This family type, in which brothers also share land, is almost certainly linked to the extreme scarcity of cultivable land in the Himalayan region, because it discourages fragmentation of holdings. The peoples of the northeastern hill areas are known for their matriliny, tracing descent and inheritance in the female line rather than the male line. One of the largest of these groups, the Khasis—an ethnic or tribal people in the state of Meghalaya—are divided into matrilineal clans; the youngest daughter receives almost all of the inheritance including the house. A Khasi husband goes to live in his wife's house. Khasis, many of whom have become Christian, have the highest literacy rate in India, and Khasi women maintain notable authority in the family and community.

Perhaps the best known of India's unusual family types is the traditional Nayar taravad , or great house. The Nayars are a cluster of castes in Kerala. High-ranking and prosperous, the Nayars maintained matrilineal households in which sisters and brothers and their children were the permanent residents. After an official prepuberty marriage, each woman received a series of visiting husbands in her room in the taravad at night. Her children were all legitimate members of the taravad . Property, matrilineally inherited, was managed by the eldest brother of the senior woman. This system, the focus of much anthropological interest, has been disintegrating in the twentieth century, and in the 1990s probably fewer than 5 percent of the Nayars live in matrilineal taravads . Like the Khasis, Nayar women are known for being well-educated and powerful within the family.

Malabar rite Christians, an ancient community in Kerala, adopted many practices of their powerful Nayar neighbors, including naming their sons for matrilineal forebears. Their kinship system, however, is patrilineal. Kerala Christians have a very high literacy rate, as do most Indian Christian groups.

In most of Hindu India, people belong not only to coresident family groups but to larger aggregates of kin as well. Subsuming the family is the patrilineage (known in northern and central India as the khandan , kutumb , or kul), a locally based set of males who trace their ancestry to a common progenitor a few generations back, plus their wives and unmarried daughters. Larger than the patrilineage is the clan, commonly known as the gotra or got , a much larger group of patrilineally related males and their wives and daughters, who often trace common ancestry to a mythological figure. In some regions, particularly among the high-ranking Rajputs of western India, clans are hierarchically ordered. Some people also claim membership in larger, more amorphous groupings known as vansh and sakha .

Hindu lineages and clans are strictly exogamous--that is, a person may not marry or have a sexual alliance with a member of his own lineage or clan; such an arrangement would be considered incestuous. In North India, rules further prohibit marriage between a person and his mother's lineage members as well. Among some high-ranking castes of the north, exogamy is also extended to the mother's, father's mother's, and mother's mother's clans. In contrast, in South India, marriage to a member of the mother's kin group is often encouraged.

Muslims also recognize kinship groupings larger than the family. These include the khandan , or patrilineage, and the azizdar , or kindred. The azizdar group differs slightly for each individual and includes all relatives linked to a person by blood or marriage. Muslims throughout India encourage marriage within the lineage and kindred, and marriages between the children of siblings are common.

Within a village or urban neighborhood, members of a lineage recognize their kinship in a variety of ways. Mutual assistance in daily work, in emergencies, and in factional struggles is expected. For Hindus, cooperation in specific annual rituals helps define the kin group. For example, in many areas, at the worship of the goddess deemed responsible for the welfare of the lineage, patrilineally related males and their wives join in the rites and consume specially consecrated fried breads or other foods. Unmarried daughters of the lineage are only spectators at the rites and do not share in the special foods. Upon marriage, a woman becomes a member of her husband's lineage and then participates regularly in the worship of her husband's lineage goddess. Lineage bonds are also evident at life-cycle observances, when kin join together in celebrating births, marriages, and religious initiations. Upon the death of a lineage member, other lineage members observe ritual death pollution rules for a prescribed number of days and carry out appropriate funeral rites and feasts.

For some castes, especially in the north, careful records of lineage ties are kept by a professional genealogist, a member of a caste whose traditional task is maintaining genealogical tomes. These itinerant bards make their rounds from village to village over the course of a year or more, recording births, deaths, and glorious accomplishments of the patrilineal descent group. These genealogical services have been especially crucial among Rajputs, Jats, and similar groups whose lineages own land and where power can depend on fine calculations of pedigree and inheritance rights.

Some important kinship linkages are not traced through men but through women. These linkages involve those related to an individual by blood and marriage through a mother, married sisters, or married daughters, and for a man, through his wife. Anthropologist David Mandelbaum has termed these "feminal kin." Key relationships are those between a brother and sister, parents and daughters, and a person and his or her mother's brother. Through bonds with these close kin, a person has links with several households and lineages in many settlements. Throughout most of India, there are continuous visits--some of which may last for months and include the exchange of gifts at visits, life-cycle rites, and holidays, and many other key interactions between such relatives. These relationships are often characterized by deep affection and willingly offered support.

These ties cut across the countryside, linking each person with kin in villages and towns near and far. Almost everywhere a villager goes—especially in the north, where marriage networks cover wide distances—he can find some kind of relative. Moral support, a place to stay, economic assistance, and political backing are all available through these kinship networks. The multitude of kinship ties is further extended through the device of fictive kinship. Residents of a single village usually use kinship terms for one another, and especially strong ties of fictive kinship can be ceremonially created with fellow religious initiates or fellow pilgrims of one's village or neighborhood.

In the villages and cities of the north, on the festival of Raksha Bandhan (the Tying of the Protective Thread, during which sisters tie sacred threads on their brothers' wrists to symbolize the continuing bond between them), a female may tie a thread on the wrist of an otherwise unrelated male and "make him her brother." Fictive kinship bonds cut across caste and class lines and involve obligations of hospitality, gift-giving, and variable levels of cooperation and assistance. Neighbors and friends may also create fictive kinship ties by informal agreement. Actually, any strong friendship between otherwise unrelated people is typically imbued with kinship-like qualities. In such friendships, kinship terms are adopted for address, and the give and take of kinship may develop.

Such bonds commonly evolve between neighbors in urban apartment buildings, between special friends at school, and between close associates at work. The use of kinship terms enhances affection in the relationship. In

Gujarat, personal names usually include the word for "sister" and "brother," so that the use of someone's personal name automatically sounds affectionate and caring.

All family members are socialized to accept the authority of those ranked above them in the hierarchy. In general, elders rank above juniors, and among people of similar age, males outrank females. Daughters of a family command the formal respect of their brothers' wives, and the mother of a household is in charge of her daughters-in-law. Among adults in a joint family, a newly arrived daughter-in-law has the least authority. Males learn to command others within the household but expect to accept the direction of senior males. Ideally, even a mature adult man living in his father's household acknowledges his father's authority on both minor and major matters.

Women are especially strongly socialized to accept a position subservient to males, to control their sexual impulses, and to subordinate their personal preferences to the needs of the family and kin group. Reciprocally, those in authority accept responsibility for meeting the needs of others in the family group. There is tremendous emphasis on the unity of the family grouping, especially as differentiated from persons outside the kinship circle. Internally, efforts are made to deemphasize ties between spouses and between parents and their own children in order to enhance a wider sense of harmony within the entire household. Husbands and wives are discouraged from openly displaying affection for one another, and in strictly traditional households, they may not even properly speak to one another in the presence of anyone else, even their own children. Young parents are inhibited by "shame" from ostentatiously dandling their own young children but are encouraged to play with the children of siblings.

Psychologically, family members feel an intense emotional interdependence with each other and the family as an almost organic unit. Ego boundaries are permeable to others in the family, and any notion of a separate self is often dominated by a sense of what psychoanalyst Alan Roland has termed a more inclusive "familial self." Interpersonal empathy, closeness, loyalty, and interdependency are all crucial to life within the family. Family resources, particularly land or businesses, have traditionally been controlled by family males, especially in high-status groups. Customarily, according to traditional schools of Hindu law, women did not inherit land or buildings and were thus beholden to their male kin who controlled these vital resources. Under Muslim customary law, women are entitled to inherit real estate and often do so, but their shares have typically been smaller than those of similarly situated males. Under modern law, all Indian women can inherit land.

Purdah System

A particularly interesting aspect of Indian family life is purdah (from the Hindi parda , literally, curtain), or the veiling and seclusion of women. In much of northern and central India, particularly in rural areas, Hindu and Muslim women follow complex rules of veiling the body and avoidance of public appearance, especially in the presence of relatives linked by marriage and before strange men. Purdah practices are inextricably linked to patterns of authority and harmony within the family. Rules of Hindu and Muslim purdah differ in certain key ways, but female modesty and decorum as well as concepts of family honor are essential to the various forms of purdah.

In most areas, purdah restrictions are stronger for women of high-status families. The importance of purdah is not limited to family life; rather, these practices all involve restrictions on female activity and access to power and the control of vital resources in a male-dominated society. Restriction and restraint for women in virtually every aspect of life are the basic essentials of purdah. In India, both males and females are circumscribed in their actions by economic disabilities, hierarchical rules of deference in kinship groups, castes, and the larger society. But for women who observe purdah, there are additional constraints.

For almost all women, modest dress and behavior are important. Clothing covering most of the body is common; only in tribal groups and among a few castes do women publicly bare their legs or upper bodies. In most of the northern half of India, traditionally dressed women cover the tops of their heads with the end of the sari or scarf (dupatta). Generally, females are expected to associate only with kin or companions approved by their families and to remain sexually chaste.

Women are not encouraged to roam about on pleasure junkets, but rather travel only for explicit family-sanctioned purposes. In North India, women do relatively little shopping; most shopping is done by men. In contrast to females, males have much more freedom of movement and observe much less body modesty. For both males and females, free association with the opposite sex is limited, and dating in the Western sense is essentially limited to members of the educated urban elite. In all areas, illicit liaisons do occur. Although the male may escape social repudiation if such liaisons become known, the female may suffer lasting damage to her own reputation and bring dishonor to her family. Further, if a woman is sexually linked with a man of lower caste status, the woman is regarded as being irremediably polluted, "like an earthen pot." A male so sullied can be cleansed of his temporary pollution, "like a brass pot," with a ritual bath.

Such rules of feminine modesty are not considered purdah but merely proper female behavior. For traditional Hindus of northern and central India, purdah observances begin at marriage, when a woman acquires a husband and in-laws. Although she almost never observes purdah in her natal home or before her natal relatives, a woman does observe purdah in her husband's home and before his relatives. As a young woman, she remains inside her husband's house much of the time (rather than going out into lanes or fields), absents herself or covers her face with her sari in the presence of senior males and females related by marriage, and, when she does leave the house in her marital village, covers her face with her sari.

Through use of the end of the sari as a face veil and deference of manner, a married woman shows respect to her affinal kin who are older than or equal to her husband in age, as well as certain other relatives. She may speak to the women before whom she veils, but she usually does not converse with the men. Exceptions to this are her husband's younger brothers, before whom she may veil her face, but with whom she has a warm joking relationship involving verbal banter.

Initially almost faceless and voiceless in her marital home, a married woman matures and gradually relaxes some of these practices, especially as elder in-laws become senescent or die and she herself assumes senior status. In fact, after some years, a wife may neglect to veil her face in front of her husband when others are present and may even speak to her husband in public. Such practices help shield women from unwanted male advances and control women's sexuality but also express relations within and between groups of kin. Familial prestige, household harmony, social distance, affinal respect, property ownership, and local political power are all linked to purdah.

Restricting women to household endeavors rather than involving them in tasks in fields and markets is associated with prestige and high rank in northern India. There the wealthiest families employ servants to carry water from the well and to work in the fields alongside family males. Mature women of these families may make rare appearances in the fields to bring lunch to the family males working there and sometimes to supervise laborers. Thus elitism is expressed in women's exclusive domesticity, with men providing economic necessities for the family.

Only women of poor and low-ranking groups engage in heavy manual labor outside the home, especially for pay. Such women work long hours in the fields, on construction gangs, and at many other tasks, often veiling their faces as they work. For Muslim women, purdah practices involve less emphasis on veiling from in-laws and more emphasis on protecting women from contact with strangers outside the sphere of kinship. Because Muslims often marry cousins, a woman's in-laws may also be her natal relatives, so veiling her face within the marital home is often inappropriate.

Unlike Hindus, Muslim women do not veil from other women as do Hindus. Traditional Muslim women and even unmarried girls, however, often refrain from appearing in public, or if they do go out, they wear an all-covering garment known as a burka , with a full face covering. A burka protects a woman—and her family—from undue familiarity with unknown outsiders, thus emphasizing the unity of the family *vis-à-vis* the outside world. Because Muslim women are entitled to a share in the family real estate, controlling their relationships with males outside the family can be crucial to the maintenance of family property and prestige.

In rural communities and in older sections of cities, purdah observances remain vital, although they are gradually diminishing in intensity. Among the educated urban and rural elite, purdah practices are rapidly vanishing and for many have all but disappeared. Chastity and female modesty are still highly valued, but, for the elite, face-veiling and the burka are considered unsophisticated. As girls and women become more widely and more highly educated, female employment outside the home is commonplace, even for women of elite families.

Stages of Life

In India, the ideal stages of life have been most clearly articulated by Hindus. The ancient Hindu ideal rests on childhood, followed by four stages: undergoing religious initiation and becoming a celibate student of religious texts, getting married and becoming a householder, leaving home to become a forest hermit after becoming a grandparent, and becoming a homeless wanderer free of desire for all material things. Although few actually follow this scheme, it serves as a guide for those attempting to live according to valued standards. For Hindus, dharma (a divinely ordained code of proper conduct), karma (the sum of one's deeds in this life and in past lives), and kismat (fate) are considered relevant to the course of life. Crucial transitions from one phase of life to another are marked by sometimes elaborate rites of passage.

Throughout much of India, a baby's birth is celebrated with rites of welcome and blessing--songs, drums, happy distribution of sweets, auspicious unguents, gifts for infant and mother, preparation of horoscopes, and inscriptions in the genealogist's record books. In general, children are deeply desired and welcomed, their presence regarded as a blessing on the household. Babies are often treated like small deities, pampered and coddled, adorned with makeup and trinkets, and carried about and fed with the finest foods available to the family. Young girls are worshiped as personifications of Hindu goddesses, and little boys are adulated as scions of the clan.

In their children, parents see the future of the lineage and wider kin group, helpers in daily tasks, and providers of security in the parents' old age. These delightful ideals are articulated and enacted over and over again; yet, a coexisting harsher reality emerges from a close examination of events and statistics. Many children lead lives of striking hardship, and many die premature deaths. In general, conditions are significantly worse for girls than for boys. Birth celebrations for baby daughters are more muted than for sons and are sometimes absent altogether. Although India was once led by a woman prime minister, Indira Gandhi, and Indian women currently hold a wide range of powerful positions in every walk of life, there is a strong cultural bias toward males. Girls are frequently victims of underfeeding, medical neglect, sex-selective abortion, and outright infanticide.

That girls are victims of fatal neglect and murder has been thoroughly discussed in the Indian press and in scholarly investigations. It has been noted that infant girls are killed with potions of opium in Rajasthan and pastes of poisonous oleander in Tamil Nadu—most especially girls preceded by the birth of several sisters. Clinics offering ultrasound and amniocentesis in order to detect and abort female fetuses have become popular in various parts of the country, and many thousands of female fetuses have been so destroyed. In Maharashtra, Rajasthan, and Punjab such selective abortions have been outlawed because of pressure from feminist groups. More usually, girls are simply fed and cared for less well than their brothers.

The sex ratio is particularly unfavorable to females in the central northern section of the country. For example, in Uttar Pradesh there are only eighty-eight females per 100 males; in Haryana, eighty-seven per 100; and in Rajasthan ninety-one per 100. By contrast, in Kerala, on the southwest coast, a region traditionally noted for matriliny, the sex ratio is reversed, with females outnumbering males 104 to 100. In Andhra Pradesh and Tamil Nadu, two large southern states, there are ninety-seven females per 100 males.

Parents favor boys for various reasons. In the north, a boy's value in agricultural endeavors is higher than a girl's, and after marriage a boy continues to live with his parents, ideally supporting them in their old age. Political scientist Philip Oldenburg notes that in some violence-prone regions of the north, having sons may enhance families' capacity to defend themselves and to exercise power. A girl, however, moves away to live with her husband's relatives, and with her goes a dowry. In the late twentieth century, the values of dowries have been increasing, and, furthermore, groups that never gave dowries in the past are being pressured to do so. Thus, a girl child can represent a significant economic liability to her parents.

In rice-growing areas, especially in the south, girls receive better treatment, and there is some evidence that the better treatment is related to the value of women as field workers in wet-rice cultivation. Throughout most of India, for Hindus it is important to have a son conduct funeral rites for his parents; a daughter, as a member of her husband's lineage, has not traditionally been able to do so. For both boys and girls, infant mortality rates tend to be high, and in the absence of confidence that their infants will live, parents tend to produce numerous offspring in the hope that at least two sons will survive to adulthood.

Family planning measures are used to a modest degree in India; perhaps 37.5 percent of couples use contraceptives at least occasionally. Abortion is legal, condoms are advertised on colorful billboards, and government health services offer small bounties for patients undergoing vasectomies and tubal ligations. In some regions, most notably Kerala, better health care and higher infant survival rates are associated with lowered fertility rates. Most children survive infancy and do not fall victim to the cultural and economic pressures alluded to above. The majority of children grow up as valued members of a family, treasured by their parents and encouraged to participate in appropriate activities. Although relative ages of children are always known and reflected in linguistic and deference behavior, there is little age-grading in daily life. Children of all ages associate with each other and with adults, unlike the situation in the West, where age-grading is common.

Young Indian child grows up in intimate emotional contact with the mother and other mothering persons. Because conjugal marital relationships are deemphasized in the joint household, a woman looks to her children to satisfy some of her intimacy needs. Her bond to her children, especially her sons but also her daughters, becomes enormously strong and lasting. A child is suckled on demand, sometimes for years, sleeps with a parent or grandparent, is bathed by doting relatives, and is rarely left alone. Massaged with oil, carried about, gently toilet-trained, and gratified with treats, the young child develops an inner core of well-being and a profound sense of expectation of protection from others. Such indulgent and close relationships produce a symbiotic mode of relating to others and effect the development of a person with a deeply held sense of involvement with relatives, so vital to the Indian family situation.

The young child learns early about hierarchy within the family, as he watches affectionate and respectful relationships between seniors and juniors, males and females. A young child is often carried about by an older sibling, and strong and close sibling bonds usually develop. Bickering among siblings is not as common as it is in the West; rather, most siblings learn to think of themselves as part of a family unit that must work together as it meets the challenges of the outside world.

Young children are encouraged to participate in the numerous rituals that emphasize family ties. The power of sibling relationships is recognized, for example, when a brother touches his sister's feet, honoring in her the principle of feminine divinity, which, if treated appropriately, can bring him prosperity. In calendrical and life-cycle rituals in both the north and the south, sisters bless their brothers and also symbolically request their protection throughout life. After about four or five years of indulgence, children typically experience greater demands from family members. In villages, children learn the rudiments of agricultural labor, and young children often help with weeding, harvesting, threshing, and the like.

Girls learn domestic chores, and boys are encouraged to take cattle for grazing, learn plowing, and begin to drive bullock carts and ride bicycles. City children also learn household duties, and children of poor families often work as servants in the homes of the prosperous. Some even pick through garbage piles to find shreds of food and fuel. In some areas, children work as exploited laborers in factories, where they weave carpets for the export market and make matches, glass bangles, and other products. At Sivakasi, in Tamil Nadu, some 45,000 children work in the match, fireworks, and printing industries, comprising perhaps the largest single concentration of child labor in the world. Children reportedly as young as four years old work long hours each day.

Education in a school setting is available for most of India's children, and many young people attend school. Officials state that education is "compulsory," but the reality is that a significant percentage of children—especially girls—fail to become literate and instead carry out many other tasks in order to contribute to family income. More than half of India's children between the ages of six and fourteen—82.2 million—are not in school. Instead they participate in the labor force, even as more privileged children study at government and private schools and prepare for more prestigious jobs. Thus children learn early the realities of socioeconomic and urban-rural differentiation and grow up to perpetuate India's hierarchical society.

For many children, especially boys, an important event of young adolescence is religious initiation. Initiation rituals vary among different regions, religious communities, and castes. In the north, girls reach puberty without public notice and in an atmosphere of shyness, whereas in much of the south, puberty celebrations joyously announce to the family and community that a young girl has grown to maturity.

Marriage system

In India there is no greater event in a family than a wedding, dramatically evoking every possible social obligation, kinship bond, traditional value, impassioned sentiment, and economic resource. In the arranging and conducting of weddings, the complex permutations of Indian social systems best display themselves. Marriage is deemed essential for virtually everyone in India. For the individual, marriage is the great watershed in life, marking the transition to adulthood. Generally, this transition, like everything else in India, depends little upon individual volition but instead occurs as a result of the efforts of many people. Even as one is born into a particular family without the exercise of any personal choice, so is one given a spouse without any personal preference involved. Arranging a marriage is a critical responsibility for parents and other relatives of both bride and groom.

Marriage alliances entail some redistribution of wealth as well as building and restructuring social realignments, and, of course, result in the biological reproduction of families. Some parents begin marriage arrangements on the birth of a child, but most wait until later. In the past, the age of marriage was quite young, and in a few small groups, especially in Rajasthan, children under the age of five are still united in marriage. In rural communities, prepuberty marriage for girls traditionally was the rule. In the late twentieth century, the age of marriage is rising in villages, almost to the levels that obtain in cities. Legislation mandating minimum marriage ages has been passed in various forms over the past decades, but such laws have little effect on actual marriage practices.

Essentially, India is divided into two large regions with regard to Hindu kinship and marriage practices, the north and the south. Additionally, various ethnic and tribal groups of the central, mountainous north, and eastern regions follow a variety of other practices. Broadly, in the

Indo-Aryan-speaking north, a family seeks marriage alliances with people to whom it is not already linked by ties of blood. Marriage arrangements often involve looking far afield. In the Dravidian-speaking south, a family seeks to strengthen existing kin ties through marriage, preferably with blood relatives. Kinship terminology reflects this basic pattern.

In the north, every kinship term clearly indicates whether the person referred to is a blood relation or an affinal relation; all blood relatives are forbidden as marriage mates to a person or a person's children. In the south, there is no clear-cut distinction between the family of birth and the family of marriage. Because marriage in the south commonly involves a continuing exchange of daughters among a few families, for the married couple all relatives are ultimately blood kin. Dravidian terminology stresses the principle of relative age: all relatives are arranged according to whether they are older or younger than each other without reference to generation.

On the Indo-Gangetic Plain, marriages are contracted outside the village, sometimes even outside of large groups of villages, with members of the same caste beyond any traceable consanguineal ties. In much of the area, daughters should not be given into villages where daughters of the family or even of the natal village have previously been given. In most of the region, brother-sister exchange marriages (marriages linking a brother and sister of one household with the sister and brother of another) are shunned. The entire emphasis is on casting the marriage net ever-wider, creating new alliances. The residents of a single village may have in-laws in hundreds of other villages.

In most of North India, the Hindu bride goes to live with strangers in a home she has never visited. There she is sequestered and veiled, an outsider who must learn to conform to new ways. Her natal family is often geographically distant, and her ties with her consanguineal kin undergo attenuation to varying degrees.

In central India, the basic North Indian pattern prevails, with some modifications. For example, in Madhya Pradesh, village exogamy is preferred, but marriages within a village are not uncommon. Marriages between caste-fellows in neighboring villages are frequent. Brother-sister exchange marriages are sometimes arranged, and daughters are often given in marriage to lineages where other daughters of their lineage or village have previously been wed.

In South India, in sharp contrast, marriages are preferred between cousins (especially cross-cousins, that is, the children of a brother and sister) and even between uncles and nieces (especially a man and his elder sister's daughter). The principle involved is that of return—the family that gives a daughter expects one in return, if not now, then in the next generation. The effect of such marriages is to bind people together in relatively small, tight-knit kin groups. A bride moves to her in-laws' home—the home of her grandmother or aunt—and is often comfortable among these familiar faces. Her husband may well be the cousin she has known all her life that she would marry. Many South Indian marriages are contracted outside of such close kin groups when no suitable mates exist among close relatives, or when other options appear more advantageous. Some sophisticated South Indians, for example, consider cousin marriage and uncle-niece marriage outmoded.

Rules for the remarriage of widows differ from one group to another. Generally, lower-ranking groups allow widow remarriage, particularly if the woman is relatively young, but the highest-ranking castes discourage or forbid such remarriage. The most strict adherents to the nonremarriage of widows are Brahmans. Almost all groups allow widowers to remarry. Many groups encourage a widower to marry his deceased wife's younger sister (but never her older sister).

Among Muslims of both the north and the south, marriage between cousins is encouraged, both cross-cousins (the children of a brother and sister) and parallel cousins (the children of two same-sex siblings). In the north, such cousins grow up calling each other "brother" and "sister", yet they may marry. Even when cousin marriage does not occur, spouses can often trace between them other kinship linkages.

Some tribal people of central India practice an interesting permutation of the southern pattern. Among the Murias of Bastar in southeastern Madhya Pradesh, as described by anthropologist Verrier Elwin, teenagers live together in a dormitory (ghotul), sharing life and love with one another for several blissful years. Ultimately, their parents arrange their marriages, usually with cross-cousins, and the delights of teenage romance are replaced with the serious responsibilities of adulthood. In his survey of some 2,000 marriages, Elwin found only seventy-seven cases of ghotul partners eloping together and very few cases of divorce. Among the Muria and Gond tribal groups, cross-cousin marriage is called "bringing back the milk," alluding to the gift of a girl in one generation being returned by the gift of a girl in the next.

Finding the perfect partner for one's child can be a challenging task. People use their social networks to locate potential brides and grooms of appropriate social and economic status. Increasingly, urban dwellers use classified matrimonial advertisements in newspapers. The advertisements usually announce religion, caste, and educational qualifications, stress female beauty and male (and in the contemporary era, sometimes female) earning capacity, and may hint at dowry size.

In rural areas, matches between strangers are usually arranged without the couple meeting each other. Rather, parents and other relatives come to an agreement on behalf of the couple. In cities, however, especially among the educated classes, photographs are exchanged, and sometimes the couple are allowed to meet under heavily chaperoned circumstances, such as going out for tea with a group of people or meeting in the parlor of the girl's home, with her relatives standing by. Young professional men and their families may receive inquiries and photographs from representatives of several girls' families. They may send their relatives to meet the most promising candidates and then go on tour themselves to meet the young women and make a final choice. In the early 1990s, increasing numbers of marriages arranged in this way link brides and grooms from India with spouses of Indian parentage resident in Europe, North America, and the Middle East.

Almost all Indian children are raised with the expectation that their parents will arrange their marriages, but an increasing number of young people, especially among the college-educated, are finding their own spouses. So-called love marriages are deemed a slightly scandalous alternative to properly arranged marriages. Some young people convince their parents to "arrange" their marriages to people with whom they have fallen in love. This process has long been possible for Indians from the south and for Muslims who want to marry a particular cousin of the appropriate marriageable category. In the upper classes, these semi-arranged love marriages increasingly occur between young people who are from castes of slightly different rank but who are educationally or professionally equal. If there are vast differences to overcome, such as is the case with love marriages between Hindus and Muslims or between Hindus of very different caste status, parents are usually much less agreeable, and serious family disruptions can result.

In much of India, especially in the north, a marriage establishes a structural opposition between the kin groups of the bride and groom--bride-givers and bride-takers. Within this relationship, bride-givers are considered inferior to bride-takers and are forever expected to give gifts to the bride-takers. The one-way flow of gifts begins at engagement and continues for a generation or two. The most dramatic aspect of this asymmetrical relationship is the giving of dowry.

In many communities throughout India, a dowry has traditionally been given by a bride's kin at the time of her marriage. In ancient times, the dowry was considered a woman's wealth—property due a beloved daughter who had no claim on her natal family's real estate—and typically included portable valuables such as jewelry and household goods that a bride could control throughout her life. However, over time, the larger proportion of the dowry has come to consist of goods and cash payments that go straight into the hands of the groom's family.

In the late twentieth century, throughout much of India, dowry payments have escalated, and a groom's parents sometimes insist on compensation for their son's higher education and even for his future earnings, to which the bride will presumably have access. Some of the dowries demanded are quite oppressive, amounting to several years' salary in cash as well as items such as motorcycles, air conditioners, and fancy cars. Among some lower-status groups, large dowries are currently replacing traditional bride-price payments. Even among Muslims, previously not given to demanding large dowries, reports of exorbitant dowries are increasing.

The dowry is becoming an increasingly onerous burden for the bride's family. Antidowry laws exist but are largely ignored, and a bride's treatment in her marital home is often affected by the value of her dowry. Increasingly frequent are horrible incidents, particularly in urban areas, where a groom's family makes excessive demands on the bride's family—even after marriage—and when the demands are not met, murder the bride, typically by setting her clothes on fire in a cooking "accident." The groom is then free to remarry and collect another sumptuous dowry. The male and female in-laws implicated in these murders have seldom been punished.

Such dowry deaths have been the subject of numerous media reports in India and other countries and have mobilized feminist groups to action. In some of the worst areas, such as the National Capital Territory of Delhi, where hundreds of such deaths are reported annually and the numbers are increasing yearly, the law now requires that all suspicious deaths of new brides be investigated. Women's groups sometimes picket the homes of the in-laws of burned brides. Some analysts have related the growth of this phenomenon to the growth of consumerism in Indian society.

Fears of impoverishing their parents have led some urban middle-class young women, married and unmarried, to commit suicide. However, through the giving of large dowries, the newly wealthy are often able to marry their treasured daughters up the status hierarchy so reified in Indian society. After marriage arrangements are completed, a rich panoply of wedding rituals begins. Each religious group, region, and caste has a slightly different set of rites. Generally, all weddings involve as many kin and associates of the bride and groom as possible. The bride's family usually hosts most of the ceremonies and pays for all the arrangements for large numbers of guests for several days, including accommodation, feasting, decorations, and gifts for the groom's party. These arrangements are often extremely elaborate and expensive and are intended to enhance the status of the bride's family. The groom's party usually hires a band and brings fine gifts for the bride, such as jewelry and clothing, but these are typically far outweighed in value by the presents received from the bride's side.

After the bride and groom are united in sacred rites attended by colorful ceremony, the new bride may be carried away to her in-laws' home, or, if she is very young, she may remain with her parents until they deem her old enough to depart. A prepubescent bride usually stays in her natal home until puberty, after which a separate consummation ceremony is held to mark her departure for her conjugal home and married life. The poignancy of the bride's weeping departure for her new home is prominent in personal memory, folklore, literature, song, and drama throughout India.

In their new status, a young married couple begin to accept adult responsibilities. These include work inside and outside of the home, childbearing and childrearing, developing and maintaining social relationships, fulfilling religious obligations, and enhancing family prosperity and prestige as much as possible. The young husband usually remains resident with his natal family, surrounded by well-known relatives and neighbors. The young bride, however, is typically thrust into a strange household, where she is expected to follow ideal patterns of chaste and cheerfully obedient behavior.

Ideally, the Hindu wife should honor her husband as if he were her personal god. Through her marriage, a woman becomes an auspicious wife (suhagan), adorned with bangles and amulets designed to protect her husband's life and imbued with ritual powers to influence prosperity and procreation. At her wedding, the Hindu bride is likened to Lakshmi, the Goddess of Wealth, in symbolic recognition of the fact that the groom's patrilineage can increase and prosper only through her fertility and labors. Despite this simile, elegantly stated in the nuptial ritual, the young wife is pressed into service as the most subordinate member of her husband's family. If any misfortunes happen to befall her affinal family after her arrival, she may be blamed as the bearer of bad luck. Not surprisingly, some young women find adjusting to these new circumstances extremely upsetting. A small percentage experience psychological distress so severe that they seem to be possessed by outspoken ghosts and spirits.

In these difficult early days of a marriage, and later on throughout her life, a woman looks to her natal kin for moral and often economic support. Although she has become part of another household and lineage, she depends on her natal relatives—especially her brothers—to back her up in a variety of circumstances. A wide range of long visits home, ritual obligations, gifts, folklore, and songs reflect the significance of a woman's lifelong ties to her blood relatives.

By producing children, especially highly valued sons, and, ultimately, becoming a mother-in-law herself, a woman gradually improves her position within the conjugal household. In motherhood the married woman finds social approval, economic security, and emotional satisfaction. A man and his wife owe respect and obedience to his parents and other senior relatives. Ideally, all cooperate in the joint family enterprise. Gradually, as the years pass, members of the younger generation take the place of the older generation and become figures of authority and respect. As this transition occurs, it is generally assumed that younger family members will physically care for and support elders until their demise.

In their adult years, men and women engage in a wide variety of tasks and occupations strongly linked to socioeconomic status, including caste membership, wealth, place of residence, and many other factors. In general, the higher the status of a family, the less likely its members are to engage in manual labor and the more likely its members are to be served by employees of lower status. Although educated women are increasingly working outside the home, even in urbane circles some negative stigma is still attached to women's employment. In addition, students from high-status families do not work at temporary menial jobs as they do in many Western countries.

People of low status work at the many menial tasks that high-status people disdain. Poor women cannot afford to abstain from paid labor, and they work alongside their menfolk in the fields and at construction projects. In low-status families, women are less likely than high-status women to unquestioningly accept the authority of men and even of elders because they are directly responsible for providing income for the family. Among Sweepers, very low-status latrine cleaners, women carry out more of the traditional tasks than do men and hold a relatively less subordinate position in their families than do women of traditional high-status families. Such women are, nonetheless, less powerful in the society at large than are women of economically prosperous high-status families, who control and influence the control of more assets than do poor women.

Along with economically supporting themselves, their elders, and their children, adults must maintain and add to the elaborate social networks upon which life depends. Offering gracious hospitality to guests is a key ingredient of proper adult behavior. Adults must also attend to religious matters, carrying out rites intended to protect their families and communities. In these efforts, men and women constantly work for the benefit of their kin groups, castes, and other social units.

Caste System

Although many other nations are characterized by social inequality, perhaps nowhere else in the world has inequality been so elaborately constructed as in the Indian institution of caste. Caste has long existed in India, but in the modern period it has been severely criticized by both Indian and foreign observers. Although some educated Indians tell non-Indians that caste has been abolished or that "no one pays attention to caste anymore," such statements do not reflect reality.

Caste has undergone significant change since independence, but it still involves hundreds of millions of people. In its preamble, India's constitution forbids negative public discrimination on the basis of caste. However, caste ranking and caste-based interaction have occurred for centuries and will continue to do so well into the foreseeable future, more in the countryside than in urban settings and more in the realms of kinship and marriage than in less personal interactions.

Castes are ranked, named, endogamous (in-marrying) groups, membership in which is achieved by birth. There are thousands of castes and subcastes in India, and these large kinship-based groups are fundamental to South Asian social structure. Each caste is part of a locally based system of interde-pendence with other groups, involving occupational specialization, and is linked in complex ways with networks that stretch across regions and throughout the nation.

The word caste derives from the Portuguese casta , meaning breed, race, or kind. Among the Indian terms that are sometimes translated as caste are varna, jati, jat , biradri , and samaj . All of these terms refer to ranked groups of various sizes and breadth. Varna , or color, actually refers to large divisions that include various castes; the other terms include castes and subdivisions of castes sometimes called subcastes. Many castes are traditionally associated with an occupation, such as high-ranking Brahmans; middle-ranking farmer and artisan groups, such as potters, barbers, and carpenters; and very low-ranking "Untouchable" leatherworkers, butchers, launderers, and latrine cleaners. There is some correlation between ritual rank on the caste hierarchy and economic prosperity. Members of higher-ranking castes tend, on the whole, to be more prosperous than members of lower-ranking castes. Many lower-caste people live in conditions of great poverty and social disadvantage.

According to the Rig Veda, sacred texts that date back to oral traditions of more than 3,000 years ago, progenitors of the four ranked varna groups sprang from various parts of the body of the primordial man, which Brahma created from clay. Each group had a function in sustaining the life of society—the social body. Brahmans, or priests, were created from the mouth. They were to provide for the intellectual and spiritual needs of the community. Kshatriyas, warriors and rulers, were derived from the arms. Their role was to rule and to protect others. Vaishyas—landowners and merchants—sprang from the thighs, and were entrusted with the care of commerce and agriculture. Shudras—artisans and servants—came from the feet. Their task was to perform all manual labor.

Later conceptualized was a fifth category, "Untouchable" menials, relegated to carrying out very menial and polluting work related to bodily decay and dirt. Since 1935 "Untouchables" have been known as Scheduled Castes, referring to their listing on government rosters, or schedules. They are also often called by Mohandas Karamchand (Mahatma) Gandhi's term Harijans, or "Children of God." Although the term Untouchable appears in literature produced by these low-ranking castes, in the 1990s, many politically conscious members of these groups prefer to refer to themselves as Dalit, a Hindi word meaning oppressed or downtrodden. According to the 1991 census, there were 138 million Scheduled Caste members in India, approximately 16 percent of the total population.

The first four varnas apparently existed in the ancient Aryan society of northern India. Some historians say that these categories were originally somewhat fluid functional groups, not castes. A greater degree of fixity gradually developed, resulting in the complex ranking systems of medieval India that essentially continue in the late twentieth century. Although a varna is not a caste, when directly asked for their caste affiliation, particularly when the questioner is a Westerner, many Indians will reply with a varna name. Pressed further, they may respond with a much more specific name of a caste, or jati , which falls within that varna . For example, a Brahman may specify that he is a member of a named caste group, such as a Jijotiya

Brahman, or a Smartha Brahman, and so on. Within such castes, people may further belong to smaller subcaste categories and to specific clans and lineages. These finer designations are particularly relevant when marriages are being arranged and often appear in newspaper matrimonial advertisements.

Members of a caste are typically spread out over a region, with representatives living in hundreds of settlements. In any small village, there may be representatives of a few or even a score or more castes. Numerous groups usually called tribes (often referred to as Scheduled Tribes) are also integrated into the caste system to varying degrees. Some tribes live separately from others--particularly in the far northeast and in the forested center of the country, where tribes are more like ethnic groups than castes. Some tribes are themselves divided into groups similar to subcastes. In regions where members of tribes live in peasant villages with nontribal peoples, they are usually considered members of separate castes ranking low on the hierarchical scale.

Inequalities among castes are considered by the Hindu faithful to be part of the divinely ordained natural order and are expressed in terms of purity and pollution. Within a village, relative rank is most graphically expressed at a wedding or death feast, when all residents of the village are invited. At the home of a high-ranking caste member, food is prepared by a member of a caste from whom all can accept cooked food (usually by a Brahman). Diners are seated in lines; members of a single caste sit next to each other in a row, and members of other castes sit in perpendicular or parallel rows at some distance. Members of Dalit castes, such as Leatherworkers and Sweepers, may be seated far from the other diners—even out in an alley. Farther away, at the edge of the feeding area, a Sweeper may wait with a large basket to receive discarded leavings tossed in by other diners. Eating food contaminated by contact with the saliva of others not of the same family is considered far too polluting to be practiced by members of any other castes. Generally, feasts and ceremonies given by Dalits are not attended by higher-ranking castes.

Among Muslims, although status differences prevail, brotherhood may be stressed. A Muslim feast usually includes a cloth laid either on clean ground or on a table, with all Muslims, rich and poor, dining from plates placed on the same cloth. Muslims who wish to provide hospitality to observant Hindus, however, must make separate arrangements for a high-caste Hindu cook and ritually pure foods and dining area.

Castes that fall within the top four ranked varnas are sometimes referred to as the "clean castes," with Dalits considered "unclean." Castes of the top three ranked varnas are often designated "twice-born," in reference to the ritual initiation undergone by male members, in which investiture with the Hindu sacred thread constitutes a kind of ritual rebirth. Non-Hindu castelike groups generally fall outside these designations.

Each caste is believed by devout Hindus to have its own dharma, or divinely ordained code of proper conduct. Accordingly, there is often a high degree of tolerance for divergent lifestyles among different castes. Brahmans are usually expected to be nonviolent and spiritual, according with their traditional roles as vegetarian teetotaler priests. Kshatriyas are supposed to be strong, as fighters and rulers should be, with a taste for aggression, eating meat, and drinking alcohol. Vaishyas are stereotyped as adept businessmen, in accord with their traditional activities in commerce. Shudras are often described by others as tolerably pleasant but expectably somewhat base in behavior, whereas Dalits—especially Sweepers—are often regarded by others as followers of vulgar life-styles. Conversely, lower-caste people often view people of high rank as haughty and unfeeling.

The chastity of women is strongly related to caste status. Generally, the higher ranking the caste, the more sexual control its women are expected to exhibit. Brahman brides should be virginal, faithful to one husband, and celibate in widowhood. By contrast, a Sweeper bride may or may not be a virgin, extramarital affairs may be tolerated, and, if widowed or divorced, the woman is encouraged to remarry. For the higher castes, such control of female sexuality helps ensure purity of lineage--of crucial importance to maintenance of high status. Among Muslims, too, high status is strongly correlated with female chastity.

Within castes explicit standards are maintained. Transgressions may be dealt with by a caste council, meeting periodically to adjudicate issues relevant to the caste. Such councils are usually formed of groups of elders, almost always males. Punishments such as fines and outcasting, either temporary or permanent, can be enforced. In rare cases, a person is excommunicated from the caste for gross infractions of caste rules. An example of such an infraction might be marrying or openly cohabiting with a mate of a caste lower than one's own; such behavior would usually result in the higher-caste person dropping to the status of the lower-caste person.

Activities such as farming or trading can be carried out by anyone, but usually only members of the appropriate castes act as priests, barbers, potters, weavers, and other skilled artisans, whose occupational skills are handed down in families from one generation to another. As with other key features of Indian social structure, occupational specialization is believed to be in accord with the divinely ordained order of the universe. The existence of rigid ranking is supernaturally validated through the idea of rebirth according to a person's karma, the sum of an individual's deeds in this life and in past lives. After death, a person's life is judged by divine forces, and rebirth is assigned in a high or a low place, depending upon what is deserved. This supernatural sanction can never be neglected, because it brings a person to his or her position in the caste hierarchy, relevant to every transaction involving food or drink, speaking, or touching.

In past decades, Dalits in certain areas (especially in parts of the south) had to display extreme deference to high-status people, physically keeping their distance--lest their touch or even their shadow pollute others--wearing neither shoes nor any upper body covering (even for women) in the presence of the upper castes. The lowest-ranking had to jingle a little bell in warning of their polluting approach. In much of India, Dalits were prohibited from entering temples, using wells from which the "clean" castes drew their water, or even attending schools. In past centuries, dire punishments were prescribed for Dalits who read or even heard sacred texts.

Such degrading discrimination was made illegal under legislation passed during British rule and was protested against by preindependence reform movements led by Mahatma Gandhi and Bhimrao Ramji (B.R.) Ambedkar, a Dalit leader. Dalits agitated for the right to enter Hindu temples and to use village wells and effectively pressed for the enactment of stronger laws opposing disabilities imposed on them. After independence, Ambedkar almost singlehandedly wrote India's constitution, including key provisions barring caste-based discrimination. Nonetheless, discriminatory treatment of Dalits remains a factor in daily life, especially in villages, as the end of the twentieth century approaches.

In modern times, as in the past, it is virtually impossible for an individual to raise his own status by falsely claiming to be a member of a higher-ranked caste. Such a ruse might work for a time in a place where the person is unknown, but no one would dine with or intermarry with such a person or his offspring until the claim was validated through kinship networks. Rising on the ritual hierarchy can only be achieved by a caste as a group, over a long period of time, principally by adopting behavior patterns of higher-ranked groups. This process, known as Sanskritization, has been described by M.N. Srinivas and others. An example of such behavior is that of some Leatherworker castes adopting a policy of not eating beef, in the hope that abstaining from the defiling practice of consuming the flesh of sacred bovines would enhance their castes' status. Increased economic prosperity for much of a caste greatly aids in the process of improving rank.

Some observers feel that the caste system must be viewed as a system of exploitation of poor low-ranking groups by more prosperous high-ranking groups. In many parts of India, land is largely held by dominant castes—high-ranking owners of property--that economically exploit low-ranking landless laborers and poor artisans, all the while degrading them with ritual emphases on their so-called god-given inferior status. In the early 1990s, blatant subjugation of low-caste laborers in the northern state of Bihar and in eastern Uttar Pradesh was the subject of many news reports. In this region, scores of Dalits who have attempted to unite to protest low wages have been the victims of lynchings and mass killings by high-caste landowners and their hired assassins.

Despite many problems, the caste system has operated successfully for centuries, providing goods and services to India's many millions of citizens. The system continues to operate, but changes are occurring. India's constitution guarantees basic rights to all its citizens, including the right to equality and equal protection before the law. The practice of untouchability, as well as discrimination on the basis of caste, race, sex, or religion, has been legally abolished. All citizens have the right to vote, and political competition is lively. Voters from every stratum of society have formed interest groups, overlapping and crosscutting castes, creating an evolving new style of integrating Indian society.

The growth of urbanization is having a far-reaching effect on caste practices, not only in cities but in villages. Among anonymous crowds in urban public spaces and on public transportation, caste affiliations are unknown, and observance of purity and pollution rules is negligible. Distinctive caste costumes have all but vanished, and low-caste names have been modified, although castes remain endogamous, and access to employment often occurs through intracaste connections. Restrictions on interactions with other castes are becoming more relaxed, and, at the same time, observance of other pollution rules is declining—especially those concerning birth, death, and menstruation. Several growing Hindu sects draw members from many castes and regions, and communication between cities and villages is expanding dramatically. Kin in town and country visit one another frequently, and television programs available to huge numbers of villagers vividly portray new lifestyles. As new occupations open up in urban areas, the correlation of caste with occupation is declining.

Caste associations have expanded their areas of concern beyond traditional elite emulation and local politics into the wider political arenas of state and national politics.

Finding power in numbers within India's democratic system, caste groups are pulling together closely allied subcastes in their quest for political influence. In efforts to solidify caste bonds, some caste associations have organized marriage fairs where families can make matches for their children. Traditional hierarchical concerns are being minimized in favor of strengthening horizontal unity. Thus, while pollution observances are declining, caste consciousness is not.

Education and election to political office have advanced the status of many Dalits, but the overall picture remains one of great inequity. In recent decades, Dalit anger has been expressed in writings, demonstrations, strikes, and the activities of such groups as the Dalit Panthers, a radical political party demanding revolutionary change. A wider Dalit movement, including political parties, educational activities, self-help centers, and labor organizations, has spread to many areas of the country.

India's complex society includes some unique members—sadhus (holy men) and hijras (transvestite-eunuchs). Such people have voluntarily stepped outside the usual bonds of kinship and caste to join with others in castelike groups based upon personal—yet culturally shaped—inclinations. In India of the 1990s, several hundred thousand Hindu and Jain sadhus and a few thousand holy women (sadhvis) live an ascetic life. They have chosen to wear ocher robes, or perhaps no clothing at all, to daub their skin with holy ash, to pray and meditate, and to wander from place to place, depending on the charity of others. Most have given up affiliation with their caste and kin and have undergone a funeral ceremony for themselves, followed by a ritual rebirth into their new ascetic life. They come from all walks of life, and range from illiterate villagers to well-educated professionals. In their new lives as renunciants, they are devoted to spiritual concerns, yet each is affiliated with an ascetic order or subsect demanding strict adherence to rules of dress, itinerancy, diet, worship, and ritual pollution.

By the twenty-first century, India's population will be more than 1 billion. Approximately one-third of this enormous population will live in urban areas, which means adding the population of another Calcutta, Bombay, or Madras to India's already overburdened cities each year into the foreseeable future. In rural areas, pressures on land and other resources will continue to intensify.

In India's democracy, ideas are often vociferously expressed, and members of different groups are increasingly demanding what they consider a fair share of resources and benefits. Tolerance for inequity is diminishing among the less privileged, even as inequity is increasing in both rural and urban areas. As competition for scarce resources and benefits grows, some political leaders have been encouraging the populace to blame these problems on religious differences.

Prosperity is available to many, and access to education and an expanding range of consumer goods is possible for an ever-increasing number of people. At the same time, the sheer numbers of the poor and less privileged are increasing as they are left behind, inadequately educated, and forced by circumstance to labor under insecure conditions. Class and gender justice, widely sought by a significant number of people, remains an elusive goal.

India is part of a much wider community of nations facing these and other problems, so it will not be alone in seeking solutions. In this endeavor, the great structural principles of hierarchy and interdependence that have held Indian society together over the millennia will be brought to the fore. Creating manageable order from complexity, bringing together widely disparate groups in structured efforts to benefit the wider society, encouraging harmony among people with divergent interests, knowing that close family and friends can rely on each other in times of stress, allocating different tasks to those with different skills, and striving to do what is morally right in the eyes of the divine and the human community—these are some of the great strengths upon which Indian society can rely as it meets the challenges of the future.

2

Mass Media in India

"Media" (originally the plural of "medium") is a contraction of the term "media of communication", referring to those organized means of dissemination of fact, opinion, and entertainment such as newspapers, magazines, cinema films, radio, television, and the World Wide Web. Writers currently vary in their preference for using "media" in the singular ("the media is...") or the plural ("the media are...").

Mass media is the term used to denote, as a class, that section of the media specifically conceived and designed to reach a very large audience (typically at least as large as the whole population of a nation state). It was coined in the 1920s with the advent of nationwide radio networks and of mass-circulation newspapers and magazines. The mass-media audience has been viewed by some commentators as forming a mass society with special characteristics, notably atomization or lack of social connections, which render it especially susceptible to the influence of modern mass-media techniques such as advertising and propaganda.

During the 20th century, the advent of mass media was driven by technology that allowed the massive duplication of material at a low cost. Physical duplication technologies such as printing, record pressing and film duplication allowed the duplication of books, newspapers and movies at low prices to huge audiences. Television and radio allowed the electronic duplication of content for the first time. Mass media had the economics of linear replication: a single work could make money proportional to the number of copies sold, and as volumes went up, units costs went down, increasing profit margins further. Vast fortunes were to be made in mass media.

During the last decade of the 20th century, the advent of the World Wide Web marked the first era in which any individual could have a means of exposure on the scale of mass media. For the first time, anyone with a web site can address a global audience, although serving high levels of web traffic is still expensive. It is possible that the rise of peer-to-peer technologies may have begun the process of making the cost of bandwidth manageable. Media in India, especially news media, are undergoing significant changes in the current liberalised environment. To understand these changes, one needs to have some idea of the road traversed so far. It is useful to look at media in the two phases of India's history - pre-colonial and post-colonial. Each medium has taken its own evolutionary path

History of Indian Media

William Bolts, an ex-employee of the British East India Company attempted to start the first newspaper in India way back in 1776. Bolts had to beat a retreat under the disapproving gaze of the Court of Directors of the Company. The Bengal Gazette by James Augustus Hicky was started in 1780. The Gazette, a two-sheet newspaper, "specialised" in writing on the private lives of the Sahibs of the Company. He dared even to mount "scurrillious attacks" on the Governor-General Warren Hastings' wife, which soon landed "the late printer to the Honourable Company" in trouble. Hicky landed himself a 4 months jail term and Rs.500 fine, which did not deter him. After a bitter attack on the Governor-General and the Chief Justice, Hicky was sentenced to one year in prison and fined Rs.5,000, which finally drove him to penury. These are the first tentative steps of journalism in India.

B.Messink and Peter Reed were plaint publishers of the India Gazette, unlike their infamous predecessor. The colonial establishment started the Calcutta Gazette. It was followed by another private initiative the Bengal Journal. The Oriental Magazine of Calcutta Amusement, a monthly magazine made it four weekly newspapers and one monthly magazine published from Calcutta, now Kolkata. Madras, now Chennai: The Madras Courier was started in 1785 in the southern stronghold of Madras, which is called Chennai now. Richard Johnson, its founder, was a government printer.

Madras got its second newspaper when, in 1791, Hugh Boyd, who was the editor of the Courier quit and founded the Hurkaru. Tragically for the paper, Boyd passed away within a year of its founding - it ceased publication too. It was only in 1795 that competitors to the Courier emerged with the founding of the Madras Gazette followed by the India Herald. The latter was an "unauthorised" publication, which led to the deportation of its founder Humphreys. The Madras Courier was designated the purveyor of official information in the Presidency. Bombay, now Mumbai: Bombay, surprisingly was a late starter - the Bombay Herald came into existence in 1789. Significantly, a year later a paper called the Courier started carrying advertisements in Gujarati.

The first media merger of sorts: The Bombay Gazette, which was started in 1791, merged with the Bombay Herald the following year. Like the Madras Courier, this new entity was recognised as the publication to carry "official notifications and advertisements". 'A Chronicle of Media and the State', by Jeebesh Bagchi in the Sarai Reader 2001 is a handy timeline on the role of the state in the development of media in India for more than a century. Bagchi divides the timeline into three 'ages'. The Age of Formulation, which starts with the Indian Telegraph Act in 1885 and ends with the Report of the Sub-Committee on Communication, National Planning Committee in 1948.

The Age of Consolidation that follows stretches from 1951, with the extension of the Indian Telegraph Act to the whole of India and ends with the promulgation of the Indecent Representation of Women (Prohibition) Act in 1985. The current age is the Age of Uncertainty, which began in 1989 with the introduction of the Prasar Bharati (Broadcasting Corporation of India) Bill. The story gets better from now. II News Agencies: PTI(Press Trust of India) and UNI(United News of India) are the two primary Indian news agencies. The former was formed after the it took over the operations of the Associated Press of India and the Indian operations of Reuters soon after independence on August 27, 1947. PTI is a non-profit cooperative of the Indian newspapers. UNI began its operations on March 21, 1961, though it was registered as a company in 1959 itself.

Media penetration as of 2003

All India Urban		
Print	25%	46%
Terrestrial television	53%	80%
Cable and satellite television	20%	46%

Radio	22%	25%
Cinema	7%	11%
Internet	1%	3%

Press Media

Compared with many other developing countries, the Indian press has flourished since independence and exercises a large degree of independence. British colonialism allowed for the development of a tradition of freedom of the press, and many of India's great English-language newspapers and some of its Indian-language press were begun during the nineteenth century. As India became independent, ownership of India's leading English-language newspapers was transferred from British to Indian business groups, and the fact that most English-language newspapers have the backing of large business houses has contributed to their independence from the government.

The Indian press has experienced impressive growth since independence. In 1950 there were 214 daily newspapers, with forty-four in English and the rest in Indian languages. By 1990 the number of daily newspapers had grown to 2,856, with 209 in English and 2,647 in indigenous languages. The expansion of literacy and the spread of consumerism during the 1980s fueled the rapid growth of news weeklies and other periodicals. By 1993 India had 35,595 newspapers--of which 3,805 were dailies--and other periodicals. Although the majority of publications are in indigenous languages, the English-language press, which has widespread appeal to the expanding middle class, has a wide multicity circulation throughout India.

There are four major publishing groups in India, each of which controls national and regional English-language and vernacular publications. They are the Times of India Group, the Indian Express Group, the Hindustan Times Group, and the Anandabazar Patrika Group. The Times of India is India's largest English-language daily, with a circulation of 656,000 published in six cities. The Indian Express , with a daily circulation of 519,000, is published in seventeen cities. There also are seven other daily newspapers with circulations of between 134,000 and 477,000, all in English and all competitive with one another.

Indian-language newspapers also enjoy large circulations but usually on a statewide or citywide basis. For example, the Malayalam-language daily Malayala Manorama circulates 673,000 copies in Kerala; the Hindi-language Dainik Jagran circulates widely in Uttar Pradesh and New Delhi, with 580,000 copies per day; Punjab Kesari , also published in Hindi and available throughout Punjab and New Delhi, has a daily circulation of 562,000; and the Anandabazar Patrika , published in Calcutta in Bengali, has a daily circulation of 435,000. There are also numerous smaller publications throughout the nation. The combined circulation of India's newspapers and periodicals is in the order of 60 million, published daily in more than ninety languages.

India has more than forty domestic news agencies. The Express News Service, the Press Trust of India, and the United News of India are among the major news agencies. They are headquartered in Delhi, Bombay, and New Delhi, respectively, and employ foreign correspondents. Although freedom of the press in India is the legal norm--it is constitutionally guaranteed--the scope of this freedom has often been contested by the government. Rigid press censorship was imposed during the Emergency starting in 1975 but quickly retracted in 1977. The government has continued, however, to exercise more indirect controls.

Government advertising accounts for as much as 50 percent of all advertisements in Indian newspapers, providing a monetary incentive to limit harsh criticism of the administration. Until 1992, when government regulation of access to newsprint was liberalized, controls on the distribution of newsprint could also be used to reward favored publications and threaten those that fell into disfavor. In 1988, at a time when the Indian press was publishing investigative reports about corruption and abuse of power in government, Parliament passed a tough defamation bill that mandated prison sentences for offending journalists. Vociferous protests from journalists and opposition party leaders ultimately forced the government to withdraw the bill. Since the late 1980s, the independence of India's press has been bolstered by the liberalization of government economic policy and the increase of private-sector advertising provided by the growth of India's private sector and the spread of consumerism.

List of popular publications in urban India in 2003

— Dainik Bhaskar (Hindi daily)

— Dainik Jagran (Hindi daily)

— The Times of India (English daily)

— Amar Ujala (Hindi daily)

— Anand Bazar Patrika (Bengali daily)

— Grihshobha (Hindi)

— Eenadu (daily)

— Lokmat (Hindi daily)

— India Today (weekly; Hindi edition most popular)

— Gujarat Samachar (Gujarati daily)

List of popular English dailies in urban India in 2003

— The Times of India

— Hindustan Times

— The Hindu

— The Telegraph

— Deccan Chronicle

— The Economic Times

— The New Indian Express

— Mid-Day

— Deccan Herald

— Indian Express

Broadcast Media

The national television (Doordarshan) and radio (All India Radio, or Akashwani) networks are state-owned and managed by the Ministry of Information and Broadcasting. Their news reporting customarily presents the government's point of view. V.P. Singh's National Front government sponsored the Prasar Bharati (Indian Broadcasting) Act, which Parliament considered in 1990, to provide greater autonomy to Doordarshan and All India Radio. The changes that resulted were limited. The bill provided for the establishment of an autonomous corporation to run Doordarshan and All India Radio. The corporation was to operate under a board of governors to be in charge of appointments and policy and a broadcasting council to respond to complaints.

However, the legislation required that the corporation prepare and submit its budget within the framework of the central budget and stipulated that the personnel of the new broadcasting corporation be career civil servants to facilitate continued government control. In the early 1990s, increasing competition from television broadcasts transmitted via satellite appeared the most effective manner of limiting the progovernment bias of the government-controlled electronic media.

Since the 1980s, India has experienced a rapid proliferation of television broadcasting that has helped shape popular culture and the course of politics. Although the first television program was broadcast in 1959, the expansion of television did not begin in earnest until the extremely popular telecast of the Ninth Asian Games, which were held in New Delhi in 1982. Realizing the popular appeal and consequent influence of television broadcasting, the government undertook an expansion that by 1990 was planned to provide television access to 90 percent of the population. In 1993, about 169 million people were estimated to have watched Indian television each week, and, by 1994, it was reported that there were some 47 million households with televisions. There also is a growing selection of satellite transmission and cable services available.

Television programming was initially kept tightly under the control of the government, which embarked on a self-conscious effort to construct and propagate a cultural idea of the Indian nation. This goal is especially clear in the broadcasts of such megaseries as the Hindu epics Ramayana and Mahabharata . In addition to the effort at nation-building, the politicians of India's ruling party have not hesitated to use television to build political support. In fact, the political abuse of Indian television led to demands to increase the autonomy of Doordarshan; these demands ultimately resulted in support for the Prasar Bharati Act.

Radio

Radio Technology was first developed during the late nineteenth century and came into popular usage during the early twentieth century. Though sometimes overshadowed by television, radio represents a medium capable of reaching a wide geographic audience at a low production cost with proven educational results. Studies by the U.K. Open University have demonstrated that radio has a greater value for weak students who benefit from radio as a supplementary learning tool. The Agency for International Development has shown that radio is more cost-effective and results in a greater learning effect size than textbooks or teacher education. Radio has the advantage of teaching subjects in which classroom teachers are deficient or untrained. An added benefit for multi-grade classrooms is that it provides instruction for one group of students while the teacher works with another group. Radio can also bring new or unavailable resources into the classroom.

Three main advantages of radio are: improving educational quality and relevance; lowering educational costs; and improving access to educational inputs particularly to disadvantaged groups. Some of the limitations of radio for education are that interaction is limited; instructor feedback and clarification is generally unavailable; the instruction is uninterruptible and not reviewable; the pace of the lesson is fixed for all students; note-taking is difficult; and that time for reflection on the content is minimal. To overcome these drawbacks, preparation, supporting materials, and follow-up exercises are recommended when possible. The popularity, availability, and low cost of radio made it a convenient and practical medium for use in programmes for learning at a distance and is mostly used in combination with other media, such as with print medium followed by face-to face teaching etc. Although, educational use of radio started around 1930, but perhaps U.K.O.U. was first make its utilization effective.

Radio is useful in providing remedial tutorials, or some other forms of tutorial based feedback; providing corrections, alterations or updating of material, where print re-make budgets are limited, or where print cannot reach students quickly enough; recordings of naturally occurring events, e.g. political speech, children talking, concerts or performances, talks previously recorded for other than Open University proposes eyewitness interviews at historical events; presenting material in a dramatized form, enabling students to identify with the emotions and viewpoints of the main participants; providing an alternative view to that presented in the correspondence text and/ or television programmes; and enabling students to perceive the different points of view that exist, and observe ideas being challenged, through discussion and interviews.

The Radio Club of Bombay broadcast the first radio programme in India in June 1923. Afterwards a Broadcasting Service was set up (that began broadcasting in India in July 1927) on an experimental basis at Bombay and Calcutta simultaneously. This was done under an agreement between Government of India and a private company called the Indian Broadcasting Company Ltd. The operations of All India Radio began formally in 1936, as a government organisation, with clear objectives to inform, educate and entertain the masses. In the year 1947 (when India became independent), the AIR network had only six Stations located at Delhi, Bombay, Calcutta, Madras, Lucknow and Tiruchirapalli with a total complement of 18 transmitters - six on the medium wave and the remaining on short wave.

Radio listening on medium wave was confined to urban limits of these cities. As against a mere 2,75,000 receiving sets at the time of Independence, now there are about 111 million estimated radio sets in about 105 million household in the country. Presently the broadcast scenario has drastically changed with 198 broadcasting centers, including 74 local Radio Stations, covering nearly cent-per-cent country's population. As of today AIR network broadcasts nearly 2000 programme hours every day in 24 languages and 146 dialects. It reaches 97.1 per cent of the population, which includes substantial population in rural area, and covers 89.7 percent of the geographical area of the country. The AIR is expected to cover an estimated 97.7 percent of population in the country on completion of various ongoing projects under the 8th Five-Year Plan.

Today, radio broadcasting is a Government of India monopoly under the Directorate General of All India Radio a government-owned, semicommercial operation of the Ministry of Information and Broadcasting. The government-owned network provides both national and local programs in Hindi, English, and sixteen regional languages. Commercial Radio services in India, which were inaugurated in 1967, are provided by Vividh Bharati Service, headquartered in Bombay. Vividh Bharati, which accepts advertisements, broadcasts from thirty-one AM and FM stations in the mid-1990s. India has an extensive network of medium wave and shortwave stations. In 1994 there were eighty-five FM stations and seventy-three shortwave stations that covered the entire country.

The broadcasting equipment is mostly Indian made and reaches special audiences, such as farmers needing agroclimatic, plant protection, and other agriculture-related information. The number of radio receivers increased almost fivefold between 1970 and 1994, from around 14 million to nearly 65 million. Most radios are also produced within India. The foreign broadcast service is a function of the External Services Division of All India Radio. In 1994 seventy hours of news, features, and entertainment programs were broadcast daily in twenty-five languages using thirty-two shortwave transmitters. The principal target audiences are listeners in neighboring countries and the large overseas Indian community.

AIR today has a network of 214 broadcasting centres with 143 medium frequency(MW), 54 high frequency (SW) and 139 FM transmitters. The coverage is 91.37% of the area , serving 99.13% of the people in the largest democracy of the world. AIR covers 24 Languages and 146 dialects in home services. In Externel services, it covers 27 languages; 17 national and 10 foreign languages.

Television

Television service in India is available throughout the country - directly as terrestrial TV and also through Cable operators, as Satellite TV. There are more than 100 Stations available for viewing. Doordarshan (DD), India's National Channel, established in 1959 as a part of All India Radio until 1976. DD consists of one national network and several regional networks. Presently, Doordarshan operates 19 channels - two All India channels, 11 Regional Languages Satellite Channels (RLSC), four State Networks (SN), an International channel and a Sports Channel. Regular satellite transmissions began in 1982 (the same year color transmission began).

Television in India has been in existence for three decades. For the first 17 years, it spread haltingly and transmission was mainly in black & white. The thinkers and policy makers of the country, which had just been liberated from centuries of colonial rule, frowned upon television, looking on at it as a luxury Indians could do without. In 1955 a Cabinet decision was taken disallowing any foreign investments in print media which has since been followed religiously for nearly 45 years. Sales of TV sets, as reflected by licences issued to buyers were just 676,615 until 1977.

Television has come to the forefront only in the past 15 years and more so in the past seven. There have been two ignition points: the first in the eighties when colour TV was introduced by state-owned broadcaster Doordarshan (DD) during the 1982 Asian Games. It then proceeded to install transmitters nationwide rapidly for terrestrial broadcasting. In this period no private enterprise was allowed to set up TV stations or to transmit TV signals.

The second spark came in the early nineties with the broadcast of satellite TV by foreign programmers like CNN followed by Star TV and a little later by domestic channels such as Zee TV and Sun TV into Indian homes. Prior to this, Indian viewers had to make do with DD's chosen fare which was dull,non-commercial in nature, directed towardsonly education and socio-economic development. Entertainment programmes were few and far between. And when the solitary few soaps like Hum Log, and mythological dramas: Ramayan and Mahabharat were televised, millions of viewers stayed glued to their sets.

When, urban Indians learnt that it was possible to watch the Gulf War on television, they rushed out and bought dishes for their homes. Others turned entrepreneurs and started offering the signal to their neighbours by flinging cable over treetops and verandahs. From the large metros satellite TV delivered via cable moved into smaller towns, spurring the purchase of TV sets and even the upgradation from black & white to colour TVs. DD responded to this satellite TV invasion by launching an entertainment and commercially driven channel and introduced entertainment programming on its terrestrial network. This again fuelled the purchase of sets in the hinterlands where cable TV was not available.

The initial success of the channels had a snowball effect: more foreign programmers and Indian entrepreneurs flagged off their own versions. From two channels prior to 1991, Indian viewers were exposed to more than 50 channels by 1996. Software producers emerged to cater to the programming boom almost overnight. Some talent came from the film industry, some from advertising and some from journalism. More and more people set up networks until there was a time in 1995-96 when an estimated 60,000 cable operators were existing in the country. Some of them had subscriber bases as low as 50 to as high as in the thousands. Most of the networks could relay just 6 to 14 channels as higher channel relaying capacity required heavy investments, which cable operators were loathe to make.

American and European cable networks evinced interest, as well as large Indian business groups, who set up sophisticated headends capable of delivering more than 30 channels. These multi-system operators (MSOs) started buying up local networks or franchising cable TV feeds to the smaller operators for a fee. This phenomenon led to resistance from smaller cable operators who joined forces and started functioning as MSOs. The net outcome was that the number of cable operators in the country has fallen to 30,000.

The rash of players who rushed to set up satellite channels discovered that advertising revenue was not large enough to support them. This led to a shakeout. At least half a dozen either folded up or aborted the high-flying plans they had drawn up, and started operating in a restricted manner. Some of them converted their channels into basic subscription services charging cable operators a carriage fee. Foreign cable TV MSOs discovered that the cable TV market was too disorganised for them to operate in and at least three of them decided to postpone their plans and got out of the market..

The government started taxing cable operators in a bid to generate revenue. The rates varied in the 26 states that go to form India and ranged from 35% upwards. The authorities moved in to regulate the business and a Cable TV Act was passed in 1995. The apex court in the country, the Supreme Court, passed a judgement that the air waves are not the property of the Indian government and any Indian citizen wanting to use them should be allowed to do so. The government reacted by making efforts to get some regulation in place by setting up committees to suggest what the broadcasting law of India should be, as the sector was still being governed by laws which were passed in 19th century India.

A broadcasting bill was drawn up in 1997 and introduced in parliament. But it was not passed into an Act. State-owned telecaster Doordarshan and radiocaster All India Radio were brought under a holding company called the Prasar Bharati under an act t1hat had been gathering dust for seven years, the Prasar Bharati Act, 1990. The Act served to give autonomy to the broadcasters as their management was left to a supervisory board consisting of retired professionals and bureaucrats.

A committee headed by a senior Congress (I) politician Sharad Pawar and consisting of other politicians and industrialist was set up to review the contents of the Broadcasting Bill. It held discussions with industry, politicians, and consumers and a report was even drawn up. But the United Front government fell and since then the report and the Bill have been consigned to the dustbin. But before that it issued a ban on the sale of Ku-band dishes and on digital direct-to-home Ku-band broadcasting, which the Rupert Murdoch-owned News Television was threatening to start in India. ISkyB, the Murdoch DTH venture, has since been wallowing in quicksand and in recent times has even shed a lot of employees. But News Corp has been running a C-band DTH venture in the country which has around 20,000 subscribers.

In 1999, a BJP-led government has been threatening to once again allow DTH Ku-band broadcasting and it has been talking of dismantling the Prasar Bharati and once again reverting Doordarshan's and All India Radio's control back in the government's hands. Some things change only to remain the same.

Doordarshan

Doordarshan, one of the largest broadcasting organizations in the world now in terms of the infrastructure of studios and transmitters, the variety of software and the vastness of the viewership, had a modest beginning. The experimental Telecast started in Delhi in September 1959 with a small transmitter and a makeshift studio and the regular daily transmission started in 1965. The TV service was extended to a second city - Bombay only in 1972. Till 1975, only seven cities were covered by Television. Television was separated from Radio in 1976 and Doordarshan came into existence. National programme was introduced in 1982 and from then onwards, there has been steady progress in Doordarshan.

On DD-1 National programmes, Regional programmes and Local Programmes are carried on time-sharing basis. Metro Entertainment channel carries Network programmes from Delhi and also Single-Metro Programmes from the four metro cities. The Regional Languages Satellite channels have two components - The Regional service for the particular state relayed by all terrestrial transmitters in the state and additional programmes in the Regional Language in prime time and non-prime time available only through cable operators. Sports Channel is exclusively devoted to the important sporting events of national and International importance. Now more than 87 percent of population of the country can receive Doordarshan programmes through a network of nearly 1044 terrestrial transmitters. About 46 Doordarshan Studios are producing TV software.

The 1990s have brought a radical transformation of television in India. Transnational satellite broadcasting made its debut in January 1991, when owners of satellite dishes--initially mostly at major hotels--began receiving Cable News Network (CNN) coverage of the Persian Gulf War. Three months later, Star TV began broadcasting via satellite tv. Its fare initially included serials such as "The Bold and the Beautiful" and MTV programs. Satellite broadcasting spread rapidly through India's cities as local entrepreneurs erected dishes to receive signals and transmitted them through local cable systems. After its October 1992 launch, Zee TV offered stiff competition to Star TV. However, the future of Star TV was bolstered by billionaire Rupert Murdock, who acquired the network for US$525 million in July 1993.

Competition from the satellite stations brought radical change to Doordarshan by cutting its audience and threatening its advertising revenues at a time when the government was pressuring it to pay for expenditures from internal revenues. In response, Doordarshan decided in 1993 to start five new channels in addition to its original National Channel. Programming was radically transformed, and controversial news shows, soap operas, and coverage of high-fashion events proliferated. Of the new Doordarshan channels, however, only the Metro Channel, which carries MTV music videos and other popular shows, has survived in the face of the new trend for talk programs that engage in a potpourri of racy topics.

Indian Cinema Audience is 2,860,000,000 (1998), News Paper circulation is 59,023,000 (1998), Radio Listeners 116,000,000 compared to that TV viewers are 63,000,000. The number of televisions in India sets increased from around 500,000 in 1976 to 9 million in early 1987 and to around 47 million in 1994; increases are expected to continue at around 6 million sets per year. More than 75 percent of television sets in India were black and white models in 1992, but the proportion of color sets is increasing annually.

Most television sets are produced in India. By 1994 some 6 million people were receiving television broadcasts via satellite, and the number was expected to increase rapidly throughout the rest of the decade. Cable television had an estimated 12 to 15 million subscribers in 1994. Doordarshan was the only network that was permitted to broadcast television signals domestically, other TV entrepreneurs were broadcasting their Indian-made videotapes via foreign transmitters.

Doordarshan Network

1. Transmitters for relay of primary channel (DD1)	As on 31.3.98	As on 31.3.99
a. High Power Transmitters	83	84
b. Low Power Transmitter	600	651

c. Very Low Power Transmitter	196	251
d. Transponders	18	18
TOTAL	897	968
2. Transmitters for relay of Metro channel (DD2)		
a. High Power Transmitter	8	8
b. Low Power Transmitter	38	43
c. Very Low Power Transmitter	3	3
TOTAL	49	54
3. Other Transmitter (LPT's)		
22 2at Delhi for relay of Parliament proceedings & one at Srinagar	3	3
4. Extent of coverage		
a. Population (%)	87.0	87.0
b. Area (%)	72.0	72.0
5. Programme Production Centres	6	42
6. Channels in operation	17	17 domestic channels

DTH satellite television

Direct-to-Home (DTH) satellite television is becoming a buzzword in the satellite broadcast industry due to the fact that DTH offers immense opportunities to both broadcasters and viewers. Thanks to the rapid development of digital technology, DTH broadcast operators worldwide have been able to introduce a large number of new interactive applications in the television market besides a large number of entertainment programmes over a single delivery platform. In addition, since digital technology permits a highly efficient exploitation of the frequency spectrum, the number of TV channels that can be broadcast using digital technology is significantly higher than with analogue technology. The increased number of television channels allows the operator to satisfy the demand of a number of niche markets with dedicated transmissions.

In general, DTH service is the one in which a large number of channels are digitally compressed, encrypted and beamed from very high power satellites. The programmes can be directly received at homes. This mode of reception facilitates the use of small receive dish antennas of 45 to 60 cm diameter installed at convenient location in individual buildings without needing elaborate foundation /space etc. Also, DTH transmission eliminates local cable operator completely, since an individual user is directly connected to the service providers. However, a digital receiver is needed to receive the multiplexed signals and view them on a TV. DTH, in sharp contrast to Cable TV, lends itself to easy monitoring and control.

Transmission in Ku band is most appropriate and widely used for the purpose. All the encoded transmission signals are digital - thus providing higher resolution picture quality and better audio than traditional analog signals. All the advantages of the digital transmission, as applicable to the terrestrial transmission are relevant in the satellite transmission also.

Doordarshan, the national broadcaster in India, at present has a network of more than 1400 transmitters spread throughout the country and its signals are available to about 90 %(DD1) and 43% (DD-News) population of country. The prime duty of any national public service broadcaster is to make the programmes of national importance available to all its people and nationals. It was estimated that the coverage of remaining 10 % population with terrestrial (single channel) broadcast would cost enormously. Besides that, setting up of terrestrial transmitters in the uncovered areas would have taken a number of years (10 to 15 years).

Also, operation of terrestrial transmission would have required a huge manpower (a few thousand persons).

With the fast developments taking place in Satellite Broadcasting, it is but natural that Doordarshan has also come up with an alternative to get the required reach with an alternate technology option "Ku-band broadcasting" which is envisaged for the coverage of remaining population. This is a much cheaper and economical option as compared to the coverage through Terrestrial transmitters. Ku-band transmission will provide coverage in all uncovered areas including remote, border, tribal, hilly and inaccessible areas in one go within a short time.

With this coverage, the national broadcaster proposes to meet its obligation of covering the whole nation and its people not only with national channels, but also make available popular Doordarshan and some other free-to-air channels on its platform. In order to meet its obligations, it has also been decided that 10,000 receive systems (Dish and Set Top Box) would be provided free of cost at public institutions like Anganwadis, Schools, Public Health Centres, Panchayats, Youth Clubs, Cooperative Societies etc. in the uncovered areas. It may be pertinent to mention here that incidentally Doordarshan would be starting DTH service with Ku band broadcasting as not only uncovered areas are covered with its commencement, but also the whole country gets multi-channel service in one stroke. The signal will be available at each home directly without the use of any cable etc. and one will be able to receive the programmes with the help of a small receive segment.

The DD DIRECT+ envisages telecast of 30 free-to-air channels (containing both Doordarshan and private channels) initially and is likely to include more channels later on. Satellite Earth Station for uplink of signals has been setup at Delhi. Test transmission has already commenced and the commissioning of the service would take place shortly. NSS 6 is the high power Ku-band satellite hosting the DD DTH services. The free distribution of the receive systems is also being expeditiously done.

Future of DTH

Opportunities for DTH in India look great. Since cable has penetrated the Indian market in a big way with roughly 40 million C&S homes, it is imperative that in its first few years of operations, paid service of DTH will be focused on a niche market. This niche would basically constitute the rich segment from urban as well as rural areas due to the primary reason of high initial costs for DTH and the associated psychology of people. Since Doordarshan will be starting its novel free-to-air service on Ku band, it is likely to give the prospective private DTH operators tremors and nightmares. The most attractive part of the Doordarshan platform is going to be its low initial cost and no recurring expenditure. Many cable homes are likely to make a shift to its platform and the service is likely to show its full impact in the rural areas where cable service is not possible.

All in all, there exists a tremendous potential for direct to home broadcast in Indian market and it is projected that within three years, there would be around 2.5 million DTH subscribers in India. This figure is likely to increase due to the increase in TV and Cable households and also the growing multiple TV households, which would form a large percentage of the total subscriber base. Since India's population crossed the one billion mark, it is no surprise that satellite operators and programmers world-wide have set their eyes on the world's largest open market for DTH satellite TV services. The growing popularity of TV as a communication medium has resulted in the TV media sectors undergoing a rapid transformation.

How to receive DD DIRECT+ ?

Receive System includes a small satellite dish (which is an antenna for receiving a satellite broadcast signal); a digital integrated receiver/decoder (IRD) also called STB, which separates each channel and decompresses and translates the digital signal for viewing over a television; and a remote control. Investment on the part of subscriber for receiving DD-DIRECT signal is only one time on receive system and no recurring monthly expenditure will have to be incurred by the viewer. As compared to other DTH systems, where a huge activation fee and a monthly subscription fee is charged, the DD DIRECT+ can be received without payment of any activation fees. Price of a receive system is around Rs 3000/ to Rs 3500/-. Once the technology gets induced the demand for the receive systems will increase and the prices would further comedown.

Installation of the Receive System is very easy and does not take much time. However the viewer has to take the services of skilled technical personnel to get the dish installed and oriented towards the Satellite which is required to be carried out before the system starts receiving the DD DIRECT+ signals. Tuning/configuring the STB also is required to be done initially. Tuning procedure is normally supplied by the manufacturer along with the STB. Some of the parameters which are required to be fed to the IRD are mentioned therein and are also given under the heading 'Satellite in use'.

Gyandarshan

Gyandarshan, a major milestone in the field of educational

TV in India is a joint venture of Ministry of HRD, Information & Broadcasting, the Prasar Bharati and IGNOU. It was launched formally on 26th January 2000. Gyandarshan is envisaged as a public co-operative in which institutions such as the UGC/CEC, NCERT/CIET constitute the major stakeholders. The Gyandarshan channel, had a modest beginning on 10th January 2000 with a 2 hours daily test transmission (5 PM to 7 PM). Then on 26th January 2000 the channel was formally inaugurated. Its duration was increased to 4 hours (5 PM to 9 PM). In mid-February 2000 the transmission rose to 9 hours a day. By st June, 2000 it was extended to 16 hours and by 1st November, 2000 it became a 24 hour channel with non-stop transmission daily offering a rich fare of multi-faceted programming.

The channel has earmarked time slots for curriculum-based as well as career based programmes targeting various groups of learners. Special programmes on art, culture, science and technology, etc., having a wider appeal across different age groups are telecast. The unique feature of the channel is the high degree of interactivity. It is a people's channel which inspires, instills hope and provides the means. Gyandarshan is all set to usher in a learning society. The channel has lent support to the students of Secondary and Senior Secondary School through specially designed programmes by NCERT/CIET, SIET, NOS and others. It also covers topics ranging from science and technology to environment, computer education to career counseling.

The channel seeks to offer alternatives and substitutes to learners of various age groups and categories in the growing demand for quality education in the country. The 24 hour Gyandarshan channel is now accessible to an estimated 20 million viewers in 40 lakh cable homes spread all over India.

Telecommunications

In 1994 the Government of India issued its National Telecommunications Policy. The policy was issued in recognition of the "urgent need" to provide universal access to basic telecommunications services by 1997 and offers guidelines for entry of the private sector into basic telecommunications services. To facilitate private-sector participation, licensing procedures were established in the Department of Telecommunications in India, and equity participation for companies registered in India (with 51 or more percent Indian ownership) was anticipated. Private-sector licenses, however, were to be granted only for local (versus long-distance) telecommunications networks. An autonomous body, the Telecommunications Authority of India, was established to regulate private-sector activity.

India's telephone system, like many other aspects of telecommunications, is in the government sector, under the control of the Ministry of Information and Broadcasting. The modernization of the telephone system in India has been underway since 1986 when Mahanagar Telephone Nigam, a government corporation, was established to operate systems in Bombay and New Delhi, and Videsh Sanchar Nigam, also government owned, was set up as the overseas carrier. Progress was slow, however; the rest of the nation's service continued as a civil-service-run operation under the Department of Telecommunications until 1994 when basic telephone services were opened to private-sector competition.

The number of telephone connections in India rose from 800,000 in FY 1968 to 8 million in FY 1994. The system remains substandard by international standards, however, and there is a waiting list for connections of 2.8 million people. Sometimes several years elapse between application and installation of a telephone line. Close to 1 million new connections a year are being established in the mid-1990s. Plans for increasing the capacity of the system to handle more directly dialed calls were being implemented in the early 1990s, and 20 million lines should be in operation by FY 2000. This number is very low for a population that by then will probably exceed 1 billion.

Telephone line density was less than 0.7 per 100 persons in 1994, one of the lowest densities among the major nations of Asia. There also are submarine telecommunications cables linking India with Malaysia and the United Arab Emirates. Although the government is a major manufacturer of telephone equipment, the private sector--especially foreign ventures--is becoming increasingly involved in manufacturing in the mid-1990s and paging, cellular phone service, and electronic mail are being introduced.

Internet

The growth of the Internet as a market and a tool in India is a development which evokes global aspirations on its 50th anniversary of independence - as well as concerns about equitable access to the technology in the country. Form a humble dial-up network in the late 1980s to prospects of upto 40 private and government ISPs unleashing over two million domestic users in the coming year or two, the Internet has come a long way in India - but can go much further than the current user base of about a million users.

Today, India has more software companies with ISO 9000 certification than any other country. Its software industry has grown more than a hundredfold over the last decade, though it has less than 1 percent of the world software market share. For the local Internet market, numerous opportunities abound in Web design and business solutions. Some Indian companies are also actively courting Web outsourcing opportunities from foreign businesses. More ambitious organisations are targeting their products at other countries seeking effective country-positioning technologies.

In 1987, the first dial-up e-mail network was set up between NCST and IIT Bombay. In 1998, an international dial-up e-mail network connected NSCT in Bombay to a host in Amsterdam. In 1994, a satellite communications network was set up with assistance from the United Nations Development Programme (UNDP). And in August 1995, VSNL introduced commercial Internet access in India, now accounting for over 100,000 subscribers. The Internet access monopoly by VSNL was lifted by the Indian government on November 6, 11998, and NASSCOM (National Association of Software and Services Companies) predicts there may be as many as 8 million Internet users by year 2002. Thirteen prospective ISPs are targeting states and the major metros like Mumbai and New Delhi, and 21 are targeting only the larger cities. One ISP each has focused on the states of Karnataka, Andhra Pradesh, Gujarat and Punjab. In 1999, the number of cities and towns in India with Internet access is expected to go up from the current 40 to over 70.

Indian news on the Net, once largely the preserve of mailing lists and Usenet newsgroups, is increasingly available directly from the Web, thanks to online editions of English and local language news media. As in countries like the U.S. and Australia, recent releases of the Indian budget have been accompanied by extensive live coverage and analysis on numerous Web sites. The National Informatics Centre has launched Web sites for various arms of the government, including the Parliament and the ministries of finance, industry, and education, as well as state governments. The Indian search engine Khoj currently lists about 7,000 websites/pages focusing in India, now growing at about 25 a day.

About 3,000 companies in India are now online, and close to 500 companies across the country offer some sort of support in Web publishing (designing and hosting Web content). In India, the most popular ad destinations are Webzines and Web sites of newspapers and magazines. High-profile advertisers tend to be banks wishing to target an NRI audience, and info-tech giants like IBM and Intel. Non-English content in languages like Japanese, German, Spanish, Chinese and Portuguese is growing on the Web; Indian languages are poised for a similar explosion, if appropriate Webware tools are made readily available.

As for governance and regulations for the Internet, unfortunately, there seems to be a legal vacuum in Indian cyberspace. In areas ranging from the use of Internet telephony to recognition of online payment architectures, much lobbying and legislation needs to be done by all concerned Internet players. And high costs of Internet access and leased lines will ensure that the growth of the 'Net, Intranets, and Extranets will be at a steady but slow - frustratingly slow for some - growth rate. While the lifting of the government ISP monopoly has been a welcome development, challenges still remain in ensuring a level playing field between government players and the private sector.

Close to 20 players in the Indian ISP market have teamed together to form the ISP Association of India, to work on areas like pooling together resources for creating independent international Internet gateways. While the Department of Electronics and the National Task Force on

IT are lobbying aggressively for Internet telephony, one faction in the Group on Telecom is convinced it should not be legalized. The group's contention is that if Net telephony is allowed, it may lead to the collapse of the Department of Telecommunications (DoT). The Department of Electronics (DoE) has prepared the draft for a Bill, which if passed, will be known as the Information Technology Act. Andhra Pradesh Chief Minister Chandrababu Naidu has urged the Central Government to frame a national policy on information security and privacy, warning of increased crime in the area.

The IITs and the IIMs have only recently begun to offer courses and modules in areas like Web publishing and e-commerce. In a country of scarce resources, the Internet can truly enhance education. The professional training institutes have already launched some offerings in this area. For instance, IBM Global Services India and Aptech have announced a strategic e-business solutions partnership. IBM and Aptech would be offering courses in IBM products such as Net.Commerce, Firewall, VA Java, Lotus Notes and concepts like Internet security and web administration. On January 26, Rediff On The Net launched content catering to the needs of students, teachers, educationists and parents. Model test papers, on-line chat session to solve problems, career counselling and links to related sites will aim at attracting eager students to the site.

Spurred by the anticipated boom in the Indian Internet user base, a number of state governments have announced local Internet initiatives, ranging from online trade and investments services to high-tech corridors conducive to foreign investments. Chandrababu Naidu is talking about getting all the companies in his state on to the Internet, and creating transparent government services accessible online. Information and services to be provided via the Net will include land records, property taxes, birth and death data, and applications for certificates. Prime Minister Atal Bihari Vajpayee has talked about having a PC in every village.

Importance of Online Content

Much of the success of the Internet as a medium and as an economy depends on universal or near-universal access for citizens to cyberspace. But unlike ordinary telecommunications service, issues relating to access to the Internet do not stop at the level of the line and the device; that is where Net access issues begin. Since the Net is a two-way communications and publishing medium, access issues (especially in emerging economies) should also take into account what publishing and communication resources are available at the user end. Internet users, after all, are not just consumers but producers and active participants in the information economy (or "prosumers").

The Six C's of a successful national Internet agenda, then, could be aptly summed up as: connectivity, content, community, commerce, capacity and culture. In other words, national and local connectivity to the Net must also be coupled with locally relevant content and community groupings. Gearing up to meet all these challenges requires local capacity in terms of technical expertise and organisational/national leadership.

Following are seven key areas of development necessary for India to emerge as a prolific generator of online content, so as to effectively and proactively harness the Net.

I. *Content Sectors*

1. Publications (newspapers, magazines, academic journals) which are not yet online must be

encouraged to publish their information on the Web, target audiences in India and abroad, and provide value-added services like access to archived material. Seminars on this topic should be provided, in conjunction with Web publishers.

2. Content must also be provided in the business sector, geared towards creating a business marketspace. Constantly updated telephone/e-mail directories and yellow pages for businesses in each city and town must be made available online. Big businesses and the SOHO/SME segment must be encouraged to set up Web sites and get access to e-mail.

3. Special attention must be paid to the export/import sector. Directories of exporters, product catalogues, customs information, shipping/transport agencies, insurance agencies, third party audit/verification information must all be compiled online for one-stop access by importers and exporters. Linkages must be provided to existing trade databases published by organisations like the United Nations.

4. Content from non-profit organisations, public health groups and social service agencies must also be published online; a special grant should be set up for this purpose.

5. Special measures must be taken for providing online content rapidly during times of disaster like earthquakes and floods (eg. lists of victims and survivors, contact numbers of relief agencies, live news updates).

6. Libraries must be given grants to publish online catalogues of their books and periodicals.

7. The travel industry must work collectively in publishing content about airfares, train schedules, hotel reservations, car rentals, visas, maps, police stations, post offices, medical services, tourism destinations, scenic points, cultural highlights and local customs. This information should also be accessible via Internet kiosks in airports, train stations, bus stations, hotels, post offices and shopping centres. Such measures must be rolled out beginning with key tourism destinations like Agra, Goa, Kerala, etc.

8. Government departments and agencies must publish extensive content online, geared towards citizen services like land registration, tax information, appointments with officials, transparent accounting practices, employment opportunities, etc. 9. Initiatives must be launched to publish education-related content and services at all levels. Online educational content and instructional delivery must be used to extend the scarce resources of educational institutes across the country.

II. *Software and Web Tools*

1. Content generation must take place in Indian languages and English. The development and standardisation of Indian language software, fonts, and Web publishing tools must be promoted aggressively.

2. Where possible, use of freeware and shareware packages and tools should be encouraged instead of relying on costly proprietary software solutions, such as in the use of the Linux operating system and Apache Web server for digital publishing.

III. *Access, Devices, Infrastructure and Interfaces*

1. Cybercafes and Internet community centres should be created, to give more people access to the Net. Such centres must also provide basic training and resources for Web publishing.

2. World-class hosting infrastructure must be created in India so that local Web content is hosted within the country and not outside, thereby saving lucrative foreign exchange revenues. Indian IDCs (Internet Data Centres) must occupy pre-eminent positions within the regional Asian market.

IV. *Capacity*

1. Training centres and seminars should be set up for generation of internal and intra-organisational Internet content, via Intranet document management systems and Extranet-oriented flow of information.

2. Computer courses and curriculum in schools and colleges must be augmented to go beyond basic word processing and programming to include Web page design and online database management.

V. *Legal Issues*

1. Legal developments concerning content classification, regulation and enforcement in countries around the world must be tracked. Indian representatives from the industry, academia and government should try to be present in forums of the UN, WTO, OECD, G-7, ASEAN, APEC, etc. dealing with cyberspace content issues like intellectual property rights, copyright protection, online privacy, online crimes, and digital watermarks.

2. Online forums and periodic seminars/briefings must be conducted at the national and state levels to invite participation in policy making regarding national online content laws.
3. Draconian content laws which require censoring of material published on Web sites in India and abroad should be avoided. Where necessary, parental filtering solutions should be used to protect children from seeing objectionable content on the Web. But laws interfering with basic freedoms of speech and expression should be avoided.

VI. *Political Will*

1. A key focus on content should be to make a difference to the way service is delivered. In areas like making government procedures transparent, a lot of political will and muscle will be needed. For instance, in areas like land records and getting power connections, some unscrupulous middlemen tend to get involved; openness and transparency will threaten them, but the government must display the political to clean up these processes via open content publishing.

VII. *International Cooperation*

Many of the concerns facing India are also encountered by other developing nations in the world. Online and offline forums must be created and sustained to encourage discussion on digital content-related activities between India and other emerging economies. Encouraging signs along these seven dimensions are already emerging. India's Centre for Development of Advanced Computing has recently launched a multilingual Webware scheme called iLEAP-ISP scheme. A multilingual word processor with Internet and e-mail support in Indian languages will be made available free to all Internet subscribers through their respective ISPs.

3

Role of Mass Media in Democracy

The mass media constitute the backbone of democracy. The media are supplying the political information that voters base their decisions on. They identify problems in our society and serve as a medium for deliberation. They are also the watchdogs that we rely on for uncovering errors and wrongdoings by those who have power. It is therefore reasonable to require that the media perform to certain standards with respect to these functions, and our democratic society rests on the assumption that they do.

The most important democratic functions include surveillance of sociopolitical developments, identifying the most relevant issues, providing a platform for debate across a diverse range of views, holding officials to account for the way they exercise power, provide incentives for citizens to learn, choose, and become involved in the political process, and resist efforts of forces outside the media to subvert their independence. However, there is a growing concern that the mass media are not fulfilling these functions properly. Media critics claim that commercial mass media controlled by a few multinational conglomerates have become an antidemocratic force supporting the status quo. The news are more entertaining than informing, supplying mostly gossip, scandals, sex, and violence. Political news are more about personalities than about their ideologies.

The media hunt for scandals in the private lives of politicians and their families, but ignore much more serious consequences of their policies. They go after wounded politicians like sharks in a feeding frenzy. All too often, the media make us afraid of the wrong things. Minor dangers are hysterically blown out of proportions, while much more serious dangers in our society go largely unnoticed. The exaggerated fears often lead to unnecessary measures and legislation and "gonzo justice".

Even more alarming is the claim that certain mass media are promoting worthless alternative health products, thereby effectively conspiring with the industry to defraud consumers of billions of dollars every year. If all these claims have any merit at all, then we have to drastically revise our view of the way our democracy works. The *Concise Encyclopedia of Democracy* makes only brief mentioning of the possibility of political, commercial or other influences on the mass media. Most other treatises on the theory of democracy make no mentioning at all of any such problems. The political and cultural consequences of this alleged misinformation of the public are not fully explored.

Media Market

Most newspapers, radio- and TV stations get most or all of their income from advertisements and sponsoring. The media will therefore seek to optimally satisfy the interests of their advertisers, which are not necessarily coincident with the interests of the readers, listeners and viewers. The predominant view among economists is that free competition generally benefits society because it provides the most differentiated supply of commodities to the optimal price. This line of reasoning dominates European as well as American media policy.

It is well known, however, that free competition does not always consider all interests. The term market failure describes the situation where the free market forces do not automatically lead to maximal welfare (often defined as the sum of benefits to all parties). Market failure may occur, for example, when consumers are unable to evaluate the quality of a commodity, when third party interests are affected (externalities), or when production has large fixed costs. In the case of media financed by advertisements exclusively, the interests served are those of the advertisers. The interests of the media consumers are satisfied only insofar as these are coincident with the interests of the advertisers. There is no guarantee that public interests are served well. This is the reason why many countries have public radio- and TV stations with public service obligations.

Liberalizing the media market and relying on the free market forces are policies that are often used for the express purpose of making sure that all interests are served. Many theorists ignore, however, that the media not only satisfy consumer preferences, but also form them. Many economists assume that competition increases diversity. Numerous policy discussions have recommended increased competition as the best way to assure diversity which, it is assumed, will make sure that all interests are served well. However, this strategy has failed time and again because the underlying assumptions are wrong. It has been known for many years that there is a strong tendency towards wasteful duplication of the most popular program forms under free competition. There is considerable uncertainty over whether competition increases or decreases the diversity and quality of media products.

While moderate competition may increase diversity, it has been found theoretically as well as empirically that excessive competition may lead to decreased diversity. Assume, for example, that a country has two competing commercial TV-stations with each one channel. In this case they will most likely both try to maximize their market share by sending the same kind of programs that appeal to the broadest possible audience. But if, on the other hand, both channels are owned by the same TV-station, then the owner will seek to minimize competition between the two channels by sending different types of programs on the two channels. Most studies of the effect of market structure on the quality of mass media products use diversity as the only measure of satisfaction of consumer needs.

Diversity is the most objective criterion and the one that is most easily measured. Some authors explicitly state their unwillingness to use more subjective quality measures, but a few scientists have demonstrated that it can be done. Diversity may indeed be a poor measure of quality. If we assume that there is a positive relationship between production costs and the quality of a media product, and if we further assume that the total revenue from a particular niche of the media market is limited, then we can conclude that the more competitors there are to share the niche, the less income will each competitor have to spend on improving quality.

A diversity of program formats is hardly related to fairness, relevance, thorough investigation, or other requirements that we expect a democratic press to meet. The available studies of diversity therefore fail to capture the central problems related to the democratic role of the media.

It is necessary that media economists introduce other quality measures in studies of the relationship between market structure and the quality of mass media products. Lacking better criteria, we may use production costs as a reasonable measure of quality. Many mathematical models are based on the assumption that a TV program or other media product satisfying a specific demand is produced at fixed costs.

The product is either produced or not produced, depending on whether it is profitable. This simplification fails to cover the easily observable fact that a media product satisfying a specific demand may be produced in varying degrees of quality at varying costs. If many competitors share the same product niche then each competitor will have less income to cover production costs and will therefore be forced to make a product of lower quality. For example, if many competitors share the market for political news, then each competitor will have few resources for investigative journalism and will only be able to uncritically relay the messages from politicians and news agencies.

Several studies have found a negative correlation between competition and news quality. You may expect that at least free competition leads at to an optimal satisfaction of the interests of the advertisers, but this is not the case according to a study of the American radio broadcasting market. Theoretical calculations show that free competition may favour products with high variable costs rather than products with high fixed costs; because as the number of suppliers gets higher, each supplier has less income for covering the fixed costs. When applied to mass media, this theory means that more competition may lead to lower quality if we assume that there is a positive correspondence between production costs and quality.

Several observations confirm this. If we assume that media products of higher quality can attract a larger audience, then we must conclude that excessive competition benefits neither consumers nor advertisers. Denmark is regarded as a good test case because it had a state monopoly TV station until 1988 when one, and later more, commercial TV stations were introduced. The introduction of competing TV stations were motivated by the desire to improve the quality and diversity of the program supply and to make sure that minority interests were satisfied.

The development of the mass media during the last several decades is characterized by the following main tendencies:

— *Convergence*: Different media like newspapers, radio, television, telephone and internet are increasingly being fused together, technologically as well as economically.

— *Concentration*: Media companies are being merged together and controlled by fewer owners. This concentration is horizontal (several media under the same owner) as well as vertical (several links in the "food chain" under the same company group). Different media bring news from the same sources.

— *Globalization*: The media are owned by multinational companies broadcasting across borders.

Commercialization: Advertisements are sneaked into entertainment as well as news stories. The distinctions between advertisements, news and entertainment are increasingly blurred. Audience groups with less spending money are not considered.

— *Commercial influence*: Advertisers and owners have influence on editorial decisions. Trivialization: More sex and violence. More prying into the private lives of celebrities. The media avoid controversial issues and serious debates. Debates are reduced to an entertaining clash between personalities, resembling a boxing match, where the issue of controversy has only secondary importance.

Several media scholars agree that the main cause of these tendencies is the liberalization of the media market. Stories are selected for profitability rather than relevance.

POPULARIZATION

The simulation of proximity is an important element in popularization. A political decision can be difficult to explain in abstract terms. It helps when the medium shows an ordinary person telling what the consequences of the decision is for him or her. The audience feel that a story is more convincing when they see an example they can identify with. But in fact it is less credible because the example may not be representative. Advertising has a profound influence on the choice of programs. TV advertisers prefer to have their commercials shown in association with soft entertainment. Ideal from the advertisers' point of view are shows such as competitions where one can win sponsored merchandise, or soap operas that portray a privileged lifestyle where luxurious goods give status. This does not provide good conditions for the political debate. It is difficult to find sponsors for serious political debates because these do not make the viewers relax and because some of the viewers will disagree with the points of view presented.

Furthermore, the commercial media are not very inclined to cover controversial issues in a balanced way.

People prefer to hear points of view that they agree with. It is therefore adverse to the media's economy to view a controversy from both sides and present alternative points of view. The media are prone to choose side in a controversy; and if later evidence should favour the opposite side, they are likely to keep silent about the matter rather than loosing face. Disclaimers are not profitable. This is a self-amplifying process. The more the media create consensus about a particular issue through biased coverage, the fewer proponents of the opposite view will there be to balance the issue, and the more difficulties will these proponents have in gaining access to the media.

Nowhere is this bias problem worse than in crime reporting. The media often take a stance on the question of guilt before a verdict has been made. The police and the prosecutor are often very willing to express themselves because it gives them a PR gain and an opportunity to ask the public for help in solving crimes, while a suspect has few, if any, possibilities and resources for replying. It is very unlikely that judges can resist being influenced by this when a media frenzy has created a public outcry against a suspect. The legal possibilities of forcing the media to publish disclaimers or to give a voice to alternative points of view are quite illusory, and the means of sanctions are far from effective.

The printed media cannot compete with the ability of the electronic media to keep their audience spellbound by strong sense impressions. The newspapers have their strength in the possibilities for in-dept analysis of social and other topics. However, this possibility is not fully exploited because the journalistic resources are limited by economic competition, and because this parameter of competition only gives access to a limited niche of the reader market. Many papers and magazines therefore compete on news about celebrities and topics that appeal to the emotions. Everything that is dangerous, deviant or wrong has a prominent place, especially in those papers that are mainly sold from newsstands. They want to have a new scandal on the front page every day in order to tempt people to buy the paper.

Radio- and TV-channels based on advertising use fewer horror effects, because this would conflict with the principle of bringing the viewers into a buying-mood. This does not improve the journalistic and artistic quality, however. Many media workers are frustrated that their creativity is curbed by the economic structures, and the situation is hardly better for advertisement-free commercial media, such as home video and pay-TV.

Selection of News

Traditionally, media scholars have described the selection of news with concepts like gatekeeping and newsworthiness. These concepts are based on a scenario where an editor or journalist sorts incoming news according to news value and political criteria. Social problems involving fear and danger are very attractive to the media and such topics often make up a significant part of the stories. The excessive focus on fear and danger has important political implications. The dissemination of news may occasionally be so selective and biased that you may accuse the media of manipulation and propaganda, for example in connection with war. But in general we do not have to impute dishonest motives on producers in order to explain media distortion.

Most cases of selection in the news media can be explained by structural factors, such as the organization of news agencies, financing, dependence on sources, and ratings competition. The news coverage is determined by such factors as the journalist's knowledge, predefined news formats, deadlines, the authority of sources, and the possibility of obtaining good pictures. The media may not publish a story if it does not fit into an existing format or if it does not relate to an existing theme. The media are self-referential to such a degree that the newsworthiness of a story may be a self-fulfilling prophecy. A topic is interesting because all the media tell about it.

Violent crimes and sex crimes are areas where the news reporting is highly selective. The media prefer emotional stories, sobbing victims, and stories that fit into the political agenda and confirm the image of the criminal as a monster. The use of expert sources has been found to be extraordinarily selective. The media play a key role in the public debate on risks and dangers, but their coverage is highly selective. At times the media exaggerate minor risks where reassurance would be more sensible. In other cases they ignore serious risks, e.g. when new technologies are uncritically described as progress. It is an essential problem when informing about risks and dangers that the concept is abstract and invisible until it manifests itself in a specific accident or disaster.

The media do not like to report on hypothetical risks. They need a real event that the theoretical discussion can be related to and real people to give the story a human-interest dimension. Risk analysts have been criticized for ignoring these problems and not focusing enough on the mass media. The media may be attracted to risks, but not unconditionally so. They are not good at maintaining attention to a theoretical risk when there are no actual events to make the topic newsworthy. There is an unusually fierce competition between sources when it comes to informing about risks, dangers and other social problems.

Various interest groups, politicians and experts seek to promote each their agenda on which dangers to fear. The media inevitably play a key role in this conflict because their choice of sources influences the definitions of dangers. The politicians have to take a stance to whatever problem the media place high on the agenda. The media's decision on who is allowed to define a problem, or whether the problem is mentioned at all, is not controlled in a democratic way.

Mass Media Influence People's Attitudes

There are many different theories about how mass media influence people's attitudes, worldview, and behaviour. While historical as well as contemporary observations are full of examples attesting to the power of the mass media to influence people, early experimental studies have failed to confirm the assumption that mass media have a strong power to change people's attitudes. This discrepancy between experiments and real world observations was solved with the introduction of theories of cognitive processing, such as agenda setting, framing, and priming.

Cognitive Processing

The human cognitive capacities are limited. The newsmedia contain huge amounts of information, much more than any person can possibly handle. It is therefore theorized that humans are economizing the processing of the information they receive from newsmedia as well as from other sources. The first step in the handling of information is selection. People chose which newsmedia to read, watch, and listen to, according to their needs and preferences. They are screening the media for interesting information, ignoring topics that appear to be irrelevant to them, redundant, boring, or too complicated to comprehend. People routinely reject stories that appear too remote or too complicated simply to save time and energy. Stories that catch people's attention are those that are relevant to their personal interests, but also general human-interest stories such as reports about crimes and accidents, health, sports, entertainment, and celebrities.

The producers of news have learned to snare people's attention by giving most stories a personal touch. Once a story has been selected for attention, the cognitive processing of the story is further economized by schematic thinking. Humans use what has been called knowledge structures or schemata as mental templates that people and events are fitted into. This process facilitates the integration of new information into existing knowledge. Since news sources usually present the news in isolated snippets without sufficient background, the schemata allow the receivers to embed the news into a meaningful context. This process also facilitates discarding redundant information that already exists in the schema as well as information that conflicts with previous knowledge that still appears to be sound.

People often misunderstand stories, either because they do not have an appropriate schema for interpreting the story, or because they apply the schema that comes first to mind rather than the schema that is most appropriate. Well-informed people have a rich collection of schemata that makes it easier to process new information. Thus, the information-rich become still richer.

Agenda-setting

The effect of agenda-setting is epitomized in the famous quote by Bernard Cohen, saying that the press "may not be successful much of the time in telling people what to think, but it is stunningly successful in telling its readers what to think about". People need to orient themselves in a complex world full of complex issues. In the absence of other cues, people tend to judge the importance of issues from their salience in the media and to focus their attention on those presumably most important issues. There is plenty of evidence that the media have a strong influence on people's perception of which issues are important and which problems they want their government to do something about.

The agenda-setting influence of the news media increases when the need for orientation among the audience is high. The agenda-setting effect is lower for obtrusive issues that people can observe directly, as well as for other issues that the audience is well informed about. The media have little power to set the agenda when people have sufficient political knowledge to counterargue the claims made by the media. Furthermore, the agenda-setting effect is stronger for concrete issues that are easy to visualize than for abstract issues.

While the powerful effect of agenda-setting is generally accepted among media scholars, there is some uncertainty about who sets the agenda. Some studies show that politicians have a strong influence on the agenda of mass media, at least in areas such as economic policy. But, as discussed in the preceding paragraphs, the media may themselves put attention-catching issues on the agenda for economic reasons, especially sensationalistic issues involving danger, crime, sex, and celebrity scandals. Access to the public agenda is a limited and precious resource that special interest groups often compete for, as discussed below.

Priming

Closely related to agenda-setting is the effect of priming. Priming refers to the fact that one piece of media information can influence how we interpret subsequent pieces of information by making us tune in to certain areas of thought. Thus, the news media can influence the criteria by which political candidates are judged by calling attention to some issues and ignoring others before the speech of the candidate. The priming effect is often explained in terms of schematic thinking. When evaluating new information or making a decision, people tend to apply the information and schemata that are most readily accessible or available in memory at that moment, rather than conduct a complete and comprehensive search and examination of information.

Framing

Another cognitive effect, which may be explained as a consequence of schematic thinking, is framing. Framing refers to the frame of reference within which an issue is described. For example, a news broadcast about the development of new nuclear weapons can variously be framed as a story about technological progress, about military budgets, about military strategy, about balance of power between nations, about arms race versus disarmament, or about radiation hazards. The way the story is framed can have a strong influence on people's attitudes towards the issue. It is often assumed that framing is a kind of second-level agenda setting in the sense that it makes certain aspects of an issue more salient in such a way as to promote a particular problem definition.

However, it has been argued that framing influences how audiences think about issues, not by making aspects of the issue more salient, but by determining which schemata are activated in the interpretation of the incoming information. While Entman's often cited definition of framing implies that the effect of framing is likely to be intentional, Scheufele's model implies that framing is based on subtle nuances in wording and syntax so that the effect of framing is most likely unintentional. Since every story must have a frame, whether the journalist pays attention to framing or not, we cannot assume that the effects of framing are always intentional. Several theorists make a distinction between frames in the media and frames in the minds of the audience.

A media frame is "a central organizing idea or story line that provides meaning to an unfolding strip of events..." Audience frames are defined as "mentally stored clusters of ideas that guide individuals' processing of information". These definitions should be preferred because they have a better theoretical foundation and because they make no assumption about whether a particular media frame is intended to promote a particular audience frame. A review of the studies on framing finds that the concept is often vaguely defined and there is more research to do. On the other hand, the review leaves no doubt that framing in some cases can have a profound effect on the attitudes, worldview, and behaviour of the audience.

The commercialization and trivialization of news media has a strong influence on how issues are framed in the commercial news media. Framing political news around the strategies of politicians rather than issues makes the audience perceive the motives of politicians as egoistic, whereby a cynical view on politics may be fostered. Stories about social problems are often framed with a focus on people rather than principles, single events rather than themes, and easily understandable proximate causes rather than deeper and more complex causes. This choice of framing influences the attribution of responsibility for the problems, the causal attribution, and the remedies that will be chosen to ameliorate the problems in question.

The media will often find some person to blame for a problem, but without a deeper focus on the social structures that caused the problem, it is unlikely that an effective solution to the problem will be found and accepted. Entertainment abhors ambiguity. Once a particular interpretation has been applied to a conflict, it is unlikely that the media will reframe the issue. Without seeing an issue from more than one side, it is unlikely that the conflict or problem will be solved in a sensible way.

Crime reporting is just one example of this effect, and admittedly a controversial one (differing frames may indeed explain why this issue has become controversial). The pervasive media focus on people rather than principles, events rather than themes, and simple rather than deep causes, is adversely affecting the problem-solving capabilities of democratic societies on a broad variety of issues, ranging from poverty to international conflicts.

Cultivation theory

Not only news and documentaries can influence people's perception of the world, but also fiction and entertainment shows. Cultivation theory is a research tradition, which assumes that there are certain repetitive and pervasive patterns of images and ideologies dominating most genres of television shows and films. If people spend several hours a day, year after year, watching television, and if every show they watch is full of violence, then people may come to believe that the world is full of violence. This is the kind of hypotheses that cultivation studies are trying to prove.

There can be no doubt that the television world is different from the real world. News and drama alike contain more crime and violence than the real world. The proportion of violent crimes to nonviolent crimes is much higher in TV than in the real world. The characters portrayed in TV drama are not representative of the population at large. There are more men than women and an over-representation of people in prestigious professions. Numerous studies have found that heavy TV-viewers tend to overestimate the amount of violence in society, the risk of falling victim to a violent crime, the fraction of the population engaged in law enforcement, the fraction of the population with prestigious professions, the fraction of the population that have marital discords and extramarital affairs, etc. The observed effects are relatively weak, but consistent and statistically significant.

The effects of receiving the high dose of crime and violence from television have been called the mean world syndrome. People become fearful of falling victim to violent crime and take drastic measures to protect themselves and their children - measures that are out of touch with the objective risk. The fearful people become authoritarian and easy victims of political manipulation. Many Cultivation theorists assume that the pervasive patterns of TV images are shaped by commercial influence.

A few studies in countries where non-commercial television has a significant impact, find the "mean world" effect to be smaller than in the USA. The hypothesis of commercial influence is further supported by a few international comparisons that find the cultivation effects to be stronger in countries where commercial television dominates than in countries with predominantly noncommercial television. The very broad-based focus has made cultivation studies vulnerable to criticism. Evidently, some TV genres contain more violence than others, and different genres have different effects on people's worldview.

Critics of cultivation research point out that the correlations may be spurious, while adherents of the paradigm emphasize that no strong mediating variables have been found and that the results are quite stable over different research conditions. Most cultivation studies are based on surveys. A survey can prove correlation, but not causation. It is theoretically impossible to tell on the basis of a correlation between TV viewing habits and attitudes whether viewing habits influence attitudes, or attitudes influence viewing habits, or whether some unidentified extraneous variable influence both.

In fact, one study, which observed an association between the viewing of crime drama and authoritarian aggression, found both directions of causality to be equally plausible. The position of cultivation theorists towards the question of causality is sometimes quite inconsistent. Leading theorists state that causal models are impossible, or even irrelevant. Yet the same theorists discuss causal models all the time. In fact, the whole paradigm rests on the assumption that cultivation is a long-term cumulative effect, and this assumption makes no sense unless a direction of causality is assumed. An irrefutable proof for the direction of causality is only possible with experimental manipulation of TV viewing patterns. Unfortunately, most cultivation researchers discount such experimental studies because experiments focus on particularistic short-term effects, while the cultivation research project emphasizes the long-term combined effect of the viewing of all TV genres.

A few experimental studies have found significant effects of relatively short-term exposure on the attitudes of

TV viewers, but most experimental studies are concerned with measuring behaviour (especially violent behaviour) rather than attitudes. A strong indication of the direction of causality has recently been obtained, however, from an improved understanding of the cognitive mechanisms underlying the cultivation effect. These mechanisms, which have been confirmed experimentally, cannot easily be accounted for if the causality is spurious or reversed. When asked to estimate, for example, the incidence of violence in society, people tend to economize their mental processing effort and give a heuristic answer based on the ease with which instances of violence can be recalled. Experimental conditions that induce a more systematic information processing can make test persons discount TV as a reliable source of information and give more accurate answers.

Likewise, it is known from cognitive psychology and endocrinology that concrete and emotional accounts make a stronger impression than abstract descriptions. In accordance with this theory, it has been found by experiments that people judge the incidence of particular phenomena by the number of examples in the media rather than by statistical accounts when both examples and statistics are presented in the media. Likewise, examples that evoke emotions or are presented in an emotional fashion make a stronger and more lasting impression than non-emotional presentations.

Many studies have found that the media have little power to change people's opinions, but more power to reinforce existing views. One may hypothesize that the media have a strong effect the first time a new issue is discussed. In fact, several studies have found that media effects are stronger for issues that people are unfamiliar with. Communication studies have traditionally been divided between the study of mass media and the study of interpersonal communication. Recently, it has been argued that this is a false dichotomy because the mass media may inspire interpersonal communication. Rogers attributes the findings of many studies that mass media effects are small to the fact that they do not include the secondary effect of interpersonal communication.

In fact, the two-step flow model of communication has been known for many years: The mass media influence some people who, in turn, influence other people. A few recent studies have found very strong media effects in cases where the media have prompted people to discuss an issue with their families and friends. The influence of the media is not unidirectional. Among the people influenced by the media are the elites and opinion leaders whose opinions appear in the mass media. This circular flow of communication may obviously amplify certain opinions. Another self-amplifying process is the "spiral of silence".

Noelle-Neumann discovered that people might be reluctant to voice unpopular opinions for fear of social isolation. This effect may cause the amplification of mainstream opinions or opinions that are perceived as growing in popularity, while minority opinions are suppressed. Such a mechanism may explain fashions and fads. Several studies have measured the "spiral of silence" effect by asking people whether they would voice their opinion in a hypothetical situation. These studies have found a quite weak, though significant, effect. One field study, which placed unsuspecting people in a situation where they were actually asked to present their opinion, found a stronger effect. These secondary effects, some stronger than others, all point in the same direction: The effect of the mass media is stronger when secondary effects are taken into account than when the direct effect of media messages on each individual are measured.

Sociological theory

In the sociological theory of Jürgen Habermas, the mass media are seen as controlled by political and economic forces, which have an interest in manipulating the audience. This compromises the legitimacy of the communicative power exercised by the mass media. The political manipulation is a kind of opinion making and PR, where the media not only transmit debates, but also create and shape them. The commercial manipulation uses the carefully designed and tested psychological methods of advertising. The media explore themes and identification possibilities that appeal to the unconscious dispositions of the audience in order to attract attention. Habermas mentions the following themes as attracting common interest: romance, religion, money, children, health, and animals.

The German political scientist Peter Klier criticizes Habermas' manipulation hypothesis because absolute objectivity does not exist. Klier thinks that the amount of information in modern society is so huge that media as well as citizens and politicians have to make a very strict selection. Members of the public can neither grasp the many topics, nor penetrate sufficiently deep into a particular topic to fulfill the role that they are supposed to, according to the norms of democracy. Klier thinks that this selection is such a big problem that no manipulation hypothesis is needed for concluding that democracy has a legitimacy problem. He stresses that people's reality image is more determined by the media-reality the more they are dependent on selective media and the less their chances are of getting corrective information from primary sources.

Niklas Luhmann, in his social systems theory, sees communication as a fundamental process in any social system. The communication forms a triple selection process:

1. selection of information at the sender,
2. selective attention at the receiver,
3. the selecting effect of the received information.

The communication is very much controlled by the media in modern society. Luhmann describes the mass media as a self-referential and self-maintaining (autopoietic), almost autonomous system. Unfortunately, Luhmann does not go very far in his analysis of how this media system is integrated into the bigger social system. Luhmann finds that the most important selection criteria of the media are the following: surprising news, topicality, conflicts, quantitative data, local relevance, as well as scandals and norm violations in relation to individual actors and moral judgments. Luhmann is not clear in the question of whether the media distort reality, because he emphasizes that there is no objective measure to evaluate the media reports against. He tries to evade the problem by saying that the media are accused of manipulating, rather than just saying that they manipulate. We also have to accept that the media fit reality into certain frames of reference, because there is no other option.

However, this relativist line of thought does not deter Luhmann from giving specific examples of how the media influence society by their selectivity. He mentions the Gulf war, AIDS, and immigrant crimes as examples. He even recognizes that the media may provide falsehoods if the need for news and sensations overweigh the risk that the deception be revealed. Unfortunately, Luhmann only mentions the role of the mass media superficially in his book on *risk sociology*. Risk is a subset of danger, and a topic that has given rise to at least three different research traditions: risk sociology, risk analysis, and risk communication. Because of the prominence of the topics of risk and danger in the mass media, and because of the important political implications of the intense focus and possible exaggeration of certain dangers, we may find it worthwhile to look more into these areas of study.

As a parallel to framing theory, there is much importance attached to the influence of semantics and symbols in risk sociology. People are not good at evaluating risks and making rational choices based on small probabilities. The choice of which risks to accept and which to combat is a social process depending on the social organization. The perception of a risk is malleable, as a result of negotiations and struggles between different experts, authorities and action groups who are providing competing views and definitions of technological risks. In these struggles, the concepts of risks are often used to legitimize or challenge hierarchies of power.

However, risk sociologists pay surprisingly little attention to the role of the media in selecting who is given the opportunity to speak and thus to gain power and influence by promoting a particular definition of a particular risk. Mary Douglas tells us that what we fear most are the things that disturb our sense of the order of nature. Her studies are based on tribal societies where modern mass media are nonexistent. Subsequently, she has tried to apply the same theories to modern societies, together with Aaron Wildavsky. The analysis of the environment protection movement performed by these two anthropologists has been interpreted as a claim that these organizations create fictive risks in order to consolidate their internal organization.

Risk sociologists may have ignored the significance of the mass media, but this is not the case for the sociology of deviance and the closely related sociology of social issues.

The objects of study of these disciplines overlap quite a lot with the aforementioned risk sociology. It is therefore very odd that these branches of sociology apparently have developed largely independently of each other with very little mutual inspiration. The sociology of deviance is a study of how society defines certain persons, phenomena or behaviors as deviant and dangerous. The dangerous is thus a social construct. Society can control unwanted behaviors by defining them as sinful or sick. Whoever has success in setting the norms for what is considered deviant and dangerous and promoting their particular interpretation of the deviance has thus gained a key position in the social power apparatus.

Sometimes, a social deviance is considered so dangerous that it must be combated with the most draconian means. Such a manifestation of exaggerated fear is called a witch-hunt or moral panic. These persecutions have been compared with magic rituals in accordance with Mary Douglas' theory. In modern society, there is a fierce competition for defining what is dangerous to society. Numerous organizations and lobbying groups compete for setting the agenda for the discussion of social problems in order to gain influence and get more resources for their particular cause. This has very aptly been called the social problems marketplace.

Throughout the times, various professions like priests, lawyers, psychologists, psychiatrists, neurologists, etc. have had monopoly on making statements about certain dangerous deviancies. Thereby they gain power and influence through what has been called issue ownership. Many sociologists have described how certain social problems get inflated to hysterical proportions because of the way they are exposed in the media. Media-created fears have made people change their lifestyles, have changed the nature of social policies and undermined the process of justice.

Suffice it to mention that the most viable approach seems to be contextual constructionism. This allows us to use statistics and other relatively more objective measures as reference when evaluating media claims. Whatever method we use for evaluating dangers, we have to accept a certain inaccuracy and admit that there are disagreements on which measures to use. This inaccuracy means that we can only detect big distortions in the media, not small distortions. Not seldom, however, the exaggerations or downplayings in the media are so gross that they will be obvious to everybody.

Risk analysis is a research tradition based on statistics, psychology and sociology. Risk analysts have found that experts evaluate risks on the basis of statistical criteria, while lay people tend to base their evaluation on political and moral criteria and on how individual risks affect people. The characteristics of different risks have been divided into two main factors according to the so-called psychometric model: Factor 1 comprises risks that are unknown to the persons affected, unknown to science, new, involuntary, and with slow effect. Factor 2 characterizes risks that have fatal, dreaded and catastrophic consequences as well as consequences for future generations. It has been found that people's fear and their demand for risk-reducing intervention is influenced much more by factor 2 than by factor 1.

Slovic finds that people's emotional response is primary to their attitude towards risks, and that their evaluation of advantages and disadvantages of risky activities is secondary and at least partially determined thereby. It is also important to what degree people have trust in the organizations or authorities that are supposed to control risks. It is noteworthy, that trust is easier to break down than to build up. Sources of bad news are regarded as more trustworthy than sources of reassurance.

A single investigation finding that a certain activity is risky has more impact than a large number of investigations finding no risk. Risk analysts have set up a model of how the social effects of a risk are amplified or attenuated when channelled through the different units of society. The direct effect of the risk factor in terms of damage or exposure to danger has influence on people's risk perception directly as well as through the mass media. The risk perception so formed gives rise to individual as well as collective reactions, which may have a range of cultural and socioeconomic consequences. These consequences often feed back on the risk factor with the effect that it is either decreased or increased.

Risk Communication: People tend to evaluate the probability associated with a risk on the basis of the amount of information they receive about the risk factor. The perception of a risk is thus shaped by the amount of media coverage and the vividness of this information. The media coverage is determined by factors such as causality, responsibility and blame, according to agenda setting research. Framing also has a strong effect. For example, people's attitude towards a risk or danger depends on whether it has been described in strictly scientific and statistical terms, or the media have focused on uncertainty, economy, health, environment, who is affected, justice, equality, etc..

Scholars of risk communication tell us that it is important how the responsible authorities inform the population about risks. The population should be kept informed about the newest knowledge about technological risks and the efforts to reduce these risks in order to build up trust. It is necessary to bridge the gap between technical descriptions and people's personal perception of security. An information vacuum is created if the responsible organizations ignore or deny a risk. The population, the media, and grassroots organizations will seek to fill this vacuum with information from other sources. The lack of trust that arises leads to an amplification of the conflict with increased media coverage and excessive fear as a result. This may often force the authorities to implement quite drastic measures against the risk that they originally tried to downplay. The handling of the mad cow disease by the British government is a good example of how a problem that the authorities originally denied developed into a major moral panic which in the end forced the society to spend enormous sums of money on fighting the problem.

Cultural selection theory is a theory that explains social change based on selection events. Humans may make conscious decisions based on intelligent planning as well as unconscious or irrational decisions. All decisions count as selection events. Selection events can also be caused by external influences, the environment, or be necessitated by the logic of the social structure. The systematic study of selection mechanisms shows that the combined effect of many small selection events can bring about macroscopic changes in the social structure. These social changes are sometimes planned and beneficial, but they may as well be unplanned, unexpected and undesired. An important advantage of cultural selection theory over other models of social change is that it better explains undesired developments.

When applying this theory to the mass media, we already know that news and stories are selected by the media, and the selection criteria have already been discussed. But there is also a selection going on at a higher level, namely the economic competition between mass media. The relentless economic competition forces the media to concentrate on those topics that immediately catch our attention and make us buy today's newspaper or stay tuned on the TV channel through the commercial breaks. Serious quality media that do not mesmerize their audience with psychological means get fewer customers and thus less revenue from advertisements. The reduced income forces them to cut down on journalistic staff whereby the quality is reduced and more readers or viewers fall away. This vicious circle continues until the medium goes bankrupt or changes its policy.

The discipline of evolutionary economics applies selection theory to socioeconomic systems. The economic selection that results from competition between news media is taking place at a higher level than the selection decisions of journalists and other gatekeepers. The economic selection may therefore be able to override the selection at the lower level by forcing those media organizations out of business that do not let economic considerations determine their selection and shaping of stories. This means that the media can, and do, develop in directions that no journalist or editor wishes. Many journalists are frustrated by the increasing tabloidization of their media and try to improve the standards, but to no avail.

We now know that those media that survive on the conditions of a free market economy are the ones that are best at catching people's attention. Some of the most important survival factors for primeval man were food, danger, sex, and children. It is deeply ingrained in every human being that these topics catch our attention wherever we meet them. For example, it has always been of vital importance to collect knowledge about everything that is dangerous. Therefore, we listen attentively when the TV tells about disasters, and we always buy the newspaper when the front page tells about dangerous criminals. Such attention-catching topics are metaphorically called buttons.

The psychological appeal in the media lies not only in the choice of topics but also in the way they are framed. A message is more appealing when it is focused on a real person that people can identify with. Therefore, the media prefer to give a story a personal angle rather than discussing abstract principles. Thus, political debates are often presented as personal conflicts between politicians rather than as discussions about ideologies. The personality, private life, and media appeal of a politician thus becomes more important than his ideological stance.

Concept of Authoritarianism

Some studies have indicated that the viewing of fear-provoking television programs cultivates authoritarianism. The concept of authoritarianism has been widely used and studied in social psychology for half a century. Unfortunately, this concept is strongly criticized for being vaguely defined and politically biased. Therefore, the cultural r/k theory is preferred here as an alternative to the theory of authoritarianism. With a theoretical basis in cultural selection theory, the r/k theory avoids the political bias and accusations of psychopathology that lies implicitly in the diagnosis of authoritarianism. The cultural r/k scale, which may be seen as a replacement for the authoritarianism scale, is applicable not only to individuals, but also to entire cultures and cultural products.

A culture and its population will, according to this theory, adapt to the environment in which the society finds itself and, more specifically, to the need for defence against factors that threaten the nation or social group. The perception of a bellicose neighbour state as a security threat will give rise to a kind of psychological armament in the citizens who see their nation or tribe as threatened. The solidarity and feeling of group identity will be strengthened. It has been discovered that these social psychological reactions give rise to a whole series of emergent cultural phenomena. The political structure will be more hierarchical because people feel the need for a strong leader.

The ideology will go in the direction of saying that individuals exist for the sake of the society, rather than vice versa. Religious life will be stricter. Discipline will be harsh and the tolerance for deviants will go down. Sexual morals will also be stricter, and the birthrate will go up. Interestingly, it has been found that these cultural changes are also reflected in the artistic production. Architecture, pictorial art, fiction, and even music becomes more formalistic, embellished and perfectionist so as to achieve a cognitive congruence between the art and the social system where political and religious leaders have a grandiose and majestic status.

Media studies clearly show the consequences of strong competition between the mass media. The media are trying to generate a sense of personal proximity. Political disagreements are presented as a clash between personalities rather than between ideological principles. The stories often appeal to the emotions rather than to the intellect. Advertisers prefer soft entertainment and shun controversy. Relaxing entertainment may not suffice for attracting the attention of viewers or readers, however. In order to survive in the competition for attention, the media often turn to emotional and attention-catching subjects involving crime, fear, danger, and of course sex and gossip. There is a remarkable consistency among different scientific disciplines in the finding that certain topics like these are used repeatedly in the media for catching attention.

Media owners define the overall editorial policy of a medium. Economic factors determine the amount of journalistic investigation and cultural production that can be afforded. A highly competitive market with wasteful duplication of the most popular genres leaves few economic resources to spend on heightening the quality of each program. Economic considerations may force the media to deploy an attention-catching strategy by emphasizing entertainment, emotional and personalized stories, sex, violence, gossip, etc. Economy determines the influence of advertisers and sponsors on the types of programs and stories that are being published. Sponsors also have an influence through sponsored cultural events and sports events that may not take place unless they are profitable to the sponsors.

The news are obtained from sources such as politicians, opinion leaders, experts, professionals, police, organizations, and ordinary people who happen to be involved in a newsworthy situation. These sources can influence the media, not only through the stories they tell, but also by rewarding or punishing certain media by providing or withholding desired information. The editors and journalists who produce stories obviously have an influence through their personal engagement as well as their professional, ideological and ethical principles. Technology determines how many media channels we can have and which formats are possible and attractive. Government regulation may impose additional ethical principles such as fairness requirements and public service obligations.

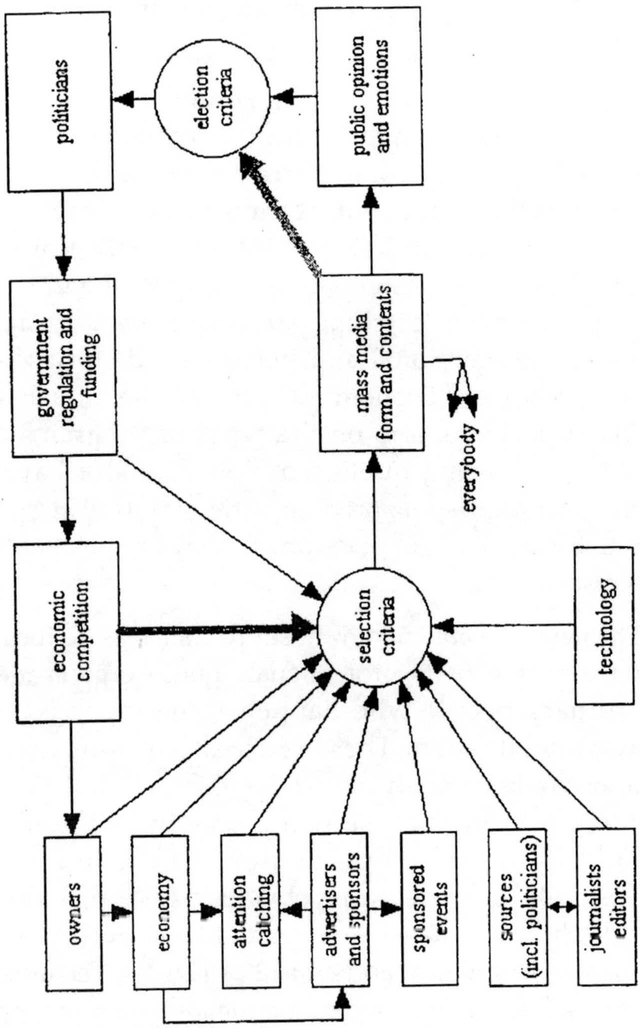

Figure 1. Integrated model showing the role of mass media in democratic society

All these factors influence the form and contents of the media products. However, the most important implication of the integrated model is that the degree of economic competition between the mass media is a meta-factor, which determines the weight of the other factors. A strongly competitive market situation may force the media producers to give more weight to considerations of attention-catching and to the wishes of the advertisers and less weight to ideology and ethics. Ideals of fairness, relevance, and thorough investigative journalism have little influence when fierce economic competition drains the media organizations of resources and forces them to compete on attention-catching stories and entertainment. Quality media that refuse to compete on these premises may simply perish unless they can rely on non-commercial sources of funding.

The media are conveying and influencing the public opinion, which in turn determines the democratic elections. The influence of the media works not only through voters' opinions. Everybody in society is influenced by the media, including politicians, opinion leaders, journalists, editors, and whoever may have the role of news sources. Furthermore, the media are influencing the criteria by which voters evaluate political candidates by means of agenda-setting, priming and framing. It is easy to see that this model has many feedback loops that provide ample opportunities for self-amplifying processes. These feedbacks are likely to make the effects stronger, reinforce existing tendencies, hide deficiencies, and make the system resistant to political intervention.

Civil Society, Mass Media and Democracy

Media are considered as the "watch-dogs" of democracy. As an integral force of civil society, the mass media is expected to play a prominent role in controlling the parliament, the government and the judiciary, in investigating whether private industrial and financial interests respect the law, sounding the alarm if the environment is polluted, and engaging in conflict prevention and resolution. Mass media are omnipresent in modern times. Perhaps, therefore, people expect omnipotence from the media.

Media are first of all enterprises to be affected by the mechanisms of the market. However, at the same time, what the media produces is important for the public. Communication channels that are established and operated by mass media are vital to society. Without free and balanced political communication, democratic institutions will corrupt. Without accurate business information, markets will collapse. Without uninhibited information about new artistic trends, culture will degenerate.

These are all truisms. It is simple to spell out what the media should and should not do in democracies, especially in post-authoritarian countries which are still building democratic institutions. However, in this paper there is little of a normative approach. It intends to offer a basic analysis of the politics of media control and the media markets in post-communist countries. The result should be an elementary overview into the complex interplay between public authorities, media owners and journalists in post-communist countries. It should offer a better understanding of the performance of mass media, as a central part of the civil society, in post-communist countries.

In many post-communist countries the concept of civil-society is still foremost associated with western democracy assistance because, evidently, most, if not all, non-governmental organisations would not survive without external financial assistance. In the case of the media in post-communist countries, it is obvious that the public does not perceive the most important non-governmental media to be working in the public interest. Most mass media are regarded as political instruments of the government or particular interest groups. Activists in non-governmental organisations, in the "third sector" are, for instance, often ridiculed in Albanian as "Sorosani", meaning off-springs of George Soros, the New York philanthropist. If they are not considered outright to be foreign-paid elements, then there is certainly a wide-spread perception of civil society in post-communist countries as a kind of Western export meant to create problems for the democratically elected government.

Many people in post-communist countries suspect that the reason the West would support NGOs, mass media and other segments of the nascent civil society, is associated with the Western conviction that there is only an imitation of democracy in the East. Democratic elections sometimes produce undemocratic politicians, or at least politicians who are not in accordance with the taste of some people in the West and, in fact, also in the East. In other words, western sponsored civil society organisations should help cover the democratic deficits of east European societies.

In some Western countries, civil society organisations, such as FAIR (Fairness & Accuracy in Reporting) in the US, monitor the media and often raise alarm about alleged or genuine bias in reporting. Objections are raised as to whether the Western prescriptions to new democracies concerning the role of mass media are not, to a certain extent, hypocritical. So, what could be the purpose of a debate about the role of mass media in building democracy if reality, also in developed democracies, is never attaining the noble norms set by political philosophers?

Transition in the Media Field

In the year1848 - the year in which the bourgeois revolutions paved the way for more civil liberties in Europe - concerning the basic condition for his trade to be really free to perform adequately its important social task. The privilege of not being a business was, according to Karl Marx, the precondition for the freedom of the press. A century and a half later, when the single-party Marxist regimes in Central and Eastern Europe and the former Soviet Union were collapsing, their opponents, the anti-communist revolutionaries, were demanding exactly the opposite: the freedom of the media to be a business. After decades of state and party dominance over every segment of public life, and especially remembering the iron grip of the security apparatus on the public sphere, it was self-explanatory that only the elimination of state control - and especially the eradication of police oppression - over the media would enable freedom of speech.

Another common demand in the post-communist countries, over the past fifteen years, has been that the media sector be reformed according to the "European" model, with matching legal regulations and administrative practices across the region. It was assumed that this model would counter the perils of the return of state control while simultaneously eliminating the pitfalls of US-type commercialisation of the media and television above all. Sporadically, one could also hear the demands that civil society wielded more influence over the media. Such propositions came primarily by the intelligentsia, who had been at the forefront of the struggle against the previous regime and rejected the thought of simply exchanging state domination for subservience to business interests.

Western media scholars looked at the back-ends of their book-shelves for dusty studies on the role of the media in development and modernisation - a topical issue in the decolonisation debate of the fifties and sixties. The mantra in that discourse was quite similar, if not identical, to the normative role currently ascribed to the media in the process of transition. Half a century ago, Western scholars expected the population in former colonies to develop an "empathy" for, Western life-style through exposure to relevant messages in the mass media and to modernise accordingly. Nowadays, the media are expected to "transmit western democratic norms and role models to the public and thus act as a major agent of political re-socialisation". However, even fifty years ago it was easy to observe that the prevalent Western media products, especially in Asia, Africa and Latin America, were cowboy serials such as Bonanza and other similar American-made entertainment.

In modern times, every accidental tourist will confirm that the most frequently shown foreign shows, between Albania and Kazakhstan were, if not Latin American telenovellas, American smash hits, portrayals of wealth, power and matrimonial crises, such as Dynasty, or the German crime evergreen Tatort. The image of the West and Western values, as transmitted by the majority of its exported programmes, seldom relates to reality and, certainly, does not intend to propagate democracy, market economy and civil society. Evidently, the prevailing picture of the world in the media of post-communist countries is not an essentially European one. In post-communist societies, there is an overwhelming presence of American fiction on the screens.

An analysis of the world-wide news-flow confirms that reporting on US politics, economy and culture remains a predominant feature in the international exchange of information. It becomes apparent that exposure to Western produced media content is definitely not the channel through which societies in transitional countries will receive a decisive impetus to modernise. Additionally, the intelligentsia's ambition to exert an influence on the shaping and running of the new media system has obviously been thwarted. Non-commercial media outlets such as Open TV channels, representation of the listeners and viewers in supervisory agencies of major public service broadcasters, and related forms of civil society representation in the organisation and creation of the public sphere have remained marginal in most post-communist countries.

The only operational criterion to measure the progress in the transition of mass media seems, therefore, to be the achieved degree of introduction of the "European" model. In essence, this would denote, on the one hand, the existence of a private media sector that is acting responsibly and respecting law, the code of journalistic ethics and the rules set out by independent broadcasting authorities and similar institutions of social control. On the other hand, the "European" way of organising the media system also postulates the existence of the public service media, mostly in the field of broadcasting. Such media is meant to provide public interest programmes that commercial media could not afford, or, for other reasons would not offer, without the negative aspects of political meddling.

At this point, it is necessary to call attention to the fact that some analysts tend to perceive public service media as "autonomous state media organisations". Also, one has to remember that the "European" model evidently exists only as a normative prescription: "Public service broadcasting is more of an ideal, more of a consummation of citizen desires and an element of a perfected democracy. "Political interfering by the public authorities and political parties as well as the influence of economic interests, irresponsible behaviour by the tabloids and other deviations from the noble postulates are daily occurrences.

In reality, the match between the norm and actual media performance differs from one polity to another and depends on many interconnected variables. Once the former regimes, to use another Marxian phrase, have landed on history's pile of rubbish, the audiences expect from the media perhaps not as much as to enlighten them, but at least not to tell untruths again. Specially when dealing with the security apparatus, which had sinned so much in the past. Nevertheless, critical, or even investigative reporting on the murky world of the "services" or the armed forces is still a risky business.

Politics of Media Control

More freedom for the press was one of the first visible changes after the breakdown of the old regimes. Actually, in the first years after the collapse of the single-party rule, the media was in a chaotic, unstructured state as much as the rest of the society. Only in the mid-nineties and later, were attempts made to regulate the media. Media developments inherently lend themselves to more public scrutiny. Therefore, the public was generally quick to react to violations of media freedoms. The Czech Republic, which was lucky enough to experience a tranquil regime change in 1989, astonished the world when on 3 January 2001, some 100 000 people took to the streets of Prague to protest against, what appeared to be, the political muzzling of the nation's public television. Similar strife, though on a lesser scale, has erupted in Hungary, Poland, Bulgaria, Slovenia and other, more or less, "settled" new democracies.

In Hungary in March 2001, an expert group from the International Federation of Journalists (IFJ) accused the then government of Prime Minister Viktor Orban of having "weakened to the point of destruction" the national system of public broadcasting through "political manipulation and wilful neglect. " "Regrettably, even those countries closest to accession to the European Union have not been able to fully transform public media into a genuinely professional and democratic institution," said the IFJ.

Authorities in Central and Eastern European countries have typically moved to transform the state broadcaster into a public broadcasting service (PBS). The British Broadcasting. Corporation (BBC) and its German offspring, the —ffentlich-rechtliche Sender, served as models for reformed radio and TV systems in most countries of that region. The BBC's celebrated autonomy was the ideal but rarely achieved goal.

In most countries facing transition, fierce disputes have broken out over issues of the influence of television, as well as over the type of media perceived to have strongest political clout. Particularly, in times of approaching elections, there were frequent clashes over the influence of TV - because it was widely assumed that voters were prone to follow the lead offered by TV stations. It was usually difficult to reach an agreement on how national broadcasting councils, editors, and executive officers of PBSs were to be appointed and supervised. More often than not, allocation of frequencies proved a divisive issue. Politicians, journalists, and civil society activists often clashed over the limits imposed on foreign investors and producers.

The fact that these questions in many cases remain unresolved indicates that the struggle for influence in the post-communist electronic media is far from over. It will be most interesting to watch the outcome of the debate reallocation of broadcasting licenses and frequencies in Serbia after the law on the national broadcasting council has finally been passed. Will Slobodan Miloševi æ 's pet TV stations, such as BK and TV Pink, that are now shamelessly supportive of the democratic government, survive or even prosper under new political circumstances? It is an alarming signal that the ruling parties have stood firmly behind the leading members of the new Broadcasting Council, although several well-known media experts resigned, pointing out that the president of this body had been elected contrary to the law.

The media in "unconsolidated presidential democracies" - and most countries in the former Soviet Union - have done far worse than its counterparts in Central and Eastern Europe. Countless incidents revealed that current governments can deal with outspoken media professionals as brutally as the previous regimes. The still unresolved disappearance of Ukrainian journalist Georgiy Gongadze in September 2000 in Kiev is one spectacular example because it involves the highest level of power at the state level. A headless corpse was later found, but there is still no confirmation that the body was Gongadze's. Since then, President Leonid Kuchma has been pressured to resign in light of audio recordings made by a fugitive presidential bodyguard, in which the president appears to order the abduction of Gongadze.

In a bizarre twist in Ukraine in May 2001, the Kuchma administration claimed that there was no political aspect to Gongadze's disappearance: criminals killed Gongadze and, in turn, they were killed. This is the account the authorities offered to a sceptical public. The most recent interpretation of the case blames initial investigators of gross errors. Nevertheless, a credible explanation of the events surrounding Gongadzes's disappearance has not been provided for by the authorities. Several other journalists have lost their lives in similarly suspicious circumstances. When asked why there was not more foreign companies willing to invest in the Ukrainian media industry, one veteran editor in Kiev recently replied, "You know, journalists get killed in this place".

A mind-boggling proliferation of broadcasters has occurred all over the post-communist realm. Even poor countries such as Serbia or the Former Yugoslav Republic of Macedonia maintain hundreds of locally owned radio and TV stations with revealing names such as TV Pink or Pop TV. As a rule, they offer programmes of the poorest quality - they do not rebroadcast without permission or without paying royalties for foreign satellite channels. In Hungary, Poland, the Czech Republic, Slovenia and some other new democracies, there is also a well-established presence of foreign commercial television.

While authorities have paid a lot of attention to retaining some leverage over public service broadcasters, commercial broadcasters have, for the most part, been spared their efforts. One likely reason for this is that commercial broadcasting in Central and Eastern Europe has yet to prove that it will be as lucrative and influential as had been assumed initially. Whatever the case may be in future, up to now foreign-owned commercial TV stations have been flooded with soaps, quiz games, B-movies and soft-porn with offensively long commercial breaks.

The largest television company in the region, the U. S. -owned Central European Media Enterprise Ltd. (CME), with stations in Slovenia, Slovakia, Romania, and Ukraine and an audience of 110 million, announced losses in last several years that were partly connected to an ongoing legal dispute over ownership of the Czech TV station Nova, once the CME flagship. CME finally won the dispute and was awarded compensation of more than US$300 million, more than the Czech state spends per year for its public health system. It remains to be seen how the Balkan News Corporation, a company owned by Rupert Murdoch, will fare after having acquired, in 2000, the broadcasting rights to the former second channel of Bulgarian state TV.

A novel approach, understood as part of democracy building through the media, has emerged in some post-conflict countries of southeast Europe where capital coming from philanthropic or other Western political motivated sources was funnelled to media pursuing pro-democracy and anti-nationalistic editorial policies. The US billionaire George Soros is the founder of the Media Development Loan Fund (MDLF) in Prague which has sponsored through soft-loans non-government media in many post-communist countries. Such loans and non-returnable grants from the Soros Open Society Institute, the European Union's Human Rights and Democratisation Initiative and other EU budget lines, the US government backed Eurasia Foundation, USAID, the Norwegian People's Aid, various German political foundations and other Western sources are, in many cases, still the most important pillar for the economic survival of pro-democracy media.

In the recent past, the MDLF has become co-owner of some media in southeast Europe such as the Rije è ki Novi List and Feral Tribune in Croatia, or the famous B92 radio and TV station, once a symbol of resistance against the previous regime. In Russia, with some 40. 000 registered media outlets, and most other former Soviet Union countries, much of the print media, especially in outlying regions, still depends heavily on state subsidies - that is, if it is not owned outright by the state. There are huge privately owned media holdings as well which usually belong to some industrial oligarch. Some of them like Gusinski and Beresovski, who were the biggest media owners in President Yeltzin's times have been in the meanwhile ousted from control over their assets - which were initially bought through loans from the state that were never reimbursed. These two mega-oligarchs have fled Russia in the meanwhile.

MediavBerlusconisation

Media transition, understood as the emphasis on private ownership and the promise to transform the former state-owned electronic media into public service broadcasters, yielded dissimilar results in different parts of the former communist world. The introduction of market mechanisms created new opportunities - and risks - for journalists and the media in post-communist societies. While private competition is certainly a most important corrective to state dominance in the public sphere, it is still not the ultimate guarantee that the noble goals of the freedom of the press will soon materialise in the predominantly pauperised world of post-communism.

In the former Soviet Union, and there is empirical proof for this statement, the state owned media are still firmly under control during elections by the parties in power. Sensitive topics, such as security issues, are difficult to discuss in the media and attempts to do so still entail considerable risks for the journalists. Even so, it is not any longer lethal to criticise the army, the police and the "services" as it used to be in not so ancient times. With the exception of some neo-Stalinist polities in Central Asia, in most part of the former Soviet Union, the interested reader and viewer can find information critical of the powers that be. Depending on the internal political situation and the pressure from the West, the rulers gauge how much liberty they will permit in the media channels.

The initial ambition, the "Europeanisation" of the media, still continues to be a distant goal in most parts of the former Soviet Union. With great speed Russia (and Ukraine that, in many aspects, demonstrates copycat similarities to Russia) has moved from an initially anarchistic media situation after the collapse of the empire towards re-asserting formal and informal control mechanisms by the Kremlin and many lower levels of the power over the media. The situation is far worse in the majority of Central Asian countries that are firmly in the grip of neo-authoritarian leaders who do not hesitate to infringe heavily the freedom of the press. The three Trans-Caucasian countries are trapped in economic misery, civil strife, lingering ethnic conflicts and unresolved wars which all reflects heavily on the plight of the media.

"Europeanisation" has become far more factual in those countries of Central and Eastern Europe that are pursuing a successful economic transformation and retain a political consensus about national priorities such as EU accession and integration into Euro-Atlantic security mechanisms. However, they are often at the verge of a new danger -the "Berlusconisation", a recently erupted European malaise, comprising the persistence of government control over TV, private monopolies in the broadcasting industry, strong overt and stealth collusion of business interests and media ownership, blatant partisanship in the media and other flaws.

The Western Balkans area - actually former Yugoslavia and Albania - displays a confusing mixture. Not so recently leading media outlets in Serbia, Croatia and other parts of the region were part of a huge propaganda and hate machinery closely reflecting the whims of their autocrats. Although all countries in the region have democractically elected new governments and have proclaimed their willingness to cast away the nationalistic past in favour of the European future, political and economic stability is far from guaranteed. As always, media reflect this precarious state.

Laws on public service broadcasting are adopted all over the region - but their implementation seems to over-stretch the political elite's enthusiasm for democracy. WAZ, Bertelsmann and some other mostly German and Austrian investors have bought off huge chunks of the print media market -but their local products such as Politika in Serbia or Jutarnji List in Croatia only faintly resemble the mainstream West European press. The proliferation of mass media continues. Whether prolific quantity will transform to pluralistic quality remains to be resolved.

4
Media and Audience

India is perceived by the world media as a country that has thrown off its isolationist mindset for the most part, is no longer wary of Western influences and is embracing globalization. According to a study of media perceptions, conducted by the multinational public relations firm Edelman and India's R&P Management Communications Pvt. Ltd., the need for planned and sustained communications can take India beyond the "outsourcing" label. In the next five years, India will emerge stronger than other emerging markets, it said.

India is also perceived to have a stronger potential in the next five years than other emerging markets such as Brazil, Russia, Poland and Mexico, according to the study."Brazil is perceived as just beginning economic reforms, Russia's economy as still weak and its government is autocratic, while Poland and Mexico are way behind in perceptions of emerging markets even in Europe and the United States," the study said. The survey pointed out that, India needs to emphasize its strong management expertise, transparency, corporate governance and leadership role in corporate social responsibility.

It also said that emerging markets are closing in on India's dominance in business-process outsourcing and posing a threat, with the Philippines offering a lower cost structure, Mexico and Canada offering greater proximity to the United States, and Ireland and South Africa being closer to Europe. These countries also enjoy time zone advantages when compared to India. India's key advantages over other emerging markets lie in its educated, English-speaking young workforce, a democratic and business-friendly government, a low-cost structure and an eager and savvy consumer market with growing buying potential, according to the study.

Print Media

National Readership Survey 2002 shows that the print media have acquired 17 million more readers since 1999. Doomsday prophets predicting the death of the print media in the electronic age can calm down. Printed periodicals do not appear to be in any danger of dying out. On the contrary, Gutenberg's medium seems to be growing. The findings of the National Readership Survey (NRS) 2002 show that India's print media readership base has expanded by 10 per cent over the last two years. Since the last NRS survey in 1999, the print media have acquired 17 million more readers. The data may indicate that different media need not necessarily substitute one another. According to the NRS estimates, India's vast media industry reaches 180 million readers, 383.6 million television viewers, 189 million radio listeners and six million Internet users.

According to the findings of the National Readership Survey 2002, newspaper readership has grown by about 20 per cent, from 131 million in 1999 to 155 million in 2002.

Despite the growth in readership, a majority of India's 428 million literate adults do not read any periodical publication. Besides India's vast illiterate adult population (252.5 million), there are 248 million literate adults who are unexposed to newspapers and magazines, in comparison to the 180 million who do read publications. Readers from nearly six lakh villages make up only 48 per cent of the readership base, although rural India is home to 62.6 per cent of the country's literate population. This could be due to the urban-centric nature of most publications, which may not cater to the interests of rural residents. The NRS points to a vast, untapped readership base in rural India, which could offer new opportunities for the Indian press.

Newspaper readership has grown by about 20 per cent from 131 million in 1999 to 155 million in 2002. Readership growth has been faster than literacy growth, which expanded by 13 per cent during the same period. Newspapers contributing to this rise in readership were mainly in English, Hindi, Marathi and Kannada. The Hindi dailies, Dainik Bhaskar and Dainik Jagran, have the highest readership, with 13 million and 12.6 million readers respectively. No English newspaper figured amongst the 10 most widely read newspapers in the country. The prominence given to the English press is disproportionate to its actual readership. Even in urban India, only one English daily, The Times of India, is amongst the top 10. The fastest growing dailies are the Assamese dailies in urban areas (51.8 per cent increase) and the Bengali dailies in rural areas (129 per cent rise). Other high growth dailies are published in Oriya, Hindi, Punjabi, Kannada and Marathi. The highest readership was found to be in Kerala.

While newspaper readership has picked up, magazines have lost some ground. Their reach fell by 22 per cent in two years (taking into account the population growth in these years) from 93.8 million in 1999 to 86.2 million in 2002. General interest, film/entertainment and sports magazines in particular have suffered declines. Bengali, Tamil and Telugu magazines are the only ones that increased their readership. Magazine readership in all other languages decreased. The Hindi magazine Saras Salil enjoys the highest readership, followed by Grihashobha, also in Hindi, and India Today.

The data reveal a clear correlation between literacy and media exposure. The reach of the press is higher in the southern, western and northeastern States, which have higher literacy rates. The northern States, apart from Punjab, Himachal Pradesh and Haryana, have lower exposure to the press. Television reach patterns are almost identical to press exposure, except in the northeastern States where television reach is low but press reach is high. Although Hindi is the most widely used language, the reach of the press in the Hindi belt remains low due to lower literacy rates. Readership mirrors literacy and educational achievements. Kerala, the State with the highest literacy rate, has a 70 per cent readership. But in Bihar, which has one of the lowest literacy levels, only 15 per cent of the population reads periodicals.

People in urban India spend less time on media - print, television, radio and the Internet. The average cityslicker is now exposed to the media for 13 hours a week, as compared to 14 hours in 1999. This decline has not affected reading time. The average urban person still reads for 18 minutes a day, which accounts for 16 per cent of his/her total media time. In rural India, an average adult is exposed to the media for just six hours a week. The media time of rural adults has remained constant since NRS 1999. Most media time is taken up by television, which commands 72 per cent of the urban Indian's time spent on media. In absolute terms, the average viewing time has fallen from 85 minutes a day in 1999 to 82 minutes in 2002. Television Audience Measurement (TAM) meter readings also show that television viewing time has fallen from an average of 140 minutes a day last year to 130 minutes a day this year.

Yet, the reach of television has grown by 12 per cent since 1999. Cable and satellite penetration has risen from 29 million in 1999 to 40 million, a 31 per cent growth, which is more than double the figure of television's rate of growth. Around half of all homes in India with televisions now have cable and satellite subscriptions. This highlights the vast potential for expansion of this already pervasive medium. Television reach has been higher in the southern States of Tamil Nadu, Karnataka and Andhra Pradesh. It has also been high in Gujarat, one of the most prosperous States.

Although it is yet to achieve as wide a reach as other media forms in India, the Internet has grown in terms of access by over 30 per cent in the last year. Currently, 6.02 million people access the Internet, as compared to only 1.4 million in 1999. Most Internet users are from urban India. Only 8 per cent of those who used the Internet over the last three months live in India's villages. The digital divide is yet to be bridged. The places from where people access the Internet have changed. The number of people surfing the Internet in the office has fallen, while there has been a sudden spurt in the growth of Internet cafes, making the WorldWide Web accessible to a larger audience. Another progressive indicator is the fact that the percentage of people accessing the Internet from schools and colleges has also seen a sharp increase.

Women's media habits have undergone a change. The number of women who read newspapers has increased by 37 per cent, but they spend less time reading magazines.

Women also spend less time watching television and listening to the radio than they did in 1999. The NRS in India is one of the largest in the world, with a reporting sample size of over 2,13,000 individuals to track media exposure and changing consumer trends in both urban and rural India. The study covers 514 publications. A useful guide for media analysts and marketing strategists, the NRS is conducted annually by three research agencies - the Indian Market Research Bureau (IMRB), TNS Mode and AC Nielsen. It is one of two readership surveys conducted in India. The other is the Indian Readership Survey.

The sample is urban-centric, with only 30 per cent of it based on people living in villages. Jammu and Kashmir, Goa and offshore territories (Andaman and Nicobar Islands and Lakshadweep) are excluded. Over the years, the survey has provided a comprehensive picture of the country's media landscape. It also highlights the vast uncharted territories and the potential of the media, which remains untapped owing to socio-economic factors such as poverty, inequality and poor access to education.

MEDIA TRENDS

The release of the 1999 National Readership Survey (NRS 99) has provided new insights into the changing character of India's media landscape. Based on surveys in 818 urban centres and 2,058 villages, NRS 99 provides a comprehensive account of the state o f India's media. It is particularly significant for being the first comprehensive survey of rural newspaper readership and television audience size in the rural areas. Each week, NRS 99 says, the print media reaches 242 million Indians, television 329 mi llion and radio 174 million. These enormous numbers, the survey suggests, represent a chain of growth, driven both by expanding literacy and improved living standards.

NRS 99 once again underlines the theory that growth in newspaper circulation has a close relationship with literacy levels. Broadly, NRS 99 shows that Indian newspapers and magazines have continued to grow in both urban and rural areas. Since 1997, when the last NRS report came out, the percentage of adults in India who read newspapers and magazines grew by four percentage po ints, from 45 to 49. Assuming a population of 620 million adults over the age of 15, as NRS 99 does, that means well over 25 million people have begun to read some newspaper or magazine for the first time in these two years. However, since NRS 97 based i ts readership figures entirely on urban residents, the real growth of print media audiences could in fact be larger than the data at first suggest. While 62 per cent of the 183 million Indians in urban areas read newspapers or magazines each week, NRS 99 records, only 29 per cent of the 437 million rural residents do so. This lower rural reach was not factored into NRS 97.

The number of adults who read a daily newspaper overall grew by one percentage point from 1997, reaching 42 per cent of all adults or some 260 million people. By contrast, evening papers, popular in urban centres, showed a decline in circulation. But the real growth in the print media was marked by magazines; many adult Indians took to reading a magazine for the first time. Magazine readers as a percentage of all adults rose from 25 per cent in 1997 to 28 per cent, which in absolute terms means there are some 174 million magazine readers today. The growth in magazine audiences was driven by news, general interest and subject-specific publications, while business magazines performed relatively poorly.

Radio is the only major medium to have seen an erosion of its audience since 1997. Radio reached 29 per cent of adults in an average week in 1997. NRS 99 records that that figure has come down to 26 per cent. Given the growth of population, however, the audience size of 161 million may not represent a significant fall in absolute terms. The decline could possibly be linked to the growth of television in rural areas, with sections of the agrarian rich switching their allegiance to the new medium.

Cinema, too, showed less than riveting results, despite some media hype about a renewed wave of blockbuster films. NRS 99 recorded that just 3 per cent of the adult population, both rural and urban, went to a cinema in an average week. Audience figures f or cinema showed no increase from 1997. Internet usage has grown, but as yet only 1.4 million adults have access to it and they are concentrated mainly in the eight principal cities. NRS 99 offers some interesting answers to this question. For one, it again underlines the argument that growth in newspaper and magazine circulations has a close relationship with literacy levels. In Kerala, a State with near-total literacy, 71 per cent read at least one newspaper or magazine. In Bihar, a State with just 45 per cent literacy, only 15 per cent of the population read newspapers or magazines. In urban Kerala, where 96 per cent of the adult population is literate, 80 per cent read publications, while in urban Maharashtra and Goa, where 84 per cent are literate, 53 per cent of the population read at least one newspaper or magazine. Growing literacy has clearly fuelle d the growth of the print media.

But the presence of television makes the media picture more complex than it perhaps was a decade ago. Conventional wisdom has it that television caters to audiences in States where literacy levels are relatively low.

But NRS 99 makes clear that that isn't the case. In Bihar, just 29 per cent of the adult population watches television. In Punjab, Haryana and Himachal Pradesh, where 67 per cent of adults are literate, just 27 per cent access a newspaper or magazine, just above the national average, while 69 per cent watch television, a good 16 percentage points above the national average.

In Assam and other northeastern States as also in West Bengal, higher than average literacy rates again do not translate into high reach for the print media. In some States and areas, both high television viewership and print-media reach go together. In Tamil Nadu, an average family spends some 3.3 hours each day watching television, while in Uttar Pradesh, such a family does so for two hours. But Tamil Nadu's figures for the percentage of adults forming the newspaper and magazine reading public are almost twice those of Uttar Pradesh. NRS 99 suggests that States like Tamil Nadu, which have seen a proliferation of satellite television channels, have seen a l ess sharp growth in newspaper circulation than those like Uttar Pradesh, where the spread of satellite television has been less marked. But the mere proliferation of television choices clearly does not explain the growth of certain media platforms - or the absence of it.

NRS 99 thus makes at least two major points clear. The first is that the growth of television has been the most marked in the relatively affluent States, not in those with the lowest levels of literacy. In one sense, therefore, if the growth of the print media is literacy-driven, that of television is affluence-driven. This tells us not a little about the breakdown of India's public service broadcasting paradigm, where the creation of state television was legitimised on the basis of the claim that it wo uld make the medium available to the illiterate rural poor. The second point is that television has not in any meaningful way emerged as a substitute for print media, in the sense that the proliferation of channels and increase in television audiences ha s not led to a reduction in the number of people reading newspapers and magazines.

NRS 95 and NRS 97 laid the foundations for this year's empirical treasure-trove. NRS 99 has several new features, among them sheer scale, spanning 192 newspapers and 265 magazines. Then, the survey has now gone six-monthly, with the next phase of NRS 99 being due by the end of this year. Two further NRS reports will be available by February 2001, enabling better trend analysis. The methodology used in the survey was also more rigorous than in the past, with three agencies, TN Sofre Mode, Indian Market Research Bureau (IMRB), and AC Nielsen cross-checking each other's fieldwork. NRS 99 is available on floppies and CD ROMs, and search engines have been developed to enable researchers to disaggregate easily media audiences by their economic status, for ex ample, or their purchasing habits.

It is important that such research be carried out by serious students of the media, and not just agencies whose primary interests lie in the commercial realm. The broad brush strokes of NRS 99 are made up of an enormous mosaic of local-level data, offeri ng insights into the relationship of the media with audiences sharply differentiated along class, linguistic and regional lines. "It's almost as if there are several countries within the country," says the head of NRS 99's Technical Committee, Ketaki Gupte. "The variations are enormous." NRS 99 contains a vast amount of information on just where the Indian mass media is headed. With its signal inclusion of data on the media's rural reach and character, the poverty of empirical material that researchers on the Indian media have long felt is at last starting to be addressed.

The National Readership Study (NRS) 2002 has some good news for newspapers; the readership of the print media has grown by 10 per cent in the last two years. According to NRS 2002, the press has added over 17 million readers in the last two years. The reader base in India has grown from 163 million to 180 million, a growth of 10 per cent. What is interesting is that there is still a significant scope for growth in this segment as 248 million adults who are literate do not read any publication.

Another interesting fact that comes to light is that there are nearly as many rural readers as urban. Of the 180 million readers, as many as 48 per cent are from six lakh villages scattered across India. According to NRS 2002, the reader base for dailies/newspapers increased from 131 million in 1989 to 156 million this year, an increase of 20 per cent. The growth in the reach of dailies is substantially higher than the literacy growth of 13 per cent in the same period. Language dailies have contributed significantly to this growth. The highest read Hindi daily in India now surpasses a readership of 13 million. The newspaper has now extended its reach to the urban housewife/FMCG decision makers.

According to NRS 2002, 25.4 million urban housewives as compared to 21.7 million in 1999, now read daily newspapers. And this comes at the cost of reading magazines which was considered a staple diet for most women. The survey shows a decline in readers of magazines. Magazines, overall, show a decline in the reader base, both in urban and rural India. The reach of magazines has declined from 93.8 million in 1999 to 86.2 million in 2002. Magazines have lost 22 per cent of their reach since 1999, taking into account the population growth over these years. The decline is mainly in the general interest, film/ entertainment and sports magazines, where the percentage decline on an average is over 25 per cent. The time spent on traditional media has marginally declined in urban markets. According to the report, in 1999 an urban adult spent on an average 14 hours a week or 2 hours a day on traditional media, that is, press, TV, radio and Internet. Since then, the time spent per week per urban adult has declined to 13 hours a week or about 7 minutes less per day per adult.

In comparison, the time spent on traditional media in villages is virtually half-6 hours per adult-and this is more or less constant since 1999. The decline in time spent on traditional media has not affected reading time in urban media. The average reader still spends about 16 per cent of his total media time, that is, 18 minutes per day, in reading a daily/magazine. Urban India now spends marginally less time watching TV although TV still commands the lion's share of media consumption. According to NRS 2002, TV still commands a 72 per cent share of the average 13 hours spent on traditional media the amongst urban audience. If taken in absolute terms, there is a slight decline in time spent on TV in this market. Despite the increasing programme options, the average viewing time has come down from 85 minutes in 1999 to 82 minutes in 2002.

The growth in C&S penetration is more than twice the growth in TV-owning homes. As per the report, TV now reaches 81.6 million Indian homes and reflects a growth of 12 per cent since 1999. Access to C&S homes jumped from 29 million in 1999 to 40 million in 2002-a 31 per cent growth rate, more than twice the growth of the TV market. C&S subscription has now penetrated 50 per cent of all TV homes. Another interesting fact thrown up by NRS 2002 is that Internet reach exceeds 6 million homes. The access to Internet in the last 3 months increased to 6 million. The growth of the Internet has stabilised at 2 million annually.

CHANGING INDIAN PRINT MEDIA

Indian print media is set for a major change following the government decision to permit 26 per cent FDI in Indian entities publishing newspapers/periodicals dealing with news and current affairs. The landmark decision, though not entirely unexpected, is a "partial modification" of the earlier 1955 Cabinet decision on the subject. The step will give a fillip to several English and regional publications waiting for funds to take on near monopolies in publishing. The Indian Newspaper Society, however maintained that "FDI will compromise national interest." It commented that it did not matter whether it was 26 per cent or 74 per cent as the foreign investor can always control policies and content.

The official press note issued by the Information and Broadcasting Ministry said - "A comprehensive review of the whole matter has been carried out now.... The policy now would provide for 26 per cent FDI in Indian entities publishing newspapers/ periodicals dealing with news and current affairs, after suitable verifications by the Central Govenment and the editorial and management control remaining fully in Indian hands." This will, in effect, open the door for Indian media houses seeking foreign investments to upgrade their infrastructure and compete with large near-monopolistic competition. The Government also allowed upto 74 per cent equity investment in Indian editions of foreign owned technical journals and speciailty 'non- news' magazines. The Indian Newspaper Society (INS) reiterated its stance opposing the decision. Citing arguments like 'threat to national interest', 'invaluable contribution to the freedom struggle' and 'FDI will jeopardise harmonious relationship among the different communities' in support of the anti-FDI rhetoric, the INS chose to distance itself from the decision. "It is a matter of surprise and consternation that the Government have overlooked the recommendation of the Parliamentary Standing Committee on IT headed by Somnath Chatterjee and allowed entry of FDI in print," commented INS President Pratap Pawar.

While the print body was circumspect, the Confederation of Indian Industry (CII) lauded the Government's decision. "Allowing FDI is a bold and significant step. This is a positive first step. It will take a year to stabilise. After discussions with major publications, CII had made a recommendation to Ministry," remarked Biren Ghosh, member of CII sub- committee on Entertainment.

At many print organisations, notably India Today, Indian Express, Mid-Day, Dainik Jagran and Business Standard, the mood is upbeat. Others like Bharat Kapadia are cautious, "There is a plus as well as a minus. Right-minded investors can improve the knowledge base and technology. But this critical medium in wrong hands can also cause serious problems." The government, on its part, has however taken a few precautions to prevent misuse. Besides, the editorial and management control remaining fully in Indian hands, the approval to allow FDI will be on a case-to-case basis giving the government time to review each proposal. To avoid effective management control by foreign players holding 26 per cent-, the Government has stipulated that the largest Indian shareholder should have 'substantially' higher holding. Detractors argue that these clauses leave much to interpretation and can lead to slow decisions.

The Government has taken a calculated risk on FDI in print media, as the RSS and Swadeshi Jagran Manch, have been opposed to the move. The Congress the government had gone ahead with a decision on which there was no consensus.The Left parties attacked the "handing over of the media to the imperialist powers." The monsoon session of Parliament could see fireworks over the issue. Dissent and brickbats aside, the Cabinet decision will set the tone for the new print media environment, more resources facilitating content generation, marketing, HR and international best practices. The move will also be a boon for journalists, who are on the lookout for greener pastures as the foreign investors, flush with money, will need quality journalists at any price.

India radio industry is undergoing huge changes with new radio licesences being issued, new radio channels springing up & the radio audience profile undergoing a change. The Madison India Radio Research reveals that consolidation and specialization are two distinct trends in the evolution of the radio business. Their in-depth survey focuses on International trends in the radio business, radio measurement and the best practices that have evolved in using the medium.It is ironical that while India has the second highest penetration of C&S homes in the world, radio has suffered from shunted growth. This can be attributed to misdirected policies by government, which did not give enough prominence to radio as a rich medium for entertainment and also for community development.

Recently though, government has liberalized radio broadcast and this has resulted in most media houses diversifying to offer radio services. In Mumbai, for instance, five private FM radio stations have been launched. Mumbai listeners can tune in to any of the seven FM stations (five from private broadcasters and two from AIR). Government has indicated that its long-term plan is to have 150 FM stations across 40 cities. There are more than 6000 radio stations in US and even a developing country like Nigeria has 18 FM stations. In most markets, radio manages to garner around 4-5% of the mass media spend. In some countries like Sri Lanka, radio accounts for 20% of ad spend. It is estimated that in 2001, American radio commanded US$3.2 Billion out of US$60 Billion spent on mass media.

In India, currently radio is able to garner less than 1% of the total ad pie of Rs.8, 600 crore. Madison media estimates that by 2004, advertisers will spend around Rs. 500 crore on radio. This will constitute around 4 % of the enlarged ad pie. While growth of the radio broadcast industry looks exciting, there are numerous issues facing the radio broadcasters. Chief of them being the license costs and licensing policy. After bidding aggressively, many players have realized that high license cost is making the business unviable. As per reports, bidders license for 37 stations. This translates to around Rs.4.2 crores as license fee per station. The broadcasters now want the government to scrap fixed license fee and move to a revenue sharing regime. However, the industry feels that these are mere start-up issues; radio should feature in the media planner's radar as a serious medium.

Today, media planners are quite at loss as there is inadequate information on this medium. There are three aspects relevant to media planners:

1) International trends in Radio Business

2) Radio Measurement

3) Best practices that have evolved in using the medium

International Trends

International experiences show two distinct trends in evolution of radio business

Consolidation - Typically, there is a surge of activity when the media is liberalized but over a horizon of five to six years, consolidation is inevitable and stations groups are formed that controls most of the revenues. For instance, in UK four media groups control nearly 60% of ad revenue. Radio stations that are part of established media houses would do well. Publications having strong city edition will do have an advantage as they already have infrastructure to marshal local advertisers and also keep a tab on the pulse of the city citizens.

Specialization - Internationally, radio stations have grown by attracting niche audiences (like a Hispanic channel in US or a Malayalam channel in gulf) and local advertisers. As of today, if one goes by Mumbai experience, the concept of niche programming has not yet caught the imagination of the broadcaster and audiences find it almost impossible to distinguish one from another. Madison Media expects that the evolutionary pressures will prevail in India and radio stations will increasingly find their own niche. For instance, we expect that by year 2004, emergence of stations that address only specialist audience groups - like a special radio station dedicated to south Indians residing in Mumbai or a station that caters exclusively to college going population. Such specialist channels will be ideal medium for advertisers, as they will have access to well defined captive audience.

Radio Audience Measurement

The question haunting most advertisers and media planners is regarding the audience measurement that will be adopted for Radio. As it is early days in India, station owners and advertising agencies on ad hoc basis are conducting research. The trend to continue for some more time till significant advertising monies are committed on radio. Even Internationally, radio audience research has not matured to the extent of television audience measurement. The popular rating system for radio that is used in US is the Arbitron's RADAR (Radio's All Dimension Audience Research) audience report. It measures National radio audiences and the audience size of radio commercials aired on 31 radio networks operated by large radio networks.

Till recently, RADAR report was based on a 12,000-person telephone survey. However, the next round of RADAR plans to shift reliance from telephone survey to diary-based panel for data collection. There has been some academic discussion on use of "meters" in radio sets to determine listnership. However, these are many years away from being put to commercial use. The prime reason for inadequate advancement in radio audience measurement technique has been the small share of ad pie that radio commands and also the vast geographic spread.

Over a period of time, audience measurement technique for radio will improve and a currency will be established for buying commercial time and selection of alternatives. Advertisers should not ignore the media owing to non-availability of any established audience measurement data. Indicative surveys are being conducted and published periodically by research agencies. Advertising agencies also conduct periodic dipstick surveys. Madison Media routinely undertakes studies on radio usage.

While the audience measurement is still in infancy, users of radio as an advertising medium can benefit from extensive work carried out in area of media effectiveness. Most of these studies have been conducted in developed markets like UK and USA. The most impressive in this genre of research has been the Radio Recall Research (RRR), which tested 1200 commercials with 200 respondents per commercial.

This exhaustive study was conducted in early 1980s and subsequent research added to the body of available knowledge. It will be incorrect to directly transplant those learning's in Indian context. However, they are invaluable in providing directions and we at Madison Media have distilled these findings, adapted to Indian context and arrived at set of best practices for radio advertising.

Create Unique Properties - studies clearly demonstrate that properties created on radio are cost effective and have advantage of high recall. International experience suggests that music oriented properties targeted at youth last long and provide immense benefit to advertisers. Closer home, "Binaca Geet Mala" on radio was as one of the best media properties. To create such high decibel properties, advertisers should be willing to enter early and commit long term investment. It might take some time before the properties start to reward the advertisers and advertisers should be willing to fork out the extra premium now before the medium gets established.

Exploit Drive Time Audiences - the traditional bastion of radio has been the "In car" listening. However, given the low penetration of ownership of personal cars in India, we do not expect car owners to be the largest audience for radio. It is not important whether in-car listeners will form the bulk of listnership base. It is more important to understand that radio will be the best medium to target upwardly mobile high spending executives and businessmen. Studies haye demonstrated that in-car listeners are light consumers of other media like television, making radio a very effective medium. A study by Voice of British Advertisers shows that radio is the most effective medium to target businessmen. There are mixed reports with regard to station switching behavior among in car listeners.

A research by Radio Advertising Bureau (RAB), UK indicates, contrary to popular myth, that nearly 85% of in-car audience do not shift stations frequently. However, other studies indicate there is extremely low loyalty among in car listeners. In any case, it is undeniable that for brands that target at affluent section of the society need to be actively associated with radio. In other markets, many successful service brands especially those in office supplies and financial services have benefited tremendously by judicious use of radio.

Exploit Imagery Transfer - a study by Statistical research Inc. shows that three out of four consumers who watch a television spot will "replay" the visual image mentally when they hear a radio commercial for the same brand. This is called Imagery Transfer. Another series of studies called "distraction study" tried to simulate the fact that radio listening is always secondary activity. These tests also indicated that listeners were able to create and keep images fresh and top-of-mind even when engaged in other task. It is through imagery transfer that radio creates a synergy with television. Recent studies shown that Sonic branding, where aural brand elements are used is very effective in sustaining brand's recall (tring tring of Britannia). Creation of sonic branding reduces long term cost of advertising, as one need not air the complete commercial to register recall. As can be fathomed, radio can be advantageously used in creating sonic elements of a brand.

Effective Radio Copy Management - studies have clearly established that length of the commercial had a positive impact on the ad. In general, spots of 45 seconds or more were effective. RRR studies also indicate that more brand mentions in the commercial were good for ad recall and was more effective when the brand was mentioned early in the ad. Moreover, fatigue factor is high with radio commercials. The ads that were repeated too often were disliked. Copy variation can offset this fatigue and it is suggested to have three variants of the same theme. Though airing multiple variants is recommended, there is evidence, which state that simultaneous airing of more than 5 executions leads to decay in effectiveness. As in any other media, ads that were liked had higher impact.

Radio Multiplier Effect - apart from RRR, another monumental study is the Millward Brown study on radio multiplier effect. Millward Brown conducted the study across October 1999 to April to find out how effective radio advertising can be relative to television. This study involved nearly 5500 interviews in continuous research to track awareness and attitudes to 17 brands. The media tested were Commercial Radio and television in the Central Region of UK.

The broad findings of the study proved that radio was, on an average, three-fifths as efficient as television at driving advertising awareness amongst radio listeners; used in conjunction with a television campaign, it proved to be an effective medium; and in general, if 10% of a given television budget is re-deployed onto radio, the efficiency of the campaign in building awareness increases on average by 15%

With privatization, radio ad spend is expected to grow at a CAGR of 45% over the next 5 years as against 15% for total ad spend. Radio is expected to follow the growth of the Television industry, which grew rapidly following the entry of private players. A look at the charts below shows that TV. ad spend grew at a GAGR of 30% over the last 8 years and TV penetration had doubled over the last 5 years.

1.	Area	89%
2.	Population	97.1%
3.	Estimated Radio Households [reach]	104mn
4.	Estimated Radio Sets	111mn
5.	Broadcasting Centres	117mn
6.	Transmitters	
	Medium Wave	146no
	Short Wave	50no
	FM	87no
7.	Commercial Stations [Medium Wave]	
	- Primary Channel	90no
	- Commercial Broadcasting services [Vividh Bharti]	30no

Source: Facts at a glance, AIR

Radio Listenership

India has 292 radio stations in comparison to 2000 in Spain and 1000 in Italy. But more significant are the differences in listenership. Despite just 52 stations in Austria, listenership there is 1,477 minutes a week, while in India, it is 15 minutes a week in the rural areas and 60 minutes a week in the semi urban areas. The United Kingdom can boast of 1,813 minutes a week, while Switzerland has listenership of 1,792 minutes per week.

Sixteen Indian companies have been issued licences to operate the country's first privatised FM radio stations. Fourteen other companies that had bid for licences defaulted in paying the fees, according to officials. There was some concern raised earlier that the firms that bid for the music only broadcasting stations had ended up having to pay huge sums for the bidding for a limited number of frequencies allotted by the government.

Companies that have been issued licences are Entertainment Network (India), Vertex Broadcasting, India FM Radio (Delhi), Radio Today (Delhi, Mumbai and Kolkata each), Music Broadcast, M/s Sun TV, Millennium Broadcast (Delhi, Chennai and Mumbai each), Udaya TV, Hitz FM Radio India, Radio Mid-Day West India (Mumbai), Mid-Day Radio North (India) and Mid-day Broadcasting South (India). Some of these firms are linked to major Indian newspaper groups. Of them, Mid-Day has gained experience in radio broadcasting through slots on the government-run All India Radio (AIR) network in the mid-1990s.

The FM Market in India seems to be maturing in line with International markets. Round 2 of DRS research on Radio Listenership in Delhi city throws up a lot of interesting insights into the current consuming habits of radio listeners, all of which seem to indicate that Indian market is maturing on similar lines as in FM markets internationally.

International Market

The international scenario indicates that four major mass commercial radio stations in London in the popular music format category—95.8 Capital FM, Heart 106.2 FM, Kiss 100 FM, Magic 105.4—enjoy almost equal listenership. The DRS Survey in Delhi City indicates that a similar trend is emerging in India as well.

In a sample of 1,069 respondents in Delhi across SEC ABC, 18-45 yrs, conducted in June 2004, indicates that there is practically equal listenership and a very high level of duplicacy of close to 70% between the three Pvt. FM stations. Only about 5% of the total sample tunes in exclusively to any one radio station, thus indicating a very high level of duplication between stations. Thus, for example, over 838 respondents (78%) tune into both RED and Mirchi, 821 (76%) tuned into RED and CITY, and 842 (78.7%) tuned into both City and Mirchi. In other words, all channels are delivering virtually similar overall numbers.

— All three stations have equal listenership

— Heavy duplicacy in listenership

Another key insight, which the survey throws up, is that while listeners can recall shows, they are unable to associate the show with the right channel. As high as 70% of respondents cannot associate a particular show with the right channel. Moreover, about one-fourth of respondents were unconcerned / don't even know which station they are listening to. A clear implication of the above insight is that listeners are consumers of programs and not channels.

Roght Channel Accociation

	Red Program	Mirchi Program	City Program
Accociation with RED	29	15	19
Accociation with Mirchi	27	39	31
Accociation with CITY	21	22	28
don't know/ Can't say	23	24	22
Total	100	100	100

A more recent development is the entry of a large number of private producers. Radio City from Star Television, Radio Mirchi from Bennett & Coleman (read TOI), Go 92.5 from the Mid Day group, Today from Living Media Group and Win from the Millennium. Like television and print this medium too is becoming more and more competitive, with all of them fighting for the top position. But what does the present scenario look like, a comprehensive account of where the new players are operating and how they plan to expand in various markets.

FM Listenership in Delhi

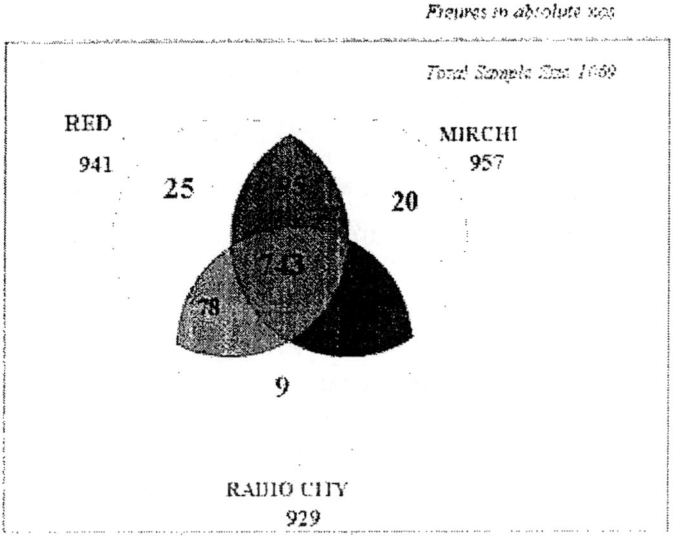

Radio Mirchi

Wholly owned subsidiary of Bennett, Coleman & Co. Ltd., Radio Mirchi is the FM brand of ENIL(Entertainment Network India Ltd.). With their past experience with Times FM and its success, BCCL launched their new radio channel Mirchi in Indore in October'01, thereby spreading its network to Pune, Mumbai and Ahmedabad. Though the programming includes regular music, chat shows, educative programs etc, the endeavor is to position the brand as 'Youthful', thus attracting a whole lot of young audiences. Which does not mean that the young executives or the housewives are to be ignored.

The programming caters to their needs as well by dishing out programmes like 'On the Move' in the morning for the executives, 'Chatpati Baatein' in afternoon for the women and Campus Fundas also in the afternoon for the youngsters. With most of the programming being Hinglish, Radio Mirchi is targeted towards the masses. So if you are addressing a large audience, Radio Mirchi is for you.

Radio City

Star Network made its foray into this medium with Bangalore. The metro just lapped up the excitement that the channel had to offer. Star known for being marketing savvy understood the requirement of the hour and set everybody's foot tapping in Bangalore, with good quality music, professional RJs and programming that met the local flavour. Then they rolled out to Lucknow and very recently to Mumbai. The programming content is similar to that of Mirchi. What sets it apart from Mirchi is City's openness towards innovations and wacky ideas. Creative packaging is its advantage. It is more cost effective and therefore is giving Mirchi a run for its money.

Radio Midday

Radio Midday with it's 'GO 92.5' is another player in Mumbai. They seem to have found a niche for themselves and clearly positioned themselves as 'the English Channel with a local/Indian image'. The channel targets the 25 year old, SEC AB, educated, white collar executive whose needs are clearly English music and programming. Therefore, a focus on international artists popular in India. Not to say that big Indian artists with big fame do not feature in their mix.

WIN

Millennium's 'WIN' launched in Mumbai towards the end of April'02. So those who thought that radio is a background medium need to think twice. The medium seems to be infested with a lot of vibrancy and there are more exciting times to look forward to. All this translates to more and better options for the listener, but this is not a hunky-dory situation for the planners. They will have to be cautious about where to invest. So gone are the days when the planners could simply rely on AIR FM - a channel with assured listenership. With fragmentation setting in and the niches emerging, it would be imperative that the right channel be chosen for the brand.

A media survey has revealed that growth in Indian cable & satellite (C&S) TV penetration is coming from small towns with populations below 100,000 and that it has petered out in urban India. Growth in smaller towns is taking place in excess of 11.5% per annum. The Indian Media & Market Studies survey - conducted annually by market research agency ORG-Marg and the Media Research Users Council - has said that there are about 5.3 million C&S homes in rural India. The survey was carried out in the period between December 1997 and June 1998 and covered 2,965 towns and villages and the sample size was more than 200,000. It covered readership patterns and habits, consumption of products, demographics, TV viewing and cable and satellite TV penetration.

DD's national network channel has turned up as the most watched channel with a 39.6% share of viewership. Hindi entertainment channel Zee TV tops in the most viewed satellite TV channel charts with a 6.9% viewership share. According to one industry estimate there are more than 22 million Indian C&S homes.

CABLE TELEVISION

Cable television is a rough business in India. Earlier this month, the news that a gang in the southern state of Kerala had set fire to the office of a cable operator, immolating two of its employees, rated a one-sentence item in the national press. That sort of thing sits ill with India's vision of itself as a knowledge-industry superpower, which expects cable to deliver much of the data and entertainment needed to justify that ambition. When international investors, such as Intel, are putting money behind the vision, the murder, piracy and cable-cutting that characterise the industry have become positive embarrassments.

Up to now, chaos has had its virtues. The land of the "licence raj" somehow forgot to regulate cable. Anybody could run wires to a few hundred houses, beam programmes and collect money. The result was a boom. Like most Indian statistics, measures of the cable industry's size are disputed, but it is certainly big. The Cable Operators Federation claims to represent 60,000-70,000 firms; others say consolidation has cut that number to around 30,000. By some estimates, India has more cable connections (about 30m) than telephone lines (about 20m).

Now big firms are beginning to attach fibre-optic wires to this snarl, to give households and businesses broadband Internet connections. And India's disparate cable operators are being pulled together into alliances which are more likely to have the money and organisation to equip the country with an up-to-date communications infrastructure. Credit Lyonnais Securities Asia reckons that the number of Internet users in India will rise 15-20-fold by 2004 to 30m, fewer than in China but many more than in any other mainland Asian country. And the key driver after 2001, the brokerage firm predicts, will be cable television.

The incentive will be the difficulty of making money from cable television as it is now structured. At present, the cable industry has the pile-'em-high, sell-'em-cheap approach of down-at-heel discount shops. Subscribers get as many as 75 channels, with new ones coming all the time (recently, HBO, an American movie channel). But, since India lacks set-top boxes that can direct programmes to subscribers who are willing to pay extra for them, most households pay a flat fee of only around 100-150 rupees ($2.30-3.40) a month for their televisual cornucopia.

In this cut-throat market, cable operators grumble that customers demand new channels but refuse to pay more for them. Broadcasters say the operators cheat by drastically understating their subscriber numbers. Multi-systems operators (MSOs), middlemen who take signals from broadcasters and pass them on to local operators, complain that neither pays them adequately. The local operators are probably the best off. They keep nearly 90% of the 40 billion-42 billion rupees of subscription revenue that they collect annually, reckons Bharat Parekh, an analyst at DSP Merrill Lynch in Mumbai. MSOs get 5-6%, which leaves 4-5% for broadcasters. The MSOs are leading the drive to send more expensive services down the cable-and they want to claim a larger share for themselves. Two prerequisites are needed if they are to succeed: the communications infrastructure must improve, and the gaggle of local operators must be wielded into obedient alliances.

The need for better communications infrastructure, and not just for cable, was noted this month by the National Association of Software and Service Companies (NASSCOM), which launched "operation bandwidth", a campaign to boost Internet bandwidth 80-fold by 2003, and to remove regulatory obstacles, such as a 49% cap on foreign ownership of telecoms ventures and a ban on Internet telephony. It has the backing of many large companies, foreign and domestic. Enron, an American energy firm, wants to install at least ten gigabits of bandwidth among seven cities within the next 18 months, by itself about a tenth of NASSCOM's bandwidth target. Hughes Tele.com, a joint venture that is part-owned by General Motors, plans to spend $750m on a fibre-optic network for business communications in Maharashtra and Goa: it already offers basic telephone service there. Last week Reliance Industries, India's biggest private industrial company, offered to raise its stake in BSES, a big power producer and distributor, from 15% to 35%: BSES's fibre-optic network in Mumbai seems to be part of the attraction.

As for the local cable operators, since the mid-1990s, MSOs such as IN CableNet, owned by the Indo-European Hinduja family, and SitiCable, part of Zee Telefilms, India's biggest private broadcaster, have been enlisting thousands, supplying them with equipment and signals and sharing their revenues. Now they are trying to turn these ramshackle federations into alliances bound together with new broadband cable that can carry two-way traffic and deliver sports, movies, online shopping and other luxuries to consumers who are willing to pay extra for them.

Thus the Hindujas' IN CableNet plans to invest up to $500m of fresh money in upgrading cable networks in 75-100 cities, and buying content to take advantage of them. It has moved fastest in Mumbai, where it has laid 150 km of fibre-optic cable and is now offering speedy Internet access to the first of its 1.9m customers in the city. Intel, the biggest chip maker, is impressed enough to have invested $49m, valuing IN CableNet at $1.5 billion. SitiCable plans to offer Internet access over cable in a dozen cities within the next six months and is pondering ways to raise the money. It claims to be worth $3.5 billion.

Such lofty valuations are based in part on the assumption that the MSOs can whip local cable operators into line. They have had some success. Thus, in Mumbai, the Hindujas have an alliance of some 900 local operators who have become little more than agents, collecting the basic subscription fees and handling customers' problems. Such practices as cable-cutting and amplifier stealing have "stopped completely", says Dileep Gupte, who runs the company's broadband services. To build such alliances, MSOs are carrying the cost of upgrading the networks, sometimes including the last mile, which the cable operators usually control.

But plenty of operators retain their wild ways. Earlier this month Bhopal, capital of the state of Madhya Pradesh, lost cable service for a week because of a dispute between an operator affiliated with Siticable and a local MSO. The police brokered a truce. Roop Sharma, president of the Cable Operators Federation, scoffs that an MSO is "just a signal provider". She sees little reason for her constituents to upgrade their networks: "Why should cable operators spend when consumers only give 100 rupees a month?"

Sceptical operators are not the only risk that the MSOs face. They are pioneers in a market with low incomes, poor technology and excessive regulation. Interactive digital television has yet to arrive in India, so the first customers for the Internet over cable will be users of its 3m-4m computers. Although MSOs expect the cost of the service-1,500 rupees a month, or ten times what most subscribers pay for cable TV-to fall quickly, along with that of cable modems, for the moment it is out of reach of all but the rich.

The quality of the service that MSOs can offer depends in part on bits of the wires that they do not control. Most Internet traffic comes from outside India, and thus hits the bottleneck of India's publicly owned telecoms companies, which have a monopoly of long-distance telephony and international data exchange. The data monopoly is about to end, and private operators will soon carry Internet traffic via satellite. But the state monopoly is keeping its grip over access to ultra-high capacity submarine cables. Yet MSOs have one great advantage, which telcos cannot rival. They already have broadband connections with millions of homes, which they can now upgrade and use to promote their new services. If they succeed, India could yet be the country that proves the Internet can benefit the poor world, and not just the rich.

Uses of the Internet

There are 300 million users worldwide today with nearly 150,000 users added everyday. Internet penetration in Asia is presently driven by business, unlike in USA, where individuals drive it. The total Internet home connections here in India are close to 1.6 million, though it is estimated that the total number of users is nearly 4.8 million.

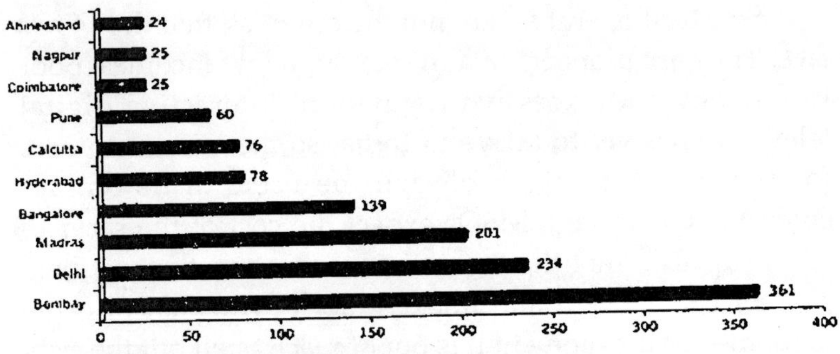

Figs in 000's Source IRS 2000

A RightServe analysis of IRS 2000 reveals interesting facets of the Internet user in India. The top 10 cities contribute to

60% of the total Internet penetration in India, with Bombay at 18%, followed by Delhi & Madras with 11% and 10% respectively.

According to IRS 2000 the average time spent on the Internet versus other media is as follows:

Time Spent on the Internet vis a vis Print & TV

	Saturday	Sunday	Weekdays
Internet	1.08	0.39	1.29
Press	1.13	1.24	1.13
TV	2.39	3.07	2.21

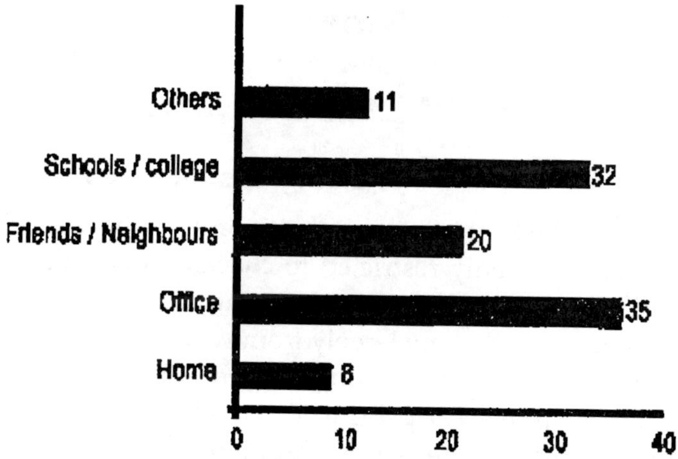

(Figures In %) Source IRS 2000

Thus, it makes innate business sense for brand managers to use the Internet, as the medium does not lag behind.

A majority of today's consumers i.e. those with disposable income, fall in the age group of 25+ and 52% of them are exposed to the Internet.Their reasons for logging on to the Internet range from e-mail to getting updates on business news, product information, political and sports news. E-mail by itself accounts for 89%. Over 35% accessed the Internet from the work place, 32% from place of study and 8% from home.

(Figures in %) Source IRS 2000

What must be kept in mind is that a person who is checking his mail is not only restricted to checking his mail. These people can be reached very easily at they have multiple points of access that are largely from work place and home. Traditionally, there was only two media vying for the consumer's time - T.V & Print. Today, the Internet has also come in and the pie is now divided between the three media, and the Internet is fast catching up.

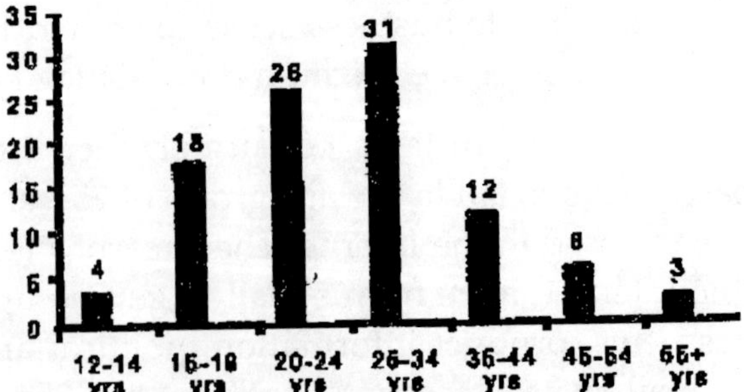

(Figures in %) Source IRS 2000

Internet Exposure by Age

Internet exposure by age shows that 75% of all adults, who accessed the Internet are in the age group of 15 - 34 years.

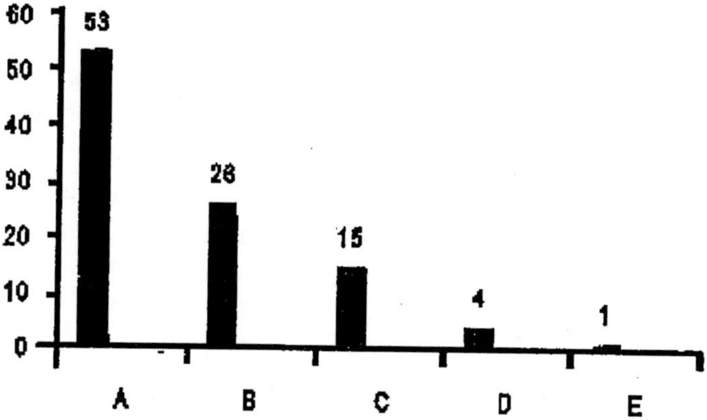

(Figures in %) Source IRS 2000

Internet Exposure by SEC

Net exposure by SEC shows that at least 79% of all adults who accessed the Internet are in SEC A and B.

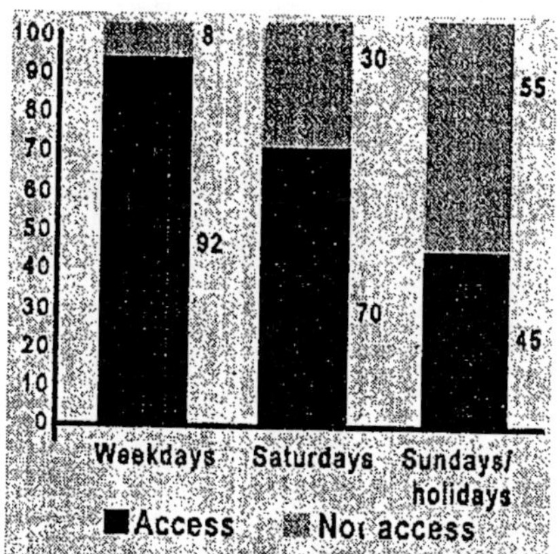

(Figures in %) Source IRS 2000

While 45% (all India) were found to access the Internet on Sundays and holidays, the figure rose to 92% during weekdays. On Saturdays the figure is 70%. Over 35% accessed the Internet from the work place, 32% from place of study and 8% from home. Industry predictions suggest that home market is likely to dominate the Internet's future in India. An IMRB study states that 97% of the users have accessed the Net out of home, at school, college, at work or a cyber cafe. According to Nasscom - Aug 2000, there are 1.6 million homes in India with Internet connections and on average at least 3 people use one system.

5

Media Influence on Society

The media - television, radio, and newspapers, is the worlds' most powerful means of communication. The media has a strong impact on our lives. In many cases, what we see in the media is not the truth. What they show is one sided-they tell what they feel is the most important. Society is being brainwashed by what they see on television, hear on the radio and read in the newspaper. Both the gangsters of the past, and todays gangsters - gangsta rappers, can be viewed in both a negative and positive light. Since power, money and success are all values that people strive for - many see them as idols. But many are against what they feel gangsters are trying to promote - Crime.

Recently gangsta rap has been playing a large role in our society. Many people feel that all gangsta rappers do, is glorify violence, rap with obscene lyrics, and totally degrade women where they are almost always always portrayed as uneducated and highly promiscuous. But more and more of the teenage population are enjoying the music and helping the sales increase. Many children look at the rappers as role models and many imitate what they see. All we know about todays gangsters is what we are taught by the media. The gangster image of today has been villianized by the media and the mass society. But what the media doesnt realize, is that even tought they are trying to portray gangsters in a negative way, all of the attention that they are giving the gangster - glorifies the criminal's life.

Media Environment in India

India is a large and diverse country with an equally sizeable and varied media. The spurt of growth in this media has a tremendous impact on shaping development values as it informs, educates and entertains. Indian government tried to control airwaves but could not hold it for a long. Today Indian sky is flooded with several channels - both Indian (Doordarshan) as well as foreign. The foreign channels combine foreign programmes with indigenous ones. There is no direct control on them. This is very clear in their carrying commercials on alcohol and a large number of soap operas round the clock, which have very little relevance with the Indian society. However they try to project their sincerity by showing some token programming having developmental messages.

Doordarshan initially started with the goal of using television for development purpose has joined in a race with the foreign channels. As a result though there are more than 50 channels and round the clock transmission is available on Indian television the actual choice of viewing is not that wide. The choice is between one sitcom to the other of the same production teams whether it is Doordarshan or any other channel. In this situation it is difficult to expect attitudinal revolution on the part of the programme makers. As a result with the quantity of the programmes the quality (not technical) has hardly improved. The people are constantly exposed to the messages majority of which are basically from the commercial houses.

Television is a major source of audio-visual images in developing countries. In general women are more regular in their television viewing compared to the men. The lower the income group, the more regular are viewers, both male and female, compared to the higher income groups. Many viewers, especially women, seem to be compulsive viewers. Similar results were obtained in American society during '80s. Television is the people's medium and the one particularly relied upon by those who for reasons of education, income or culture, have limited access to or make little use of other sources - the poor, blacks and other minorities and the elderly. These groups voluntarily or involuntarily are dependent on television and a sizeable population is totally and involuntarily so".

On the other hand in USA for the past ten years research has consistently come up with the same result that of male characters out-numbered female by two to one on television. Only a minority of the women portrayed is mature adults, compared to 70 percent of the men portrayed. Two out of three men are depicted in some occupational context compared to only two out of five women.

Media reform

While the direction of media reform in India has often been viewed in the context of demand and supply, its exclusionary and piece meal characteristics would appear to have been relegated to the background. These have significant fall-outs in terms of media democratization in the country. Even a cursory look at the pace of decentralization would take cognizance of its selective and reactive characteristics. If the first is predictable under a 'market is the mantra' regime, the latter is worrying as it raises a larger question: Does the course of the reforms conform to a larger and cogent media policy, or are they symptomatic of a crisis - management and reactive culture? While there are no easy answers, community would appear to have paid the heaviest price in an ambivalent and unlevelled media playing field.

In a county of daunting socio-economic divides accompanied by a formidable diversity of languages, dialects and cultures, the potential for community media should have assumed critical significance. Unfortunately, the gap between potential and practices would appear to have widened, judged by the media trends. Community voices, if at all, struggle at the periphery of a contrasting and often iniquitous media landscape. In contrast to the government's efforts to bridge the digital divide and take information technology to the masses, the colonial and fossilised Indian Telegraph Act of 1885 continues to hold sway over the broadcasting arena.

On the one hand, the Supreme Court Judgement of 1995 has endorsed that 'airwaves are public property.' However, in the practical realm, lines between public and privately remain conveniently blurred. While Private Radio has made an entry into the Indian broadcast arena, community radio remains to find legitimacy by the law of the land, notwithstanding New Delhi's recent New Year gift enabling residential educational institutions to be eligible for 'campus community radio.'

In terms of reach and access, India's print and broadcast media manifest - very substantially - the characteristics of mass media. 'While newspapers elsewhere struggle to hold readers, Indian daily circulation has increased by close to 500% in 20 years. Two all-India readership surveys conducted in 1999-2000, estimate that the press as a whole reaches between something 200 and 240 million persons. Translated in terms of percentages this means that about 60% of urban Indians and 25% of rural Indians read print media regularly. Radio's reach is even more comprehensive covering about 96% of the country. But, notwithstanding this growth in terms of reach, media's impact on development and governance remains, at best, tenuous. In fact there would appear to remain a substantial gap between potential and experience.

Paradoxically, in terms of need, the role of media in bridging the development gap is more keenly felt today than ever before. The 1990s, especially in the socio-economic context, yields a disquieting picture. Globalisation's impact on the poverty map leaves much to be desired. Even World Bank statistics point to a rise in the number of poor, with '40 million people' in India having joined their ranks during the 1990s. The latest Human Development Report statistics point to India slipping further down the ranks to stand at 127, three notches down from the previous year.

The situation is elaborated by development economist and head, human development programme, National Council of Applied Economic Research, Abusaleh Shariff. In a recent interview he asserted that 'if the definition of poverty were expanded to incorporate the human development parameters, the world poverty level would touch 60%.' In the Indian context, '70% of our people will qualify as poor,' while the below poverty line figures indicated 26% to be 'worse than chronically poor.' Other observations and commentaries merely accentuate the argument.

India also enters the "millennium" with hundreds of millions of illiterates. Again, spending on education in India is less than 4% of GDP. Far less than the 6% that the government itself says is the minimum required. In terms of quality of life the picture is far from rosy. New nutritional data at the all India level show that average calorie intake declined steadily in both rural and urban areas between 1973 and 1994. The threat of political conflict, communalism and terrorism has also palpably impacted on the notion of a democratic nation state.

The media's response to these trends has been a mixed bag. A study conducted by the Centre for Development and Learning, Bangalore, in 2000 focussed on media coverage of development issues in newspapers. The data was based on coverage spread over the period of one year. It noted that if 'development news can be defined as "information that has social consequence", priorities were startling. For instance, in the Times of India (one of the largest dailies in the country), 4% of a total of 24 pages were devoted to development news. This percentage proved to be more or less representative in terms of coverage in many other dailies.'

Media's relationship with governance is equally tenuous. Media coverage of the recent communal strife in Gujarat has, in the main, been positive. But disparities do exist. As Mukul Sharma points out, 'both media and governance in India suffer from serious problems, which at times, even feed into each other. Suspension of civil liberties, excessive militarisation, communal assertions and homogenising tendencies have too often spelled doom for Indian democracy. Media become more sensitive on issues of democratic governance, people's struggle against social injustice, and so on...' This, however, is only part of the picture. If the media are effectively to mirror society, then 'the role of people's organisations, social movements, voluntary organisations and other civil society formations in monitoring the functioning of the media and making it more people centred is critical.' It is here, that the rub comes.

Unlike the government or political parties and sections of the corporate sector who have developed the own press and media channels, voluntary organisations, social groups and activists, have not been able to develop their own press and television channels in a sustained manner. The exceptions that exist are usually journals/newsletters of development organisations which cannot in terms of size or scope make a sustained dent at the macro level. What is required is an active tradition of community/peoples media. Unfortunately, we do not appear to be moving in that direction.

The promise of media reform which gathered momentum in the 1980s and 90s unfortunately did not actualize into performance. The journey from the Broadcast Bill to the Convergence Bill generated considerable expectations in the public domain - only to fritter away into cynicism. While the Broadcast Bill suffered an untimely death, the Convergence Bill (notwithstanding the hype it initially evoked) remains to be tabled in the Lok Sabha despite the passage of three years. Clearly, an overt lesson would indicate a reluctance, at the policy level, to 'walk the talk'. This weakness in political will towards media reform per se becomes more evident in taking a closer look at broadcast legislation.

The Prasar Bharati Act, which in many ways provides a watershed in media legislation in the country, demonstrates this substantially. While the Bill was based on the Verghese Committee Report of 1978 there were significant differences. The Verghese Committee had favoured the creation of a 'Trust' in the service of the public, as against the Prasar Bharati Bill which proposed a

Corporation which did not have the same statutory dignity and power. While the objectives of the corporation are virtually the same as the Verghese Committee's objectives for the National Broadcast Trust, they would appear to fall short of the Verghese Report's recommendations, which wanted the Ministry of Information and Broadcasting to shed its responsibility for broadcasting altogether. The Bill has provisions for a representative of the MIB as a part time Governor which is at variance with the 'full autonomy' suggested by the Verghese Committee.

The Verghese Committee Report also underlined the need for a decentralized structure with powers delegated at regional and local levels. In sharp contrast, the Prasar Bharati bill says little about the devolution of the powers of the Government of India and executive boards. Consequently, despite obtaining 'autonomous status' under this Act, the Prasar Bharati Corporations's functioning has been described as 'de facto under the influence of the Government of India' in various ways. For instance, the Ministry of Information and Broadcasting has the ability to intervene and provide inputs to Prasar Bharati. The Convergence Bill, however, vests powers of regulation and licensing for communications in a Communications Commission. In doing so, it would, in effect, take away those very powers from the Ministry of Information and Broadcasting.

In many ways, the radio broadcasting scenario in the country provides an apt benchmark to view the case for community media reform. Unlike India's neighbours, - Sri Lanka and Nepal - community radio broadcasting remains outside the pale of legitimacy. Despite advocacy initiatives which have articulated the need for a three-tiered media structure - public (government), private and community -

the latter remains to be endorsed by law. After a virtual decade of lobbying, in early 2003 the Government allowed residential educational institutions to apply for licenses to operationalise what it defined as community radio stations. It took nearly a year before the government upheld one of the licence applicants.

At the end of 2003, community Anna University was given the green light by the Government of India to implement the country's first 'campus community' radio programme. Reportedly, the Indian Institute of Technology, Kanpur, is likely to closely follow-on Anna University's heels. So far,so good. But a closer look would indicate that it is far too early to cheer the new year gift. For instance, New Delhi's decision to allow residential educational institutions recognized by the state and central governments to apply for licenses to broadcast would appear to have completely overlooked the proven credentials of community based NGOs and CBOs who have demonstrated the viability and impact of community participation in radio. It needs stressing, that in terms of grass roots experience these NGO and Community based initiatives are demonstrably ahead of the educational institutions that have no tradition or practical experience of community broadcasting. Further, many of these initiatives have applied for licenses as early as 2000, long before the campus community initiative was conceptualized.

Community radio initiatives

One of the reasons cited by official quarters for the absence of community radio legislation is the lack of demand. While it is true that community radio advocacy needs to go beyond preaching to the converted, it is not realistic to restrict it to a clutch of initiatives any longer. Post New Delhi's campus radio initiative in early 2003, there have been several universities across the country which have not only evinced interest, but introduced community radio as a part of their media pedagogy. These include Anna University in Tamil Nadu, Indira Gandhi National Open University, Jamia Millia and the Indian Institute of Mass Communications in New Delhi. At the same time, several development NGOs at the grass roots level have initiated or facilitated endeavours which demonstrate community participation in radio. Notwithstanding the need for the recommendations to receive the official stamp of approval, their provisions palpably demonstrate the contrast between private and community broadcasting. These, in turn, effectively mirror the overall media climate in the country.

If the writing on the media reform wall is clear, it also needs reiteration if community voices are to move from the margins towards the centre:

1. The current media climate needs to be reviewed in the context of not only strengthening the public domain, but bringing community into the centre stage. This calls for a closer and more interactive link between media and development in the country which in turn warrants an appraisal not only of processes in the existing media traditions, but also widening the scope and legitimacy of media democratisation in the country. If deregulation is the buzzword, we need to ensure that its vision goes beyond the pale of strategic mergers and corporatisation. This, in turn, demands a review of the notion of access. Access without inclusiveness could be akin to information without communication and handicap the development and governance process. Inclusion of Community Media would demonstrate a way forward.

2. The two tiers of public (government) and private media are already a legitimate part of media processes

in the country. However, a third tier - that of community media - needs to be legitimized. A community media tradition has, unfortunately, not been firmly rooted in the Indian landscape. Priority needs to be given in issuing of community broadcasting licenses to rural areas and other regions and communities that are least developed in terms of various socio-economic indicators. This is also based on the fact that the least developed regions and communities of the country are also least served by media.

3. While the crux of the problem in several instances might lie with a reluctant state, civil society needs to get its act together. This, in turn, demands a review of the demand-supply equation. For instance, the observation that the demand for community radio is restricted needs to be questioned and dispelled by effective documentation, networking, capacity building, strategic alliance building. Specifically, this could mean: collaborations between universities and community media advocates/practitioners to ensure that community media is part of the curriculum and pedagogy; capacity building awareness programmes to widen the relevance of community media in the country in general and the social sector in particular; using traditional and new media to document and disseminate best practices.

4. Synergise the Right to Information with the Right to Communicate as enshrined in Article 19 of the Universal Declaration of Human Rights. The recent endorsement of a freedom of information act by the Lok Sabha and the increasing popularity of the movement across the country (five states already have the Right to Information Act in place) needs to be

integrated into community media advocacy agendas. If the denial of information aggravates the poverty gap, information without communication could be dead wood. Producers of information need to be able to communicate it in a manner they deem appropriate.

Media and Education

Communication includes all methods of disseminating information, knowledge, thought, attitudes, and beliefs. Modern mass media like newspapers, cinema, and television, and traditional media of social communication like the bazaar, puppet show, drama, dance, local meetings, as well as inter-personal communication media like posts and telegraphs, teleprinters, and telephones all impact language use. The underlying and basic factor of these categories of mass media is language. Hence for the effectual and proper utilisation of these mass media, language education is very essential and material.

Inter-personal communication media helps meet the demand for mutual communication and exchange of information among people and institutions. In recent years, the use of computer has far reaching effect on language education and communication. In this field also language education is of paramount importance. The special feature of radio, television, and cinema is that they serve the needs of both literates and illiterates. They will also entertain people in remote areas not within the reach of newspapers. On the other hand, newspapers present the 'written word' and serve as 'record,' while at the same time give local coverage. Language education to the audience, readers and spectators is very essential.

Language and Communication

In India, various forms of language are in competition with each other to draw the attention of the public. These forms range from the extremely informal style of speech found in the radio and the cinema to the formal styles found in newspapers and news broadcasts. Different language styles perform different functions in society. The styles of standard languages constantly undergo changes and development through the impact of various mass communication media. Formal public education is one of the most powerful tools that influences linguistic norms and linguistic attitudes. Another important aspect of language education in India is culture learning. One learns a language through being culturally aware. Thus there is inter-relationship and reinforcement between language and culture. They are inter-dependent. News texts are part of what a particular culture thinks of as significant, and show a hierarchy of values.

The newspaper is 'talk' about world affairs and current events, having multifarious functions in society such as disseminating information, socialisation, motivation, education, cultural learning, entertainment, integration, etc. Most newspapers in Indian languages appear to focus on the readability of the material or news they present. They recognize that the way language is used is an important factor in enabling their readers to come back to them. But language alone does not help a newspaper to increase its sale in the market place. In a country where everything is looked at from a political angle, the support base for a newspaper in Indian languages often comes from the shades of political opinion that a newspaper supports and highlights.

The manner a news item is presented and highlighted depends on the "ideology" of the newspapers. This "ideology" controls and regulates language use. Of the different mass media, newspapers assume great importance as they deal every day with dissemination of current information pertaining to different aspects of human life, such as social, economic, political and cultural, both at national and international levels. In a newspaper, headlines occupy a prominent position by summarising the most important news of the day in a nutshell, which facilitates the reader with quick reading and comprehension.

The choice of expression plays a vital role in making the headlines more effective. Thus language plays a prominent part and it aims at educating the reader. At present Indian language newspapers show a tendency to use simpler and colloquial forms of expression more frequently. Newspapers in Indian languages at present have also begun to use loaded expressions with sarcasm and cynicism, because the growing middle class around the nation that buys and reads the newspapers is basically cynical about politics and politicians. The newspapers are educators of the literate and not so literate public. Now-a-days newspaper reading habit is growing rapidly and widely. Thus there is the steady and expanding process of language education through newspapers. The educated families in south India a generation ago made it a point to read THE HINDU daily newspaper as part of their daily English education.

History reveals that the Press Acts against vernacular press in British India actually helped the people to seek greater freedom and ultimately independence from Britain. Political, social, and economic revolutions in India are closely related to the active involvement and development of newspapers in Indian languages. The prose of every Indian language is critically developed and guided by the language style used in the newspapers published in these languages. In order to establish their own identity, newspapers deliberately coin and choose their own language expressions. For example, there is a great tendency these days to combine various native words with English words to create special expressions. Translation is no more a fashion with most Indian languages newspapers. Some thirty years ago, most Indian languages newspapers made special effort to translate words and phrases in to Indian languages. Now they tend to simply transcribe foreign words in the native script. This tendency is supported by the spread of cable TV as well as by the globalization process.

Further in a democratic country like India, the newspaper acts as a powerful weapon in exposing the irregularities, shortcomings, and failures of government policy and also function as an eye-opener of the public. But newspapers should not abuse their status and functions. They should be above bias and should be fair and impartial. The language used should be of high standard aiming at educating the public not only in terms of news content but also in terms of language use. This twin function is not wholly appreciated or even discerned in some newspapers that seek only sensationalism in content and expression.

Radio has greater potential in mass communication than the newspaper for two reasons. Firstly, it reaches even the remote corners of the country and has no physical impediments. Secondly, it imparts language education and provides entertainment and disseminates information to both literate and illiterate listeners. Radio is under government control for fear of its misuse and powerful influence. There are indications that soon we will have privately owned radio stations with their own programs of broadcasts all over the country. The range of programmes includes a wide variety of educational, cultural and entertainment items, aimed at a broad spectrum of classes of people.

The type of language used in government-controlled radio stations, unfortunately, seems to be artificial in its idiom in the broadcasts done in all Indian languages. The broadcasts for farmers and workers try to use a style that is supposedly understood by less literate groups. We are yet to find a balance in the broadcasts that suit the audience for which these are intended. But the broadcasts are not as appropriate as these should be for the simple reason that these broadcasts are still largely government-controlled. Radio has a major role to play in language.

The language used in radio impacted the previous generation very much. News broadcasts introduced chaste language, closely modelled after the written variety. The newsreaders introduced standard pronunciation values to the phonemes, words, phrases, and sentences. The impact of radio language was heavy upon the written style, rather than on the spoken idiom. This is somewhat strange, considering the fact that radio is mainly an audio form. It appears that Indian radio is more closely associated with news and music than with dialogue.

Television is the audio-visual non-literary media having the additional advantage of being able to use visual cues to reinforce the information being presented in spoken form. Thus even in this field language education plays a vital role, because additional cues compensate for dialectal differences between speakers and hearers. The potential of television as an educative device is very great. But exploiting this potential depends upon the choice of appropriate language. TV programs are telecast through satellites. The satellite TV offers a dazzling array of channels and programme choices in many different languages. The divide between the literate and less literate or non-literate classes is covered up in the television media.

Media discourse provides a fertile ground for traditional cultural learning, even as it provides opportunities to entertain and educate the viewers in novel and wholly modern ways that work against traditional values. Unfortunately, TV is more cinema-centered than radio. Entertainment takes precedence in TV. The impact of TV on Indian languages, in terms of their lexicon and structure, so far seems to be negligible. Privately owned TV channels often follow the models set by the leading newspapers in their coverage.

The language of cinema, on the whole, is more accessible to the average person than that of other media. The movies, in general, make use of colloquial style of speech. The language of the cinema, like that of other media, also shows considerable variation. The cinema, being closer to informal popular speech, has two advantages:

1. It appeals to mass audience, and
2. it portrays everyday situations wherein popular language is more appropriate than the more formal variety.

In the village context the cinema competes with other forms of entertainment because it assesses a more popular language. There is, however, a serious problem. Until early seventies, most movies in Indian languages often followed a style that was closer to the written style. These days, movies are produced mostly in the colloquial idiom, except those movies that try to depict the heritage through mythology, etc. A movie viewer does not get introduced to the written variety now a day. Since in many Indian languages the distinction between the formal and informal styles of language or the distinction between the colloquial/

spoken and written styles are still maintained, the usefulness of watching a movie in order to improve the competence in mother tongue is practically less significant.

Computer revolution

The computer Revolution in teaching Indian languages is still not yet widespread, despite the fact that computer software engineering is the most preferred profession for the educated young men and women in India. Driven by economic pursuits and greed, Indians seem to be competing with one another in offering their services to enrich the already rich nations. And yet, it is a fact that the presence of Indian languages in the world-wide-web is more significant than any other group of languages in the developing world.

Certain Indian linguistic groups such as Kannadigas, Telugus, and Tamils seem to be more advanced in taking advantage of the computer revolution to improve their language education. There is a significant impact in language use brought out by the use of e-mail. Abbreviations even in Indian languages seem to be used more commonly these days. Once upon a time, inscriptions in copper plates and stones used abbreviations as a means to communicate information in short sentences, etc. Time was not the main consideration when a few generations ago Indians used lots of abbreviations in spelling and combination of letters in their written documents. But, for this generation, time is an important consideration and they use abbreviations of different sorts in their e-mails, and chats.

People want to be different from one another, especially from one generation to another. Wireless, cell phone abbreviations become the dominant feature of urban young men and women these days. Languages are mangled or deconstructed in an idiosyncratic manner. Indian languages find a significant place in the Unicode. This is a great contribution from the energetic Indian software engineers. However, just like the technical terms created by committees constituted by various governments and their agencies, the use of Unicode characters allotted to Indian languages are not yet popular with the Indian public.

Computers store material and keep them in memory. They express the correct use of language. They furnish valuable information concerning various subjects. They operate at high speed and provide opportunity for rectifying and correcting mistakes and errors. Thus the computer, mainly having literary merits, plays a very significant role in language education. It provides knowledge and information in almost all the major languages, both national and international.

Major Educational Radio Projects in India

The main projects that describe the growth of educational radio are:

School Broadcast Project: This project was commissioned in 1937 and the target group was School students. This programme started from Delhi, Calcutta, Madras and Bombay. In the beginning the school programme were not strictly governed by the curriculum. With the passages of time and acquisitions of more experience, the AIR tried to make its radio broadcasts more curriculum oriented, but in absence of common syllabi and time tables in schools, even within the same state, it could not succeed in it's aim.

Adult education and community development project (Radio Forum): Commenced in 1956, the Villagers of 144 villages in the vicinity of Poona (in Maharastra state), were the main beneficiaries of this project. This was agriculture-based project, which was originally designed and tried out in Canada. With the help of UNESCO, it was tried in 144 villages of Poona and was named as ' Radio forums Project' (defined as a listening cum-discussion-cum-action group). The members of the forum could listen thirty-minute radio programme on some agricultural or community - development programme, then discuss and decide regarding it's adoption in their own village. This project was a great success. Many action programmes were planned and put into practice.

Farm and Home Broadcast Project: This project was commenced in 1966 and again targeted at Farmers and villagers. These broadcasts were designed to provide information and advice on agricultural and allied topics. The aim was to educate the farmers and provide them assistance in adopting innovative practices in their fields as per the local relevance. The experts also conducted occasional farm radio schools, which proved to be very effective.

University broadcast project: This project for University students was initiated in 1965, with an aim to expand higher education as widely as possible among the different strata of society. The Programme consisted of two types- 'General' & 'enrichment'. The general programmes included topics of public interest and enrichment programmes supported correspondence education offered by universities in their respective jurisdictions. School of Correspondence studies, University of Delhi and the Central Institute of English and Foreign Languages, Hyderabad is well known for preparation and broadcast of their programmes through AIR.

Language Learning Programme: The project, popularly known as 'Radio Pilot project' was started in 1979-80 jointly by AIR and Department of Education Government of Rajasthan, with an aim to teach Hindi to School going children as first language in 500 primary schools of Jaipur & Ajmer districts on experimental basis. The project was found useful in improving the vocabulary of children. With its success, similar project was repeated in Hoshangabad district of Madhya Pradesh with some modifications but had limited success.

IGNOU-AIR Broadcast: In collaboration with IGNOU, AIR stations of Mumbai, Hyderabad and Shillong started radio broadcasts of IGNOU Programmes from January 1992. Main target group of this project were students of Open / Conventional Universities. Although Shillong started this but discontinued later on. Therefore presently it is being broadcast from AIR Mumbai and AIR Hyderabad only. This programme is still popular in the respective region.

IGNOU-AIR Interactive Radio Counselling (IRC): Started in 1998 for students of Open / Conventional Universities, this project is also very successful. In order to bridge the gap between Institutions and learners by instantly responding to their queries and also to provide Academic Counselling in subject area, IGNOU in collaboration with AIR Bhopal started this project in May 1998 as an experimental programme for one year. With the success of the experiment, it was extended to 8 other AIR stations (Lucknow, Patna, Jaipur, Shimla, Rohtak, Jalandhra, Delhi and Jammu). Presently Interactive Radio counseling is being provided on every Sunday for one hour from 186 radio stations of All India Radio. This includes two Sundays on the National hook-up. Toll-free telephone facility is available from 80 cities enabling the learners to interact with experts and seek clarification, without paying for their telephone calls. The first and third Sundays of the month, AIR stations of Delhi (Hindi) and Kolkata (in English) broadcast from national hook-up, which 186 radio stations relay either of them. The 2nd and 4th Sunday are slotted for programmes of various regional centers of IGNOU and State Open universities respectively. The slot of 5th Sunday (if any) has also been given to region-based programmes of IGNOU. This programme is gaining popularity day by day.

Gyan-Vani (Educational FM Radio Channel of India): This project is recently launched (in year 2001) and again the target group is students of Open / Conventional Universities. Gyan Vani (Gyan = Knowledge, Vani = aerial broadcasting) is Educational FM Radio Channel of India, a unique decentralised concept of extending mass media for education and empowerment, suited to the educational needs of the local community. It is operating presently through Allahabad, Banglore and, Coimbatore FM stations of India on test transmission mode. The network is slotted to expand to a total of 40 stations by June-2002.

Gyan Vani stations will operate as media cooperatives, with day-to-day programmes contributed by different Educational Institutions, NGO's and national level institutions like IGNOU, NCERT, UGC, IIT, DEC etc. Each stations will have range of about 60-KM radius, covering the entire city /town plus the surrounding environs with extensive access. It serves as ideal medium addressing the local educational developmental and socio cultural needs (IGNOU, 2001). Gyan Vani is not only for the conventional educational system but also a main tool in making available the dream of education for all come true. Gyan Vani's main intention is to take education to the doorsteps of the people.

Gyan Vani, in addition to giving the hardcore education will also deal with awareness programmes including the ones for Panchayati Raj Functionaries, Women Empowerment, Consumer Rights, Human Rights, the Rights of the Child, Health Education, Science Education, Continuing Education, Extension Education, Vocational Education, Teacher Education, Non-formal Education, Adult Education, Education for the handicapped, Education for the down trodden, education for the tribals and so on. Gyan Vani is available through commercial FM radio set.

Radio-Vision (Multimedia through Digital Radio): Pioneered by the BBC, the technique of radio-vision allows the subject matter to be presented through two channels, the audio and the visual. The visuals are presented in the form of still filmstrips, charts, slides, models, etc, while the explanation is given through recorded narration. Educational institutions use this as a substitute for educational television. Radio-vision has its own advantages:

— It is economical

— It can cater to different categories of learners

— It is easy to produce such programmes at the institutional level or at the learning centers

— It provides visual support to the concept that is taught.

A small experiment in the use of radio-vision technique was carried out by The National Council of Education Training and Research, India in 1975-76 using it as one of the components of the multi-media package for in service teacher training designed and operated during SITE. A series of charts and picture cards were presented to about 24,000 participating teachers 2400 centres alongwith verbal explanation provided through specially prepared radio broadcasts. The results were found to be encouraging.

A pilot project was carried out in IGNOU in 2001 under UNESCO support for testing the feasibility of using the new digital technology for cost effective transmission of audio-visual courseware. The project proved that FM Radio transmitters and Satellite Radio transponders can be used successfully to transmit, downlink and download multimedia courseware, in this case using the Asia Star of WorldSpace.

Radio-text: Radio has been used along with textual data transfer via computer networks simultaneously to create a 'radio-text' environment. The teaching end is normally a FM radio station having data broadcast facility through a computer network. The main points of the radio broadcast are sent through textual mode to the receiving end via a computer network. The learning end has radio listening facility as well as a computer screen to receive the textual data. Since both audio and text are broadcast simultaneously, the learner at the receiving end gets high quality and low cost teaching. An experiment on the use of radio-text at Yashwant Rao Chavan Maharashtra Open University, Nasik, India resulted in the satisfaction of more than 80 percent the learners. It also used for peer group discussion at the receiving end after the broadcast, which indicates radio-text could be used for varieties of objectives.

Women in Media

Stereotyped portrayal of women in media messages is a universal axiom, though definitions of what constitutes a stereotype way vary across cultures. Likewise one can find similarities in feminist reactions towards advertise-ments across cultures and geographical boundaries. So much so that portrayal of women in media has become a global sensitivity. Furthermore, in the past decade media analysis has become an important agenda of action for many women activists groups and other organisations.

Among young women (college going) there is a strong perception that obscene film songs lead to eve teasing and harassment. The positive sign in this situation is some increase in women's programmes of greater variety. But these kind of positive efforts have always remained limited. Hence we are one step forward but two steps backward. There is manifold increase in vulgarity in the programmes and using women as commodity that cannot shape the attitude of gender equality. It is generally perceived that the main reason for exploitation of woman is her lack of control over these media. There is a constant demand to increase the representation by hiring and promoting more and more women at least in the government owned media organisations. However studies have indicated marginal or no improvement in this sector.

It had been estimated that women formed 25 per cent in broadcasting in India in 1979. A need to increase women's participation was felt by all the concerned hence greater participation in the future was expected. Especially when new developments had taken place like the development of the television. Instead the percentage of women in television centres was found lower than in `broadcasting ` in 1979. Among full time permanent employees 84-88 per cent are men and only 12-15 per cent are women in Doordarshan in 1994. However it seems that there is no substantial difference over the period of five years as the sample study states the range of 7% to 13% of women in administrative and 11% to 15% in production jobs in Doordarshan during 1989.

Media and Crimes Against Women

There is no simple explanation for the frequency of violent crimes against women, but it has been suggested that one contributing factor may be the way women are portrayed in the media. Women are often depicted as victims of violence or as sexual objects, and researchers have found that these media portrayals may influence how women are viewed and treated in society. Film, television, music, music videos and computer games have all been criticized for content considered demeaning to women, such as sexual objectification, depictions of violence against women, and the frequent association of violence with sexuality. Over 40 years of scientific investigation has led researchers to conclude that media violence significantly contributes to aggressive attitudes and behavior in society.

Mounting evidence suggests that negative perceptions of women in entertainment can affect women in real life. Research examining onscreen violence toward women finds that emotional desensitization can occur after viewing as few as two films with sexually degrading and violent themes. Studies also show that men who view a number of films in which women are portrayed in sexually degrading or violent situations become increasingly less disturbed by violence against women and less sympathetic toward female victims of violence. In addition, films initially found demeaning to women are judged to be less so after prolonged exposure. Some people target pornography as the medium most likely to depict women in an offensive manner.

Mainstream films and magazines are often more violent than pornography. In fact, the American public considers many movies demeaning to women; a survey found that 68% of the public believes sexual portrayals of women in American movies "often" amount to exploitation. Recent studies have found that college men exposed to just a few of these films tend to lack empathy towards female victims of rape, believing she "deserved what she got." In addition, these men often do not believe the rapist should be punished. On television, a disproportionate amount of violence is directed toward female victims. For every 10 male characters on primetime network TV who commit violence, 11 other male characters fall to violence, but for every 10 women who inflict violence, 16 women become victims. Studies have shown that viewers who strongly associate with the victims (i.e., women) feel more susceptible to violence in the real world. More often than not, these viewers become the "real life" victims.

Movies and television alone do not foster changes in attitude. Other media, including music and music videos, may also contribute to negative perceptions of women. Researchers have found an average of 18 instances of aggression each hour on Music Television (MTV), 35% of which depict sexual violence against women. One study of 144 undergraduate males determined that after watching a significant amount of violent or demeaning music videos, desensitization occurs which may foster an antagonistic attitude toward women. Forty percent (40%) of the men in this study indicated some likelihood of committing rape if they could be assured of avoiding punishment.

Studies show that the dominating theme of "love relationship" in songs has increasingly shifted to include explicit sexual references that are often demeaning to women. In particular, gangsta rap, a popular West Coast music style distinguished by lyrics that graphically describe scenes of gunplay, sex, drug use and violence, often depicts women negatively; their roles rarely extend beyond being kidnapped, held hostage, brutally gang raped at gunpoint, or murdered. Studies have found that exposure to rap music does, in fact, "tend to lead to a higher degree of acceptance of the use of violence (including violence against women)."

These types music videos communicate a dangerous message to both men and women - that the invasion of the female body is welcomed and desired, which may translate to rape in the real world.

Video games can also portray violence against or degradation of women. In many, "women are usually cast as persons who are acted upon rather than as initiators of action; in extreme cases, they are depicted as victims." A study of 47 popular Nintendo games revealed that among 115 male and 9 female characters, 20 male and zero female characters had dominant roles. Twenty-eight percent (28%) of the games in the study contained scenes depicting women as inferior and powerless. Some video games also perpetuate negative stereotypes about women and encourage players to participate in violence against them. In Duke Nukem, 3D players earn points by killing prostitutes. In addition to presenting women as sex objects, the game awards players for harassing women by throwing cash at them.

One icon in computer games is the animated fantasy girl Lara Croft, who stars in Playstation's Tomb Raider. She is a female referred to as a "sex symbol with attitude." According to sociologists, games such as Tomb Raider encourage sexism and condition adolescents to view the world as they do the computer screen: with female sex symbols, female kidnapping, and female rescue and submission. In one study, up to one-third of parents were concerned about possible anti-social behavior (i.e., violence) influenced by these games.

Internet

As computers and Internet access become widespread, real-world crimes of harassment and stalking have moved online. It is estimated that one in twenty women will become targets of stalking behavior at least once during their lifetimes, and evidence suggests that the majority of cyberstalkers are men victimizing women. The Internet makes stalking, or "cyberstalking," much easier for the perpetrator than off-line stalking. The anonymity of e-mail and chat rooms cloak stalkers well, and stalkers can easily access private information about their victims via the Internet. Many on-line services and directories also enable individuals to obtain e-mail addresses, home addresses, and phone numbers without their intended victims knowing, since few people realize that their personal information is publicly listed online.

Cyberstalking is a relatively new phenomenon, but occurrences are becoming more frequent. In a national survey of college women during the 1996-97 academic year, 13% were stalked and 25% of those incidences reportedly involved cyberstalking. The Web Police, an international crime fighting agency, also estimated that about 30% of the 47,000 complaints it received in 1998 involved harassing or threatening e-mail, and seventeen states now have laws against on-line stalking and harassment. The Clinton administration has called for tougher laws against on-line stalking and encourages Internet companies to launch a web site to educate people about cyberstalking and how to protect themselves.

Influence of TV On Children's

Children internalize gender role stereotypes from books, songs, television, and the movies. Television, however, is perhaps the form of media most influential in shaping ideas of appropriate sex roles. Research on television viewing and the socialization of children indicates television has a great impact on the lives of children. Studies have shown preschoolers spend an average of nearly 30 hours a week watching television; it is suggested children spend more time watching television than they spend on anything else except sleeping.

By the time children are sixteen years old, they have spent more time watching television than going to school. Children are exposed to about 20,000 advertisements a year. By the time children graduate from high school, they have witnessed 13,000 violent deaths on television. Prosocial and antisocial behaviors are influenced by television. Also, television influences attitudes about race and gender.

As children grow and develop, they are taking in information and acquiring knowledge at a rapid pace. As children develop their cognitive abilities, they assimilate new information into their existing knowledge base and adjust to the new information by accommodating it to what they already know. Children's ideas about how the world works come from the experiences they have and the attitudes and behaviors they see around them. The young child who comes to understand women are nurses and men are doctors may have come to the realization because the first doctor he or she saw was a man, and he was assisted by a female nurse. This man as doctor, woman as nurse idea may have reinforced by parents reading books; conversations with friends and television may reinforce also.

If the child frequently is faced with gender biases and gender stereotypes, this knowledge will be incorporated and influence perceptions regarding men and women. Keeping in mind young children with developing minds watch many hours of television, and recalling television reinforces gender stereotypes, it is not surprising children come away from this television experience with firmly held beliefs. Frequently these beliefs are stereotyped with regard to gender. Of the various factors which help shape gender-typed behaviors, role models and imitation are extremely influential.

Children are exposed to models throughout their environment, including those on television. Research suggests children who view violent programming on television will behave more aggressively with peers. It is also true children who view prosocial behaviors on television are likely to exhibit those types of behaviors themselves. Young children will imitate and repeat behaviors they see on television. Because children are influenced by gender stereotyped role models they see on television, they will also exhibit gender biased behaviors and develop gender biased attitudes that they see modeled on television.

Positive developmental outcomes for young children during their growing-up years include developing autonomy, initiative, and a sense of industriousness. Children who witness female characters on television programs who are passive, indecisive, and subordinate to men come to understand this is the appropriate way for females to behave. It is less likely for female children to develop autonomy, initiative and industriousness when they rarely see it modeled in those around them. Similarly, because male characters on television programs are more likely to be shown in leadership roles and exhibit assertive, decisive behavior, children learn this is the appropriate way for males to behave.

What Children are Watching

Regarding gender role development on television, the National Institute of Mental Health has determined:

1) In male-female interaction, men are usually more dominant.

2) Men on television are rational, ambitious, smart, competitive, powerful, stable, violent, and tolerant, while women are sensitive, romantic, attractive, happy, warm, sociable, peaceful, fair, submissive, and timid.

3) For men, the emphasis is on strength, performance, and skill; for women, it is on attractiveness and desirability.

4) Marriage and family are not important to television's men. One study found that for nearly half the men, it wasn't possible to tell if they were married, a fact that was true for only 11% of the women.

While some children's programming has come under attack for being violent, irrelevant, or sexist, other programs for children, such as Sesame Street, are regularly lauded for attempting to meet the developmental needsof children. Sexism, however, can be found even among the Muppets, who all have male names or male voices. A study of Saturday morning cartoons found females were pictured less often than males, were less active than males, played fewer roles than males, played fewer lead roles than males, and worked primarily in the home. Although these findings were obtained two decades ago, there has been no improvement.

Females are not more fairly represented in children's programming. Recent studies of Saturday morning programs for children demonstrated males are featured in dominant roles, while females are shown in peripheral roles. Children's programs on the Public Broadcasting System have consistently shown fewer females than males. Further, television programs evidence a greater range of occupations for males than females. This discrepancy in occupations between males and females is shown on music television, where it was found that more than nine out of ten occupational roles classified as stereotypically male (e.g., physician, mechanic, firefighter) were played by male actors.

It has been suggested the preferences of boys are given precedence over those of girls because boys represent 53% of the Saturday viewing audience. Those who make decisions regarding children's programming have determined action and violence should dominate children's television.

Gender Stereotypes

Gender stereotypes occur with frequency on daytime soap operas; women are often shown as hopeless individuals, unable to solve problems without assistance. Both males and females are shown in gender stereotypic roles on many music television programs. Children frequently watch these programs after school, and receive reinforcement for the notion women are subordinate, passive, and indecisive. About two-thirds of characters in television programs are male. From the 1950s through the 1990s, this figure has remained stable. There is more interaction shown with men (with both men and women) than there is with women. Further, interactions between men and women frequently indicate women are defined by their relationships with men.

Television often does not reflect reality when it deals with the occupations of men and women. For example, programs depict 75% of women as being in the labor force, compared with the truer figure of about 56%. The primary job setting for most women on television is as a professional. Most women in real life, however, are in low paying, low status jobs. Lessthan 10% of women in the United States make more than $50,000 a year. Most females on nighttime television are young, attractive, thin, and ornamental. Most female characters are either under 35 or over 50. Middle-aged women are rare.

Females are consistently placed in situations where looks count more than brains, and helpless and incompetent behaviors are expected. Men are twice as likely as women to be shown as competent and able to solve problems. Gender stereotypes abound on television, with women being depicted as sex objects more frequently than men, and men portrayed as inept when handling children's needs.

On music television, a popular program choice among young viewers, females are often shown in degrading positions. Music videos frequently show women as sex objects. Females are also shown as trying to gain the attention of a male who ignores them. Rap music videos are also popular with young television viewers. Frequently women are portrayed as objects of lust. Women are four times more likely than men to be provocatively dressed; while men are almost always fully clothed.

While early television commercials were criticized for being overwhelmingly biased in favor of males, a study of commercials broadcast between 1971 and 1985 indicated improvement regarding numbers of male and female main characters. However, even though there is currently more equity in the number of men and women appearing in commercials, women are most often shown in the role of wife and mother, or in demonstrating products for the home. Another aspect of television advertising which is overwhelmingly a masculine province is voiceovers and narration, in which 83-90% of the voices are male.

In commercials for children's programs, boys are shown more frequently and in active roles; girls' behavior is much more likely to be passive. Advertisers indicate male models generate more product sales to children of both sexes than female models. It has also been suggested girls watch male-dominated programs and commercials because there are few other options. Girls will become loyal to programming that is more gender fair. Interestingly, children without television have been shown to be less stereotyped in their gender role attitudes. Children who view programs with non-traditional gender roles tend to have non-traditional gender role perceptions. Because children model behavior they see on television, they are likely to perpetuate gender stereotypes they view.

Influence of Media on Youth

The media executives are quick to defend their role in youth violence and bullying while selling millions of dollars in add space focused on youth. Lets take a closer look at the reality of this issue. TV producers, network executives, motion picture companies and others in the media world downplay and deny any impact of their programs on the attitudes and actions of youth. Meanwhile they continue to spend millions on special effects and marketing geared to increase appeal to youth markets. While corporations spend millions on market research and advertising to create products and campaigns targeted at a youth demographic, they still deny their ability to influence youth attitudes and culture.

If this were true to fact, would Nike continue spending millions every year on product development, marketing and advertising? Would McDonalds still be using cartoon like characters to sell hamburgers? Would music labels be increasing the level of violence and sexual content in the music geared towards the youth audience? Would liquor companies be using youth oriented activities in their advertising? Of course it works on influencing youth attitudes and ideals advertising would not be a multi-billion dollar a year business. If it had no influence, M-TV would not have consultant on staff spending huge amounts of money to ensure they keeping up with youth culture.

Clothing companies are spending millions to get young good-looking individuals to make plain and boring clothes look appealing to youth. Youth respond to visual advertising more than other forms. This is due to the fact that youth want to visualize them selves using the product or service. An example of this would be simply as follows. Even adults are manipulated by these practices. For example, Roots comes out with a new hat. You hear an ad for this hat on the radio. You may be curious but you cannot visualize the actual style or yourself wearing this item. Next you see the ad in a newspaper. Now you can visualize the product but it is only a photo. Now you see a television commercial.

The persons in the commercial are snowboarding and having fun. A song is playing in the ad that catches your ear. Now you subconsciously associate the product with fun, excitement and style. Now you want to go and purchase that hat. This is a plain and straight example of how the media in it's simplest for influences youth culture. Now if you consider how often youth are subjected to the idea that you need to look perfect, be thin, use violence and smoke cannabis etc. it is a powerful and effective influence or it would not be such big business. If they took more responsibility in the attitudes they are creating they are scared that they would not make the revenues that they currently enjoy.

This has an effect on society on a whole because of the younger kids looking up to the older youth for guidance. They want to mimic the older youth as they see as "cool". Adults have a desire to look and feel younger and therefore they tend to follow youth trends in order to facilitate this behaviour. Thus the media has a large influence on society as a whole. They effectively manipulate and create false perception to further their own financial objectives.

Influences of Media on Adolescents

The mass media is a big part of our culture in terms of entertainment, yet it can also be a helper, adviser and teacher to our young generation. The mass media affects the lives of our young by acting as a substitute for a number of institutions and social contacts, by providing information and entertainment, by creating and mediating art, etc. In this way, it fulfills a variety of functions in human life.

The time spent in front of the television screen is usually at the expense of leisure: there is less time for games, amusement and rest. Most often children look upon television as a certain kind of socially beneficial instrument, an open door into the world of the imagination. Attracted by what is happening on the screen, children not only imitate what they see but directly identify themselves with different characters. The Surgeon General also states that Americans have been concerned about the prevalence of violence in the media and its potential harm to children and adolescents for at least forty years. During this period, new media emerged, such as video games, cable television, music videos, and the Internet. Current psychological theory suggests that the interactive nature of many of these new media may affect children's behavior more powerfully than they have thought in the past. As they continue to gain popularity, these media, along with television, prompt public concern and research attention.

Body Image

Another large societal concern on our young generation inflicted by the media, is body image. External forces can influence body image positively or negatively. For one, societal and cultural norms and mass media marketing impact our concepts of beauty. In the mass media, the images of standardized beauty fill magazines and newspapers, beam from our televisions and entertain us at the movies. Even in advertising, the mass media plays upon accepted cultural values of thinness and fitness for commercial gain. Young adults are presented with a narrowly defined standard of attractiveness, an ideal that carries unrealistic physical expectations.

According to The Dairy Council of CA-Educators, both boys and girls are told that they should look like a model, but only one in forty-thousand people, naturally have a model's body shape. This is a problem because adolescence is a time when young adults begin to separate from their parents and identify their own identities. Acceptance by their peers is of utmost importance. This can make teens vulnerable to ideals embraced by our culture and reflected in the media. To obtain the fashionable, ultra thin look, many young men and women restrict their food intake. Sometimes, men or women will result to drastic measures to fit the image they want to be, or the image that they feel society will accept them.

In doing so, disorders can develop, such as Anorexia nervosa and Bulimia nervosa. Anorexia nervosa generally starts between 12-18 years of age, and is characterized by restrictive food intake, weight loss and excessive exercise. One half to one percent of adolescent girls develops anorexia. Another eating disorder that is common is Bulimia nervosa, which is the binge/purge syndrome. It typically develops between sixteen to twenty years of age. Approximately three percent of teenage girls develop bulimia. These percentages do not include all those who have these disorders, only those that have reported their' eating disorders. Many people can hide their disorder very well, and can result in death.

The mass media can affect children's thinking and behaviors. For many young people, the world on the television screen is a more frequent topic of conversation than events and unpleasant moments in school or at work, than the opposite sex, and what friends are doing, etc. Compared with television, the other mass communication media form a substantially smaller part of the daily topics of conversation. Also, television watchers can be influenced positively or negatively by what they see on the screen and can go out into the world, imitating these acts.

Also, the media portrays an unrealistic body image for adolescents and all of society. This struggle to be accepted by society can lead to feelings of depression, anger, and anxiety and even direct to eating disorders. Two common known eating disorders prevalent in society are Anorexia nervosa and Bulimia nervosa. Both disorders are common in society and can result in death if not treated. In closing, the media should be of great concern to our society. What our youth see and view, is what they feel society wants from them. Delivering wrong messages and unrealistic images by the media can only cause problems and trouble for our youth. Although the sole purpose of the media is enjoyment for society, the public should be aware that it could sometimes cause negative effects on its viewers.

Effect of Media Violence

The effect of media violence on the human mind has been a subject of debate over decades. Newspaper headlines have linked bizarre crimes to specific examples of media coverage, and the protection of children from media violence crops up periodically as a media issue. Yet although the debate seems no closer to being resolved than it was back in the 1950s, there is a substantial body of research on the patterns of media violence and the possible effects of media violence on the consumer.

Global Patterns of Media Violence

The findings of content analysis studies carried out e.g. in the USA, the UK, Israel and Germany all point almost identically in the same direction. The major criteria can be summarised as follows:

Structural violence (social injustice) is of only subordinate importance in entertainment broadcasts. Violence is presented almost exclusively in connection with individual fates, with no insight into possible socio-structural determinants of the violence. The most violent protagonists by far are unmarried men of middle age. Violence is shown as typically linked with the masculine role. As a rule, aggressive dynamic men aged 30 to 40 are surrounded by beautiful soft women aged 20 o 30. In TV entertainment an image of women is drawn that has predominated in European art since the Middle Ages; the woman is passive and seductive.

Typically violent acts occur in the TV broadcasts between protagonists who are strangers to each other, in speaking distance of one another. This depiction is most unrealistic as in most cases violence is the result of an interaction sequence between individuals who know each other, e.g. members of a family. The most frequently shown form of violence is that of a clearly dominant attacker who damages and/or overpowers another. Depiction of the violence itself is extremely unrealistic. Although an act of violence can cause death of the recipient, the suffering of the victim, blood and wounds are shown only rarely.

In the world of TV entertainment hardly a protagonist dies a natural death. The focus is on the performing of violence, i.e. on "action". As a rule the victim is presented only briefly. Violence is shown as an efficient instrument for attaining goals or solving conflicts, When a negative main protagonist who uses violence is punished, this mostly happens at the end of a film plot, after violent behaviour was previously successful in many individual sequences. Violence is not only used by "negative" protagonists but also just as often by representatives of law and order (police or private detectives) to help uphold the law. Whoever becomes violent because of loyalty to the law as a rule has nothing to fear.

Witnesses to violent events as a rule do not try to mediate or help but usually remain passive. In summary, TV violence is linked to the masculine role and is (carried out) between strangers. Although violence can be fatal for the recipient, it is very rarely painful. Television offers behaviour models demonstrating how with illegitimate means (violence) aims recognised as legitimate (prosperity, power, prestige, justice) are achieved. There are, of course, detractors from the notion that media violence causes harm to viewers and readers. A major criticism of the "media effects" theory is that it assumes that readers and audiences are passive sponges, unable to sift what is within a media genre from what is real life.

Active audiences, this theory maintains, are trained through a lifetime of viewing to tell screen violence from real violence, to enjoy the first as a form of entertainment but to naturally eschew the second. Traditional definitions of "violence" have also been criticised. According to Martin Barker the expression "media violence" has to be one of the most ill-informed of all time: "It is supposed to encompass everything from cartoons (ten-ton blocks dropped on Tom's head by Jerry, children's action adventure films (the dinosaurs of Jurassic Park...) news footage from Rwanda and Bosnia; documentary footage showing the police attacking Rodney King in Los Angeles; horror films from Hammer; the range from Clint Eastwood as the voiceless hard man of Dirty Harry to Arnie as the violent humorist of almost any of his films, etc, etc. No single ground has ever been given for us to suppose that such a list has any single property in common...it is a useless conflation of wholly different things."

Yet another exception generally taken is that research methods are crude and you cannot measure human reaction the way you observe Pavlovian dogs. But crude or not, a substantial body of research does exist to show that media violence has definite effects on consumers. Edward Donnerstein found that the level of aggression of male subjects toward females increased after they had been exposed to violent pornography in which a female rape victim was portrayed as becoming aroused by the end of the movie. (Aggression was measured by the intensity of electric shock that subjects were willing to administer.) Violent films that were non-pornographic (depicting, for example, a man hitting a woman) also increased subjects' levels of aggression toward hitting women, but not to the same extent as violent pornographic films.

Other studies have found that prolonged exposure to filmed violence desensitizes subjects. In one particular study, subjects were exposed to five consecutive days of viewing violent films. Subjects' perceptions of the violence portrayed in the films also changed over the five days. The films were perceived to be significantly less violent by the last day of viewing. Ratings of how degrading the film was to women and of its offensiveness were also significantly lower by the last day. There is a tendency for such desensitisation to "spill over" into subjects' judgements of a female victim in another context. Men who were exposed to the large doses of filmed violence against women judged the victim of a violent assault and rape to be significantly less injured and evaluated her as generally less worthy tan the control group of subjects who saw no films.

Subjects who rated the material as less offensive or violent and more enjoyable by the last day of viewing were much more likely to judge the victim as more responsible. These findings add strength to the mounting evidence that sustained exposure to filmed violence may lower sensitivity to victims of violence in other contexts." If such findings are applied to the news coverage of violence against women, it becomes clear that it is the media's responsibility not to identify, blame or judge female rape victims and not to make judgements of domestic abuse survivors. It also becomes important not to eroticise violence. Some guidelines like those put out by the Philippine Journalism Review go as far as to recommend that reports of violence are not placed next to pin-ups and other items which heighten their titillating value.

Ethnic Relations

In a rapidly changing social, political, economic scenario the world over and also shrinking world the media have to play a dynamic role. Dynamic in the sense that it has to be constantly changing and evolving to suit the needs and requirements of the society. In order to have a common understanding the word ethnic identity is defined as follows: Ethnic identity is defined to broadly include religious, linguistic, ethnic, communal, caste and other historical and cultural definitions that provide a deep rooted social identity to a community and help to separate it from other communities living in India.

India is not only a very big and populous country; it is also a very diverse country. There are about 16 main languages and a large number of dialects. Hindus form over 80 per cent of the population. But there is a fair number of several other religions like Muslims (about 12 per cent), Christians (about 4 per cent), Sikhs, Buddhists and Jains being the other religions though on a smaller extent. There is a prevalence of hierarchical caste system within the Hindus.

In addition, there is enormous geographical diversity with climates varying from extremely hot to extremely cold, variation in food habits, cultural forms of art and performance, social practices, etc. There is also diversity in terms of the levels of developments in the country. On the one hand India has the third largest scientific manpower in the world and on the other nearly 48 per cent of the population is illiterate. There are research and academic institutes of a very high order and at the same time there are several villages deprived of the basic amenities like elementary schools, primary health centres, clean drinking water, etc.

In spite of all these differences and diversity, there is a common element of "Indianness" binding the country together. This common binding can only be described as "Indianness" because it rises beyond the boundaries of religious, languages, castes, geographical or even political barriers. It may be composed of all these elements but is not circumscribed by it. The end product is clearly more than the mere sum total of different elements. The oft-mentioned Indian unity in diversity is not a mere slogan or cliché, because India has a very long history of harmonious co-existence between different ethnic groups. It is true that there are occasional conflicts, sometimes very virulent and long persisting, but by and large, the society has displayed remarkably harmonious relations.

In a sense there is a constant interplay between assertion of individual or group identity and being part of the national mainstream or even belonging in some way to the international community in today's global village. This interplay between assertion of individual identity and being part of a mainstream may lead to stress or conflicts. But they are not necessarily contradictory or conflicting. Every individual belongs to a small ethnic group - linguistic, regional, religious, etc. and at the same time is a citizen of the country, is a member of international group and thus wears multiple roles but they are not necessarily conflicting.

Another important feature of the Indian nation is that it is a democracy. In spite of several pulls, pressures, stresses and occasional distortions in its functioning, it has remained an active and a vibrant democracy for more than 50 years. The country has endowed itself with a very liberal constitution where equality under the law and the freedom to practice one's religion has been guaranteed. Freedom of expression and the rule of law have been ensured in the constitution. While certain amount of conservatism may be a part of the Indian ethos - as is likely to be the case with any ancient civilisation - it has always been receptive to new ideas and new technologies.

The role of the media has to be understood in this overall socio, cultural, political context. The Indian media scene is also extremely diverse. India is the producer of largest number of feature films in the world, publishes a very large number of newspapers and magazines in different languages (300 English dailies and 3936 regional language dailies), the reach of the electronic media of radio and television has been expanding at a very rapid rate (57.7million TV households in 1996 and an estimated 111 million radio sets). The Indian television landscape shows that the penetration of the foreign satellite channels is expanding very fast (with 14.2 million Satellite households having access to 4 English, 22 Indian language and 5 channels in both languages). At the same time the reach and popularity of the national television system has continued to hold sway.

There are several people who read foreign magazines but also read Indian magazines. Thus the Indian audience is open to both domestic and international media consumption. It is inherent to any medium that it plays a very significant dual role. The media have to reflect the reality as well as shape and change it. It cannot go overboard in attempting to shape the reality for that will distance it from the social and cultural ethos with the eternal danger of being rejected nor can it be a passive spectator and merely reflect or reinforce the realities.

The media have to contribute to the individual, local, regional, national and international needs. It has to actively participate in assertion of the ethnic identities and ethnic demands and also being participatory and non-parochial. There has to be a fine balance between the group rights and the larger social good. In reality which media play what type of a role has been a question bothering social scientists and communication researchers and people at large especially in today's context of the communication revolution.

In order to understand the role that the media played in ethnic relations in India, a study was conducted. The study had several components like literature review, content analysis of selected newspapers and selected television programmes and findings of anthropological case study and an audience survey. This study was funded by Asian Media Information and Communication Centre, Singapore. The study was carried out in two cities of India, namely, Ahmedabad and Pune. Both the cities are located on the Western part of the country, but are diverse in terms of the major spoken languages. Ahmedabad has a population of about 3.5 Million people. The main language is Gujarati, but a large number of people speaking different languages also reside in the city.

The predominant population is of Hindus with a very substantial population of Muslims. The other major religious groups include Christians, Jains and a small number of Sikhs. Pune has a population of 2.45 Million and like Ahmedabad, is also a highly industrialised city. It is known as the cultural capital of the state of Maharashtra. The majority language is Marathi but is also cosmopolitan city. The city has a rich history of filmmaking and has a premiere film and television institute of India. Both the cities have a large number of television sets and access to foreign television networks provided through distribution by local cable operators.

The survey included proportionate representatives of the four major religions, namely, Hindus, Muslims, Christians and others (Jains, Parsis etc). The total sample was of 400 respondents of whom 200 were college students and other 200 were working adults. There was equal distribution between men and women. A self administered questionnaire was prepared which consisted of:

(1) Personal biographical information about the respondents,

(2) Media habits in terms of their exposure to print as well as electronic media,

(3) Views and knowledge regarding the main ethnic issues and problems of the country and

(4) Opinions regarding the role that the media played.

The specific media about whom questions were asked were

(1) Doordarshan - the television authority of India,

(2) BBC World TV,

(3) Regional language newspapers and

(4) English language newspapers.

The views regarding the perceived characteristics associated with the media in terms of accuracy and completeness of information, promotion of ethnic harmony or sensitisation of issues and bridging the gap between different communities, etc. was obtained. There were specific media related questions regarding their roles in dealing with ethnicity.

The audience survey shows a very striking insight of respondents both regarding ethnic issues and the role played by different media. Nearly 70 per cent of the respondents stated that in spite of diversity, there is a clear commonness in the Indian society. Both advantages as well as disadvantages of the pluralistic society were perceived. Over 60 per cent of the respondents felt that plurality added variety to life and enriched Indian culture. However, only 40 per cent of the respondents agreed that pluralistic society enhanced national unity.

Nearly 68 per cent of the respondents felt that major disadvantage of plurality are chances of conflicts. The other disadvantages mentioned were that it divided Indian society and there was increased possibility of interference by foreign countries and that the minorities were treated as vote banks by the politicians. It is of significance to note that the opinion hardly varied according to religion or from students and other adults.

Respondents were asked to list some of the major ethnic issues of the country and also give an opinion whether they had improved or deteriorated. There was a great deal of similarity about perception of these issues irrespective of the religion of the respondents. There was also a great deal of similarity among all respondents i.e. irrespective of the religions followed by them regarding the specific role played by different media. Occasionally the same individual held contradictory opinions about a medium. Some times there was an element of ambivalence, but on the whole the respondents had a very clear opinion regarding the role played by different media. A very large number of respondents felt that the regional language newspapers sensationalised issues and created stereotypes. Many of them believed that they give biased and inaccurate information.

Against this the official media of Doordarshan was characterised for adequately providing information about other cultures and promoted ethnic harmony. But it was felt that it often gave accurate, but incomplete information or one-sided information. BBC World TV was ranked last as far as promoting ethnic harmony was concerned, but was credited with giving a very comprehensive and complete information. The English newspapers were considered least biased and did not create stereotypes or sensationalise issues. However, they did not provide enough information about different cultures within the country. Doordarshan was given highest rating regarding playing of unifying role while BBC TV was ranked last. All religious groups considered Doordarshan to be best in terms of playing a unifying role. The Hindus and Muslims ranked BBC TV last on this while Christians ranked regional language newspapers last.

6

Influence of Internet on Society

After 50 years of controversy over the impact of television on children, a new world of online media is emerging that may have even greater impact on them. Almost one million children in the United States are now using the World Wide Web, according to a research and consulting firm specializing in interactive technology, and 3.8 million have Web access-a figure that will grow rapidly in coming years. Like adults, children will increasingly be connected to a vast digital universe that transcends the family, the local community, and even the nation. Education will expand beyond the classroom and other traditional settings, as more interactive "edutainment" becomes available. New personal and portable technologies will enable children to inhabit their own separate electronic worlds.

The dazzling graphics and engaging interactivity of the new multimedia technologies will make them potent forces in the lives of children. If harnessed properly, the new media could enhance their drive to learn, provide them with access to a rich diversity of information and ideas, and enable them to reach across community and national borders. But there is also peril: Video game channels, virtual shopping malls, and manipulative forms of advertising targeted at children could further compound the problems in the existing media that have troubled parents, educators, and child advocates for decades.

We are in the midst of the formative stage of this new digital age. Government policies are being debated and enacted, marketing and programming strategies are being developed, and services for children are being designed. If we are to believe some hyperbolic visions of cyberspace, the information superhighway will be a great equalizing force that will bring unprecedented opportunity for all. Improvements in education and other benefits for children are often at the center of these visions. But history offers us cautionary lessons. In this century enthusiasts have hailed every new medium-from radio to FM to television to cable to satellites-with claims that it would reinvigorate our culture, expand educational opportunities, and enhance the democratic process. None has lived up to these claims. In each case, powerful commercial forces have used civic values to gain support for the new medium-and then squelched the very policies necessary to serve the public good.

While traditional media are sometimes viewed as unnecessary diversions, digital media will soon become an integral part of daily life. Those without access to the communications system are likely to fall behind in education and be unable to compete in a highly selective job market. Yet just as access is becoming imperative, the number of children living in poverty, with little or no access to technology, is growing at an alarming rate. Access isn't the only challenge; the quality of the new media culture for children also raises concern. Unlike TV, online media are dynamic and two-way. This participatory quality makes them particularly compelling to children. Such technological breakthroughs as real-time audio, real-time video, and virtual reality modeling language are transforming online media. Eventually, this interactive online world could supplant traditional television as the most powerful and influential medium in children's lives.

Many online services are now available that seek to challenge children by exposing them to places, people, and ideas far outside their everyday experiences. For example, Plugged In, a Web site created by a community computing center in Palo Alto, California, allows poor children to explore the Internet, produce their own art, and display it to other children around the world. Another Web site, CyberKids, enables children to write and share their own stories in an online magazine. Special networks have been established to foster online communities for children.

These educational and civic services, however, are in danger of being overshadowed by a powerful interactive commercial culture with an unprecedented ability to capture children's attention. Marketing to children has become a multibillion-dollar business. The direct spending power of children, almost all of it discretionary, has risen rapidly in recent years. In 1995, according to Interactive Marketing News and Youth Markets Alert, children under 12 spent $14 billion, teenagers another $67 billion, and together they influenced $160 billion of their parents' annual spending.

In the last decade, these trends triggered a proliferation of new TV networks aimed at capturing a segment of the hot children's market, including the controversial classroom news service Channel One, the highly profitable Nickelodeon cable channel, CNN's Cartoon Channel, and the Fox Children's Network. Character licensing has become the driving force not only in children's television, but also in much of the rest of children's culture. Cross-promotion of licensed products through TV, movies, magazines, discount stores, and fast food restaurants has produced a proliferation of licensed characters that permeate every facet of a child's life.

The new online services for children are being developed in the context of this highly commercialized children's media culture. Children are a disproportionately important market for the new interactive media because they are early adopters of high-tech products. Marketers who view children as the "lucrative cyber-tot category" see the emerging media as a fertile new frontier for targeting children. As an executive from Saatchi and Saatchi, a leader in the online kids' marketing field, recently proclaimed, "There is nothing else that exists like it for advertisers to build relationships with kids."

Advertisers are already aggressively moving into cyberspace.In US a Coalition for Advertising Supported Information and Entertainment (CASIE), led jointly by the American Association of Advertising Agencies and the Association of National Advertisers, is spearheading lobbying efforts to ensure that advertising becomes the dominant mode for funding online content and to ward off government restrictions. The coalition claims that advertiser support for online services is the only way to make information services affordable to all. But the consequences of making advertising the key to universal access for children are troubling.

Advertisers are not just supporting online content; they are shaping much of the virtual landscape for children. At Saatchi and Saatchi, psychologists and cultural anthropologists have perfected a variety of techniques-including play groups, art, and games-to probe children's feelings and behavior when they go online. They are also studying the nature of "kids' culture" as a separate set of experiences and values from that of adults. Knowing that children often use computers alone, marketers are carefully cultivating this separateness in the design of online services that circumvent parental authority. One online children's service recently published results from a survey that asked children whom they trusted more-their parents or their computers. The majority of respondents said they put more trust in their computers.

According to advertising researchers, going online quickly puts children into a "flow state," that "highly pleasurable experience of total absorption in a challenging activity." This is an optimal condition for advertisers to reach children. Traditional commercials will not work online. "Anything that is perceived as an interruption of the flow state," explained a Saatchi and Saatchi executive, "whether it's artwork being downloaded or an ad that is obtrusively splattered on a screen, is going to get a negative reaction." So the solution is the seamless integration of content and advertising in "branded environments." The goal of these environments is to "get kids involved with brands"-including "brand characters, brand logos, brand jingles, and brand video."

Major children's advertisers have Web sites where children are encouraged to come and play for extended periods of time with such product "spokescharacters" as Ronald McDonald, Kellogg's Snap, Crackle, and Pop, and Chester Cheetah. The aim is to encourage children to develop ongoing relationships with the characters-and the products. Within days of visiting the Kellogg's Web site recently, for example, one child received unsolicited e-mail from Snap, Crackle, and Pop, urging her to return for more fun.

The new interactive media are being designed to compile personal profiles on each child to help in developing individually tailored advertising known as "microtargeting" or "one-to-one marketing." The sites get children to volunteer such personal data as e-mail address, street address, the identity of other family members, and purchasing behavior and preferences. Sophisticated computer software can track every move a child makes online and give marketers "clickstream data" or, in the vernacular of the business, "mouse droppings."

American Federal regulations limit TV advertising to children, but no such rules exist in cyberspace. Marketers can pursue children with few restraints. Nothing prevents them from collecting personal information from children and selling it to third parties. The lines among advertising, entertainment, and information-already dangerously blurred in television and other media-are likely to disappear entirely in the new online environment. "What is really happening," explains one industry expert, "is what will ultimately happen on interactive television: the infomercialization of all programming." Adds another: "The blending of entertainment with advertising will work if packaged correctly: just look at how the toy industry has taken over production of Saturday morning cartoons."

Even traditionally noncommercial services are likely to be shaped by the norms of this new unregulated media environment. While laws prohibited from most forms of advertising on television, there are no restrictions on its use of advertising online.

Online Hate

The Internet has been rightly hailed as a groundbreaking

interactive marketplace of ideas, in which anyone with the necessary hardware and software can set up a cyber-stall. But the downside of this unparalleled information exchange is that, alongside its many valuable online resources, the Net also offers a host of offensive materials - including hate materials - that attempt to inflame public opinion against certain groups of people.

This section explores the ways in which hate-mongers use the Internet to promote their agenda, examines the line between hate speech and free speech, provides an overview of relevant legislation and voluntary industry codes, and suggests ways in which to safeguard children and teens. It is also the place to find seminal articles and the latest reports and surveys on the above issues.

Most definitions of hate focus on the ways in which hate-mongers see entire groups of people as the "Other." For example, U.S.-based Tolerance.org argues that "All hate groups have beliefs or practices that attack or malign an entire class of people, typically for their immutable characteristics." Raymond A. Franklin, author of The Hate Directory, focuses on groups that "advocate violence against, separation from, defamation of, deception about, or hostility towards others based on race, religion, ethnicity, gender, or sexual orientation."

Canadian communications scholar Karim Karim points out that the "Other" is one of a number of human archetypes common to all cultures. When people transfer their fears and hatred to the "Other," the targeted group becomes less than human. Hate-mongers can then "justify" acts of violence and degradation because they have denied the humanity of their victims.

Hate and Free Speech

The line between hate speech and free speech is a thin one, and different countries have different levels of tolerance. The line is even thinner on the Internet, where hateful comments posted lawfully in one country can be read in other countries where they may be deemed unlawful. Many pundits argue that the best response to hate speech is not criminalization, but more speech. Philosopher Pierre Lévy reminds us that:

> More and more, on the Web, ideas are being expressed by the people who are thinking them, and not by journalists who are obliged to simplify or caricature debate because of lack of time or incompetence or, even worse, the political powers that be. The new medium is therefore particularly conducive to the creation of a public space in the classical sense.

Public debate on the early Net indeed proved frustrating for those who tried to argue that the Holocaust did not occur, or that certain racial groups were inferior. The interactive nature of Usenet newsgroups ensured that false claims were challenged by healthy and vigorous debate. As a result, hate-mongers soon retreated into less interactive areas of cyberspace. Ironically, the free speech environment that characterized discussion forums in the late 1980s and early 1990s made many Internet service providers (ISPs) uncomfortable.

CompuServe was one of the first ISPs to be confronted with a vigorous debate about hate, when a revisionist began to pepper an online discussion with racist comments. The forum soon became one of the most frequently visited on CompuServe. However, the discussion ended when CompuServe created its acceptable use policy, which prohibited people from posting racist or offensive comments. It is now standard practice for ISPs to require online users to adhere to acceptable use policies.

Hate-mongers also learned a lesson about the perils of free speech. Canadian Ken McVay, founder of the Nizkor Project, has spent over a decade attempting to engage hate-monger Ernst Zundel in an online discussion. McVay notes, "It is well-established that the Zundelsite refuses to participate in the interactive forums of the Internet."

Web Sites and Private Forums

The Web has become the online forum of choice for hate groups precisely because it allows them to avoid interacting with those who disagree with their views. The Anti-Defamation League notes, "Organized haters complain about civil rights activists who critique their manifestos in Usenet newsgroups and other interactive forums. In contrast, haters can refuse to publish critical messages on their Web sites."

Web sites also help groups identify potential recruits who can be brought into the hate community through private chat rooms and e-mail, well away from the public eye. However, many activists suggest that the public nature of the Web still works against hate-mongers because their activities can be monitored and brought into the public domain. David Goldman, creator of the now defunct site Hatewatch (the first major site dedicated to tracking the activities of online hate groups) argues:

From the beginning, these organizations' self-proclaimed desire to create a digital "white revolution" was carefully monitored and documented by civil rights organizations, Hatewatch among them. The standard and often repeated quote was the "Internet is the greatest thing to happen to hate." Much to our joy it has in fact been one of the worst. Early fears that the unrestricted nature of online speech would provide haters with an effective recruitment tool appear to be unfounded. The number of hate sites on the Web are increasing day-by day. There is no evidence that the presence of these sites has led to an increase in the number of people who belong to hate groups

Nonetheless, hate groups continue to refine their online strategies.A number of sites encourage their visitors to hack anti-hate Web sites and crash the server or replace the content with hateful messages. For example, hacker Doctor Nuker broke into the American Israel Public Affairs Committee Web site in 2002 and posted anti-Semitic comments on the home page.In another incident, a hate-monger redirected Web traffic so that surfers looking for German government pages were automatically rerouted to pages containing Nazi propaganda.

A growing number of countries, including France and Australia, are beginning to exert jurisdiction over online speech in an attempt to curtail hate activities.

For example, a French court ordered California-based Yahoo.com to block the auction of Nazi paraphernalia in 2003. Although the decision is likely to be unenforceable in U.S. courts, it was enough to encourage Yahoo to reconsider its policies. As more countries seek to enforce their own laws in cyberspace, it is likely that hate groups will continue to test the limits of freedom of online expression.

Law and the Online Hate

Freedom of expression is central to a healthy democracy. Accordingly, although racist and hateful comments are offensive to the vast majority of people, they are not necessarily illegal. In many developed countries there are laws to prohibit some forms of hate speech. For example let us look at federal law system of Canada which prohibits forms of hate speech. Sections 318 and 319 of the Criminal Code of Canada make it a criminal offence to:

— advocate genocide

— publicly incite hatred

— wilfully promote hatred against an "identifiable group."

An identifiable group is defined as any section of the public distinguished by:

— colour

— race

— religion

— ethnic origin

Hatred directed against others groups (such as women, or gays and lesbians) is not punishable under sections 318 and 319. The Canadian Criminal Code provisions are intended to prohibit the public distribution of hate propaganda. Private speech is not covered by the provisions. For example, "advocating genocide" includes publicly arguing that members of an identifiable group should be killed. Wilfully promoting hatred can only be committed by communicating statements other than in a private conversation. And inciting hatred is only prohibited if statements are communicated in a public place.

Online communications that advocate genocide or wilfully promote or incite hatred are likely to fall within the provisions because the Internet is a public network. Under section 320.1 of the Criminal Code, a judge has the authority to order the removal of hate propaganda from a computer system that is available to the public. Such authority extends to all computer systems located within Canada.

Section 2 of the Canadian Charter of Rights and Freedoms guarantees freedom of thought, belief, opinion and expression to all Canadians. However, all Charter rights are subject to reasonable limits that can be demonstrably justified in a free and democratic society. In 1990, the Supreme Court of Canada considered whether or not section 319(2) of the Criminal Code (the crime of wilfully promoting hatred) violates our constitutional right to freedom of expression, in the Keegstra case. James Keegstra was an Alberta high-school teacher who taught his students that the Holocaust did not occur and was part of a Jewish conspiracy. The Court held that, although section 319(2) does limit free speech, it is a reasonable limit consistent with a democratic society, and is therefore constitutional.

Section 13 of the Canadian Human Rights Act prohibits the communication by means of a telecommunication undertaking (including the Internet) of messages that are likely to expose a person to hatred or contempt on the basis of:

- race
- national or ethnic origin
- colour
- religion
- age
- sex
- sexual orientation
- marital status
- family status
- disability
- conviction for which a pardon has been granted

In January 2002, the Canadian Human Rights Tribunal ordered Ernst Zundel to cease and desist from publishing hate messages on the Zundelsite because his writings violate section 13. However, the Zundelsite continues to post hateful messages because it is located in the United States and is, therefore, outside the jurisdiction of the Canadian tribunal.

Regulations under the Broadcasting Act prohibit any licensee from broadcasting or distributing programming that contains abusive comments about individuals or groups - comments that would expose an individual, group, or class of individuals to hatred or contempt on discriminatory grounds. These regulations apply to radio, specialty services, broadcast television and pay television. However, as it now stands, Internet-based communications do not readily fit the definition of "broadcasting."

Under the Immigration Act, customs officials have the authority to stop hate material from entering Canada, and to refuse entry to individual hate-mongers. Bigotry and hatred thrive on ignorance, fear, false information and half-truths. But if readers are able to deconstruct any messages of hate that come their way, much of the messages' power is reduced. This makes critical thinking skills an indispensable part of an anti-hate tool kit.

Common Characteristics

1. Capitalize on Paranoia

Conspiracy theories abound on hate sites, which often blame the groups they target for any number of social, economic or political problems. Such theories rely on their readers' ignorance, plus invented "evidence," to back up their claims. One of the most infamous conspiracy theories is contained in the Protocols of the Elders of Zion. The book was written by agents of the Russian czar at the end of the 19th century, and falsely "documents" the existence of a Jewish conspiracy to take over the world. Although such a theory has been thoroughly debunked, hate-mongers continue to invoke the Protocols.

2. Suggest Sanction from Above

Hate sites often make use of scriptural references, religious writings and holy tracts to give the impression that their claims are sanctified by moral righteousness and guided by a higher power. For example, the site God Hates Fags portrays gays and lesbians in a hateful and demeaning way. Embedded in its homophobic rhetoric are scriptural references to support the position that God has "given up" on gay persons.

3. Exploit Fear of Armageddon

Hate groups take advantage of people's fears of social and economic uncertainty by blaming the woes of modern society on the particular group they target. Canadian sites like National Skinhead Front, CFAR and the Canadian Heritage Alliance focus on the "dangers" of immigration and the need to return to a "traditional European way of life."

Common Strategies

Racialism: White power and white supremacy sites typically deny that they are racist organizations. Instead, they focus on the need to protect white people from assimilation and/ or direct threats from non-white groups. They call this perspective "racialist" as opposed to racist.

Pseudo-Science and Intellectualism: Many hate-mongers use pseudo-scientific intellectualized language and incorporate the work of university-based academics to make their views seem more credible.

Canadian professor Phillip Rushton's work on the different intellectual and physical abilities of different "races" is a case in point. In addition, the late Dr. William Pierce operated a publishing company that released a steady stream of neo-Nazi literature. Pierce's fictionalized account of racialist revolution in The Turner Diaries is said to have inspired the Oklahoma City bombing in 1995.

Historical Revisionsim: Holocaust denial is a frequently used strategy. Haters who "revise" history argue that the Holocaust either did not occur, or was less significant than the historical record indicates. The Zundelsite, for example, houses a collection of revisionist writings, including Zundel's pamphlet Did Six Million Really Die?

Patriotism: A number of hate sites clothe their messages in patriotic language. For example, the High Desert Militia of Southern California includes quotes from Thomas Jefferson and Ben Franklin on their home page, beside the "Patriot's Prayer".

Misinformation: A number of hate groups seek to embed their messages in sites that purport to exist for non-hateful purposes. At first glance, the site martinlutherking.org appears to contain historical information about King and the civil rights movement; however, it in fact promotes racism and anti-Semitism. Similarly, the Canadian Association for Free Expression purports to advocate for civil liberties, but its founder, Paul Fromm, admits that the site was created to promote "conservative discussion especially of race and immigration."

Nationalism: Sites such as the U.S.-based League of the South and the Canadian Heritage Alliance use the language of national pride and heritage to advocate for a return to white, "anglo-Celtic civilization."

Hate Symbols: The hate movement continues to use well-known symbols such as the Nazi swastika and the KKK's burning cross to "brand" its message. However, it is increasingly common for hate groups to co-opt mainstream symbols such as the Celtic cross and pagan runes, re-signifying them as emblems of white supremacy.

The Anti-Defamation League argues that hate symbols are more than mere signs: "These symbols are meant to inspire a sense of fear and insecurity. [They] give haters a sense of power and belonging, and a quick way of identifying with others who share their ideology."

Recruiting Young People

White supremacist groups and hate groups depend upon recruitment for survival-and their primary target is often teenagers. In their view, impressionable youth represents the only hope for the future of the "white race." Hate groups concentrate their recruiting efforts primarily in high schools (and, to some extent, in colleges and universities). Traditionally, hate groups have had to approach this group with their message by distributing pamphlets on school grounds and in neighbourhood mailboxes. But these tactics are not always successful: too many adults (principals, teachers and parents) are able to intervene to protect the kids.

But the Internet seems tailor-made for reaching disaffected young people: teenagers spend far more time on it than their parents do, and many teens consider the virtual world of the web their "home away from home."

Hatemongers now target young people directly, through hate "music" and special web sites. Young people may be susceptible to online racist propaganda because they don't have the experience or facts at hand to refute the lies and myths being fed to them.

Lonely, marginalized youth, seeking a sense of identity and belonging, are both the most attractive targets for racists and their most useful tools, once recruited. It's a common belief that youths who join hate groups are mainly poor, uneducated and alienated. Although the Internet is a new way to reach young people, the techniques hatemongers use to attract them are still very traditional. Here are some of the strategies hate groups use to attract young people on the Internet:

Music: Music is a compelling way to influence young people. When kids surf the Net for music, they may chance on sites that sell hate music, or even offer it free for downloading. Such Web sites often also provide links to hate-promoting brochures, pamphlets, newsgroups, chat rooms or Web sites. One of the most popular forms of racist music is "white power" rock 'n' roll-loud and violent, with hostile lyrics that call for the murder of black people, or the start of a racial holy war. Every year in North America, more than 50,000 white power CDs are sold; and journalist Jay Dixit reports that Resistance Records (the largest North American distributor of hate music) was expected to gross more than $1 million (U.S.) in 2001.

Games. Another strategy used to attract young people is white-power versions of popular computer games. Teens may go online looking for the latest cool game, and may find the "hate version" instead. For example, Resistance Records has produced Ethnic Cleansing-a computer game whose object is to kill "subhumans" such as Blacks and

Latinos, and their "masters," the Jews, who are portrayed as the personification of evil. Players can choose between dressing as KKK members or skinheads.

Activities for kids. Some hate sites offer special sections for kids containing games and activities. For example, on the "Creativity for Kids" section of the neo-Nazi World Church of the Creator Web site, children can try their hands at crossword puzzles with racist content. The purpose of the children's section is "to help the young members of the white race understand our fight." Cartoon spokescharacters. Some hate sites use cartoon-like or animated characters, similar to (or identical to) those used in children's media to attract young audiences.

Protecting Children and Teens

As young people surf the Net in ever-increasing numbers-from schools, libraries and their homes-the risk of them accidentally encountering hate material grows-as does the issue of how to shield them from undesirable online content.

Filtering Software: One technical solution often recommended for protecting children is filtering software. Parents and educators can install this software onto their computers, and program it (usually via keywords or phrases) with the type of material they don't want kids to access. The filtering software then "filters out" sites with that kind of content, and blocks the computer browser from going there. Such software is certainly an option for parents of young surfers, who aren't yet adept enough to turn off the filtering software. But as kids get older and more tech-savvy, they can easily find out how to override certain programs. And, of course, filtering software isn't particularly selective: if a parent programs it to block all references to "hate" or "Holocaust," for example, the software will certainly screen out most hate Web sites-but it will also block access to valuable and legitimate resources such as sites dedicated to anti-racism, Jewish culture, war museums, and even discussions of anti-hate legislation.

Another option is to block access to Internet areas that have already been identified as hate sites. The Anti-Defamation League, a U.S. non-profit human-rights group, has developed a product called HateFilter that specifically targets several hundred such Web sites. But regardless of the potential benefits and the drawbacks of such technology, the larger issue is whether to use it to censor young people's access to the Internet in the first place. Filtering software is not a complete solution: hate often comes in subtle forms that filters would not pick up.

Parental Guidance: The first and best defence for kids on the Internet is always adult guidance. Kids need to know the historical facts about racism and world events, and to talk with parents and teachers about the claims made by hatemongers. Adult involvement is rarer than we might think. MNet's 2001 survey "Young Canadians In A Wired World" revealed that many kids surf the Net at home with little or no parental supervision or awareness. Seventy per cent of the kids surveyed said their parents "rarely" or "never" ask them about the sites they visit.

Hate on the Net is not always obvious: although hard-core sites are easy to detect, some hatemongers use more subtle tactics to attract new blood. They create fun-and-games sites for children and music sites for teens; infiltrate chat-rooms and newsgroups frequented by kids; and even set up sites where children might go for homework assignments. The most effective long-range strategy for helping young people is to give them lots of information about online hate-as well as the critical thinking skills to decode messages of hate, and read between the lines.

A teen might reasonably expect, for instance, a Martin Luther King site to be a place where they could find information on a significant figure in American history. But this Martin Luther King site serves up a potent brew of racism, anti-Semitism and Communist conspiracy theories-all in the guise of historical data. Young people need to understand that the Internet has no gatekeepers and they need to be able to distinguish between such biased prejudicial material, and fair and accurate information.

Online Privacy

Privacy is a fundamental human right. It underpins human dignity and other values such as freedom of association and freedom of speech. It has become one of the most important human rights of the modern age. Privacy is recognized around the world in diverse regions and cultures. It is protected in the Universal Declaration of Human Rights, the International Covenant on Civil and Political Rights, and in many other international and regional human rights treaties. Nearly every country in the world includes a right of privacy in its constitution. At a minimum, these provisions include rights of inviolability of the home and secrecy of communications.

Most recently written constitutions include specific rights to access and control one's personal information. In many of the countries where privacy is not explicitly recognized in the constitution, the courts have found that right in other provisions. In many countries, international agreements that recognize privacy rights such as the International Covenant on Civil and Political Rights or the

European Convention on Human Rights have been adopted into law.

Definitions of privacy vary widely according to context and environment. In many countries, the concept has been fused with data protection, which interprets privacy in terms of management of personal information. Outside this rather strict context, privacy protection is frequently seen as a way of drawing the line at how far society can intrude into a person's affairs. The lack of a single definition should not imply that the issue lacks importance. As one writer observed, "in one sense, all human rights are aspects of the right to privacy."

Privacy can be divided into the following separate but related concepts:

Information privacy, which involves the establishment of rules governing the collection and handling of personal data such as credit information, and medical and government records. It is also known as "data protection";

Bodily privacy, which concerns the protection of people's physical selves against invasive procedures such as genetic tests, drug testing and cavity searches;

Privacy of communications, which covers the security and privacy of mail, telephones, e-mail and other forms of communication; and

Territorial privacy, which concerns the setting of limits on intrusion into the domestic and other environments such as the workplace or public space. This includes searches, video surveillance and ID checks.

The World Wide Web is an exciting new marketplace for consumers. It offers easy access not only to a vast array of goods and services, but also to rich sources of information that enable consumers to make better-informed purchasing decisions. It also offers the convenience of shopping from the office or home. This information-rich medium also serves as a source of vast amounts of personal information about consumers. Commercial Web sites collect personal information explicitly through a variety of means, including registration pages, user surveys, and online contests, application forms, and order forms. Web sites also collect personal information through means that are not obvious to consumers, such as "cookies."

The online consumer market is growing exponentially. In early 1997, 51 million adults were already online in the U.S. and Canada, and 73% reported that they had shopped for product information on the World Wide Web. By December 1997, the number of adults online in the U.S. and Canada had climbed to 58 million, and 10 million had actually purchased a product or service online. Analysts estimate that Internet advertising— which totaled approximately $301 million in 1996—will swell to $4.35 billion by the year 2000. While these figures suggest that the online marketplace is growing rapidly, there are also indications that consumers are wary of participating in it. Surveys have shown that increasing numbers of consumers are concerned about how their personal information is used in the electronic marketplace.

In fact, a substantial number of online consumers would rather forego information or products available through the Web than provide a Web site personal information without knowing what the site's information practices are. According to the results of a March 1998 Business Week survey, consumers not currently using the Internet ranked concerns about the privacy of their personal information and communications as the top reason they have stayed off the Internet. Clearly, consumers care deeply about the privacy and security of their personal information in the online environment and are looking for greater protections.

Consumers will continue to distrust online companies and will remain wary of engaging in electronic commerce until meaningful and effective consumer privacy protections are implemented in the online marketplace. If such protections are not implemented, the online marketplace will fail to reach its full potential.

Privacy Online of Children

Children represent a large and rapidly growing segment of online consumers and are being actively targeted by commercial Web sites. Children use the Web for a wide variety of activities, including homework, informal learning, browsing, playing games, corresponding with electronic pen pals by e-mail, placing messages on electronic bulletin boards and participating in chat rooms. Among the activities most attractive to children are those that allow them to communicate directly with their peers, for example, chat rooms, bulletin boards and e-mail.

Almost 10 million of America's 69 million children are now online, with over 4 million accessing the Internet from school and 5.7 million from home. Children are also avid consumers and represent a large and powerful segment of the marketplace. They are estimated to spend billions of dollars a year, and to influence the expenditure of billions more. Their growing presence online, therefore, creates enormous opportunities for marketers to promote their products and services to an eager audience. At the same time, the Web offers an easy way to collect large amounts of detailed marketing data from and about children.

Safety and Privacy Concerns

A wide variety of detailed personal information is being collected online from and about children, often without actual notice to or an opportunity for control by parents. This information may be collected from children at various places on a site: when the child is registering for a contest, enrolling in an electronic pen pal program, completing a survey, or playing a game. A child may also reveal such personal information in the course of participating in chat rooms or posting messages on electronic bulletin boards—areas that are publicly accessible to anyone surfing the Web. These practices present unique privacy and safety concerns because of the particular vulnerability of children, the immediacy and ease with which information can be collected from them, and the ability of the online medium to circumvent the traditional gatekeeping role of the parent.

The most potentially serious safety concern is presented by the posting of personal identifying information by and about children—i.e., information that can be used to identify children, such as name, postal or e-mail address—in interactive public areas, like chat rooms and bulletin boards, that are accessible to all online users. These activities enable children to communicate freely with strangers, including adults.

The FBI and Justice Department's "Innocent Images" investigation has revealed that online services and bulletin boards are quickly becoming the most powerful resources used by predators to identify and contact children. Further, anecdotal evidence indicates that many children surfing the Web claim to have experienced problems such as attempted password theft and inappropriate advances by adults in children's chat rooms.

Traditionally, parents have instructed children to avoid speaking with strangers. The collecting or posting of personal information in chat rooms and on bulletin boards online runs contrary to that traditional safety message. Children are told by parents not to talk to strangers whom they meet on the street, but they are given a contrary message by Web sites that encourage them to interact with strangers in their homes via the Web. The dangers in the Web environment are heightened by the fact that children cannot determine whether they are dealing with another child or an adult posing as a child.

In addition to these safety issues are privacy concerns raised by commercial Web sites' collection of personal information from children for marketing purposes. As described below, the practice is widespread and includes the collection of personal information from even very young children without any parental involvement or awareness. There is considerable concern about online collection practices that bypass parents, who have traditionally protected children from marketing abuses. Children generally lack the developmental capacity and judgment to give meaningful consent to the release of personal information to a third party. This is an even greater problem when children are offered an incentive for releasing personal information, or when release of personal information is a prerequisite to registering for a contest, joining a kid's club, or playing a game.

In sum, the immediacy and ease with which personal information can be collected from children online, combined with the limited capacity of children to understand fully the potentially serious safety and privacy implications of providing that information, have created deep concerns about current information practices involving children online.

Fair Information Practice Principles

Over the past quarter century, government agencies in the United States, Canada, and Europe have studied the manner in which entities collect and use personal information -- their "information practices"—and the safeguards required to assure those practices are fair and provide adequate privacy protection. The result has been a series of reports, guidelines, and model codes that represent widely-accepted principles concerning fair information practices. Common to all of these documents are five core principles of privacy protection:

(1) Notice/Awareness;

(2) Choice/Consent;

(3) Access/Participation;

(4) Integrity/Security; and

(5) Enforcement/Redress.

1. Notice/Awareness

The most fundamental principle is notice. Consumers should be given notice of an entity's information practices before any personal information is collected from them. Without notice, a consumer cannot make an informed decision as to whether and to what extent to disclose personal information. Moreover, three of the other principles discussed below—choice/consent, access/participation, and enforcement/redress—are only meaningful when a consumer has notice of an entity's policies, and his or her rights with respect thereto.

While the scope and content of notice will depend on the entity's substantive information practices, notice of some or all of the following have been recognized as essential to ensuring that consumers are properly informed before divulging personal information:

— identification of the entity collecting the data;

— identification of the uses to which the data will be put;

— identification of any potential recipients of the data;

— the nature of the data collected and the means by which it is collected if not obvious (passively, by means of electronic monitoring, or actively, by asking the consumer to provide the information);

— whether the provision of the requested data is voluntary or required, and the consequences of a refusal to provide the requested information; and

— the steps taken by the data collector to ensure the confidentiality, integrity and quality of the data.

Some information practice codes state that the notice should also identify any available consumer rights, including: any choice respecting the use of the data; whether the consumer has been given a right of access to the data; the ability of the consumer to contest inaccuracies; the availability of redress for violations of the practice code; and how such rights can be exercised. In the Internet context, notice can be accomplished easily by the posting of an information practice disclosure describing an entity's information practices on a company's site on the Web. To be effective, such a disclosure should be clear and conspicuous, posted in a prominent location, and readily accessible from both the site's home page and any Web page where information is collected from the consumer. It should also be unavoidable and understandable so that it gives consumers meaningful and effective notice of what will happen to the personal information they are asked to divulge.

2. Choice/Consent

The second widely-accepted core principle of fair information practice is consumer choice or consent. At its simplest, choice means giving consumers options as to how any personal information collected from them may be used. Specifically, choice relates to secondary uses of information—i.e., uses beyond those necessary to complete the contemplated transaction. Such secondary uses can be internal, such as placing the consumer on the collecting company's mailing list in order to market additional products or promotions, or external, such as the transfer of information to third parties.

Traditionally, two types of choice/consent regimes have been considered: opt-in or opt-out. Opt-in regimes require affirmative steps by the consumer to allow the collection and/or use of information; opt-out regimes require affirmative steps to prevent the collection and/or use of such information. The distinction lies in the default rule when no affirmative steps are taken by the consumer. Choice can also involve more than a binary yes/no option. Entities can, and do, allow consumers to tailor the nature of the information they reveal and the uses to which it will be put. Thus, for example, consumers can be provided separate choices as to whether they wish to be on a company's general internal mailing list or a marketing list sold to third parties. In order to be effective, any choice regime should provide a simple and easily-accessible way for consumers to exercise their choice.

In the online environment, choice easily can be exercised by simply clicking a box on the computer screen that indicates a user's decision with respect to the use and/or dissemination of the information being collected. The online environment also presents new possibilities to move beyond the opt-in/opt-out paradigm. For example, consumers could be required to specify their preferences regarding information use before entering a Web site, thus effectively eliminating any need for default rules.

3. Access/Participation

Access is the third core principle. It refers to an individual's ability both to access data about him or herself —i.e., to view the data in an entity's files—and to contest that data's accuracy and completeness. Both are essential to ensuring that data are accurate and complete. To be meaningful, access must encompass timely and inexpensive access to data, a simple means for contesting inaccurate or incomplete data, a mechanism by which the data collector can verify the information, and the means by which corrections and/or consumer objections can be added to the data file and sent to all data recipients.

4. Integrity/Security

The fourth widely accepted principle is that data be accurate and secure. To assure data integrity, collectors must take reasonable steps, such as using only reputable sources of data and cross-referencing data against multiple sources, providing consumer access to data, and destroying untimely data or converting it to anonymous form.

Security involves both managerial and technical measures to protect against loss and the unauthorized access, destruction, use, or disclosure of the data. Managerial measures include internal organizational measures that limit access to data and ensure that those individuals with access do not utilize the data for unauthorized purposes. Technical security measures to prevent unauthorized access include encryption in the transmission and storage of data; limits on access through use of passwords; and the storage of data on secure servers or computers that are inaccessible by modem.

5. Enforcement/Redress

It is generally agreed that the core principles of privacy protection can only be effective if there is a mechanism in place to enforce them. Absent an enforcement and redress mechanism, a fair information practice code is merely suggestive rather than prescriptive, and does not ensure compliance with core fair information practice principles. Among the alternative enforcement approaches are industry self-regulation; legislation that would create private remedies for consumers; and/or regulatory schemes enforceable through civil and criminal sanctions.

Self-Regulation: To be effective, self-regulatory regimes should include both mechanisms to ensure compliance (enforcement) and appropriate means of recourse by injured parties (redress). Mechanisms to ensure compliance include making acceptance of and compliance with a code of fair information practices a condition of membership in an industry association; external audits to verify compliance; and certification of entities that have adopted and comply with the code at issue. A self-regulatory regime with many of these principles has recently been adopted by the individual reference services industry.

Appropriate means of individual redress include, at a minimum, institutional mechanisms to ensure that consumers have a simple and effective way to have their concerns addressed. Thus, a self-regulatory system should provide a means to investigate complaints from individual consumers and ensure that consumers are aware of how to access such a system. If the self-regulatory code has been breached, consumers should have a remedy for the violation. Such a remedy can include both the righting of the wrong (e.g., correction of any misinformation, cessation of unfair practices) and compensation for any harm suffered by the consumer. Monetary sanctions would serve both to compensate the victim of unfair practices and as an incentive for industry compliance. Industry codes can provide for alternative dispute resolution mechanisms to provide appropriate compensation.

Private Remedies: A statutory scheme could create private rights of action for consumers harmed by an entity's unfair information practices. Several of the major information practice codes, including the seminal 1973 HEW Report, call for implementing legislation. The creation of private remedies would help create strong incentives for entities to adopt and implement fair information practices and ensure compensation for individuals harmed by misuse of their personal information. Important questions would need to be addressed in such legislation, e.g., the definition of unfair information practices; the availability of compensatory, liquidated and/or punitive damages; and the elements of any such cause of action.

Government Enforcement: Finally, government enforcement of fair information practices, by means of civil or criminal penalties, is a third means of enforcement. Fair information practice codes have called for some government enforcement, leaving open the question of the scope and extent of such powers. Whether enforcement is civil or criminal likely will depend on the nature of the data at issue and the violation committed.

The fair information practice codes are, however, applicable to parents, in light of the special status that children generally have been accorded under the law. This status as a special, vulnerable group is premised on the belief that children lack the analytical abilities and judgment of adults. It is evidenced by an array of federal and state laws that protect children, including those that ban sales of tobacco and alcohol to minors, prohibit child pornography, require parental consent for medical procedures, and make contracts with children voidable. In the specific arenas of marketing and privacy rights, moreover, several federal statutes and regulations recognize both the need for heightened protections for children and the special role that parents play in implementing these protections.

Principles of Participation and Integrity

Since parents may not be fully aware of what personal information a site has collected from their child, the access/participation principle is a particularly important one with respect to information collected from children. To provide informed consent to the retention and/or use of information collected from their children, parents need to be given access to the information collected from their children, particularly if any of the information is collected prior to providing notice to the parent. The principle of integrity, which addresses the accuracy of the data, is also important for children's information.

Parents have an interest in assuring that whatever information Web sites collect from children or have otherwise obtained about their children is accurate. This is particularly important in contexts that involve decisions that impact on the child or family, such as educational or health decisions. In addition, since children's information is considered to be a more sensitive type of information, sites should take the same steps identified above to assure that children's data is secure from unauthorized uses or disclosures.

Privacy Protection Models

There are four major models for privacy protection. Depending on their application, these models can be complementary or contradictory. In most countries reviewed in the survey, several are used simultaneously. In the countries that protect privacy most effectively, all of the models are used together to ensure privacy protection.

Comprehensive laws

In many countries around the world, there is a general law that governs the collection, use and dissemination of personal information by both the public and private sectors. An oversight body then ensures compliance. This is the preferred model for most countries adopting data protection laws and was adopted by the European Union to ensure compliance with its data protection regime. A variation of these laws, which is described as a "co-regulatory model," was adopted in Canada and Australia. Under this approach, industry develops rules for the protection of privacy that are enforced by the industry and overseen by the privacy agency.

Sectoral Laws

Some countries, such as the United States, have avoided enacting general data protection rules in favor of specific sectoral laws governing, for example, video rental records and financial privacy. In such cases, enforcement is achieved through a range of mechanisms. A major drawback with this approach is that it requires that new legislation be introduced with each new technology so protections frequently lag behind. The lack of legal protections for individual's privacy on the Internet in the United States is a striking example of its limitations. There is also the problem of a lack of an oversight agency. In many countries, sectoral laws are used to complement comprehensive legislation by providing more detailed protections for certain categories of information, such as telecommunications, police files or consumer credit records.

Self-Regulation

Data protection can also be achieved, at least in theory, through various forms of self-regulation, in which companies and industry bodies establish codes of practice and engage in self-policing. However, in many countries, especially the United States, these efforts have been disappointing, with little evidence that the aims of the codes are regularly fulfilled. Adequacy and enforcement are the major problem with these approaches. Industry codes in many countries have tended to provide only weak protections and lack enforcement.

Technology-based Privacy

With the recent development of commercially available technology-based systems, privacy protection has also moved into the hands of individual users. Users of the Internet and of some physical applications can employ a range of programs and systems that provide varying degrees of privacy and security of communications. These include encryption, anonymous remailers, proxy servers and digital cash. Users should be aware that not all tools effectively protect privacy. Some are poorly designed while others may be designed to facilitate law enforcement access.

Right to Privacy

The recognition of privacy is deeply rooted in history. There is recognition of privacy in the Qur'an and in the sayings of Mohammed. The Bible has numerous references to privacy. Jewish law has long recognized the concept of being free from being watched. There were also protections in classical Greece and ancient China. Legal protections have existed in Western countries for hundreds of years. In 1361, the Justices of the Peace Act in England provided for the arrest of peeping toms and eavesdroppers.

In 1765, British Lord Camden, striking down a warrant to enter a house and seize papers wrote, "We can safely say there is no law in this country to justify the defendants in what they have done; if there was, it would destroy all the comforts of society, for papers are often the dearest property any man can have." Parliamentarian William Pitt wrote, "The poorest man may in his cottage bid defiance to all the force of the Crown. It may be frail; its roof may shake; the wind may blow through it; the storms may enter; the rain may enter - but the King of England cannot enter; all his forces dare not cross the threshold of the ruined tenement."

Various countries developed specific protections for privacy in the centuries that followed. In 1776, the Swedish Parliament enacted the Access to Public Records Act that required that all government-held information be used for legitimate purposes. France prohibited the publication of private facts and set stiff fines for violators in 1858. The Norwegian Criminal Code prohibited the publication of information relating to "personal or domestic affairs" in 1889.

The modern privacy benchmark at an international level can be found in the 1948 Universal Declaration of Human Rights, which specifically protects territorial and communications privacy. Article 12 states: No one should be subjected to arbitrary interference with his privacy, family, home or correspondence, nor to attacks on his honour or reputation. Everyone has the right to the protection of the law against such interferences or attacks.

Numerous international human rights treaties specifically recognize privacy as a right. The International Covenant on Civil and Political Rights (ICCPR), Article 17, the United Nations Convention on Migrant Workers, Article 14, and the UN Convention on Protection of the Child, Article 16 adopt the same language. On the regional level, various treaties make these rights legally enforceable. Article 8 of the European Convention for the Protection of Human Rights and Fundamental Freedoms 1950 states:

(1) Everyone has the right to respect for his private and family life, his home and his correspondence.

(2) There shall be no interference by a public authority with the exercise of this right except as in accordance with the law and is necessary in a democratic society in the interests of national security, public safety or the economic well-being of the country, for the prevention of disorder or crime, for the protection of health of morals, or for the protection of the rights and freedoms of others.

The Convention created the European Commission of Human Rights and the European Court of Human Rights to oversee enforcement. Both have been active in the enforcement of privacy rights and have consistently viewed Article 8's protections expansively and interpreted the restrictions narrowly. The Commission found in 1976:

For numerous Anglo-Saxon and French authors, the right to respect "private life" is the right to privacy, the right to live, as far as one wishes, protected from publicity. In the opinion of the Commission, however, the right to respect for private life does not end there. It comprises also, to a certain degree, the right to establish and develop relationships with other human beings, especially in the emotional field for the development and fulfillment of one's own personality.

The Court has reviewed member states' laws and imposed sanctions on numerous countries for failing to regulate wiretapping by governments and private individuals. It has also reviewed cases of individuals' access to their personal information in government files to ensure that adequate procedures exist. It has expanded the protections of Article 8 beyond government actions to those of private persons where it appears that the government should have prohibited those actions.

Article 11 of the American Convention on Human Rights sets out the right to privacy in terms similar to the Universal Declaration. In 1965, the Organization of American States proclaimed the American Declaration of the Rights and Duties of Man, which called for the protection of numerous human rights, including privacy. The Inter-American Court of Human Rights has begun to address privacy issues in its cases.

Data Protection

Interest in the right of privacy increased in the 1960s and 1970s with the advent of information technology. The surveillance potential of powerful computer systems prompted demands for specific rules governing the collection and handling of personal information. The genesis of modern legislation in this area can be traced to the first data protection law in the world enacted in the Land of Hesse in Germany in 1970. This was followed by national laws in Sweden, the United States, Germany, and France.

Two crucial international instruments evolved from these laws. The Council of Europe's 1981 Convention for the Protection of Individuals with regard to the Automatic Processing of Personal Data and the Organization for Economic Cooperation and Development's (OECD) Guidelines Governing the Protection of Privacy and Transborder Data Flows of Personal Data set out specific rules covering the handling of electronic data. These rules describe personal information as data that are afforded protection at every step from collection to storage and dissemination.

The expression of data protection in various declarations and laws varies. All require that personal information must be:

— obtained fairly and lawfully;

— used only for the original specified purpose;

— adequate, relevant and not excessive to purpose;

— accurate and up to date;

— accessible to the subject;

— kept secure; and

— destroyed after its purpose is completed.

These two agreements have had a profound effect on the enactment of laws around the world. Nearly thirty countries have signed the COE convention and several others are planning to do so shortly. The OECD guidelines have also been widely used in national legislation, even outside the OECD member countries.

Rationales for Adopting Comprehensive Laws

There are three major reasons for the movement towards comprehensive privacy and data protection laws. Many countries are adopting these laws for one or more reasons.

— To remedy past injustices. Many countries, especially in Central Europe, South America and South Africa, are adopting laws to remedy privacy violations that occurred under previous authoritarian regimes.

— To promote electronic commerce. Many countries, especially in Asia, have developed or are currently developing laws in an effort to promote electronic commerce. These countries recognize that consumers are uneasy with the increased availability of their personal data, particularly with new means of identification and forms of transactions. These countries recognize consumers are uneasy with their personal information being sent worldwide. Privacy laws are being introduced as part of a package of laws intended to facilitate electronic commerce by setting up uniform rules.

— To ensure laws are consistent with Pan-European laws. Most countries in Central and Eastern Europe are adopting new laws based on the Council of Europe Convention and the European Union Data Protection Directive. Many of these countries hope to join the European Union in the near future. Countries in other regions are adopting new laws or updating older laws to ensure that trade will not be affected by the requirements of the European Union Directive.

In 1995, the European Union enacted the Data Protection Directive in order to harmonize member states' laws in providing consistent levels of protections for citizens and ensuring the free flow of personal data within the European Union. The directive sets a baseline common level of privacy that not only reinforces current data protection law, but also establishes a range of new rights. It applies to the processing of personal information in electronic and manual files.

A key concept in the European data protection model is "enforceability." Data subjects have rights established in explicit rules. Every European Union country has a data protection commissioner or agency that enforces the rules. It is expected that the countries with which Europe does business will need to provide a similar level of oversight. The basic principles established by the Directive are: the right to know where the data originated; the right to have inaccurate data rectified; a right of recourse in the event of unlawful processing; and the right to withhold permission to use data in some circumstances. For example, individuals have the right to opt-out free of charge from being sent direct marketing material. The Directive contains strengthened protections over the use of sensitive personal data relating, for example, to health, sex life or religious or philosophical beliefs.

In the future, the commercial and government use of such information will generally require "explicit and unambiguous" consent of the data subject. The 1995 Directive imposes an obligation on member states to ensure that the personal information relating to European citizens has the same level of protection when it is exported to, and processed in, countries outside the European Union. This requirement has resulted in growing pressure outside Europe for the passage of privacy laws. Those countries that refuse to adopt adequate privacy laws may find themselves unable to conduct certain types of information flows with Europe, particularly if they involve sensitive data.

In 1997, the European Union supplemented the 1995 directive by introducing the Telecommunications Privacy Directive. This directive established specific protections covering telephone, digital television, mobile networks and other telecommunications systems. It imposed wide-ranging obligations on carriers and service providers to ensure the privacy of users' communications, including Internet-related activities. It covered areas that, until then, had fallen between the cracks of data protection laws. Access to billing data was severely restricted, as was marketing activity. Caller ID technology was required to incorporate an option for per-line blocking of number transmission. Information collected in the delivery of a communication was required to be purged once the call was completed.

An essential aspect of any privacy protection regime is oversight. In most countries with an omnibus data protection or privacy act, there is an official or agency that oversees enforcement of the act. The powers of these officials, Commissioner, Ombudsman or Registrar, vary widely by country.Several countries including Germany and Canada also have officials or offices on a state or provincial level. Under Article 28 of the European Union Data Protection Directive, all European Union countries must have an independent enforcement body. Under the Directive, these agencies are given considerable power: governments must consult the body when the government draws up legislation relating to the processing of personal information; the bodies also have the power to conduct investigations and have a right to access information relevant to their investigations; impose remedies such as ordering the destruction of information or ban processing, and start legal proceedings, hear complaints and issue reports. The official is also generally responsible for public education and international liaison in data protection and data transfer. Many authorities also maintain the register of data controllers and databases. They must approve licensing for data controllers.

Several countries that do not have a comprehensive act still have a commissioner. A major power of these officials is to focus public attention on problem areas, even when they do not have any authority to fix the problem. They can do this by promoting codes of practice and encouraging industry associations to adopt them. They also can use their annual reports to point out problems. For example, in Canada, the Federal Privacy Commissioner announced in his 2000 report the existence of an extensive database maintained by the federal government. Once the issue became public, the Ministry disbanded the database.

In several countries, this official also serves as the enforcer of the jurisdiction's Freedom of Information Act. These include Hungary, Estonia, Thailand and the United Kingdom.On the sub-national level, many of the German Lund Commissioners have recently been given the power of information commissioner, and most of the Canadian provincial agencies handle both data protection and freedom of information. A major problem with many agencies around the world is a lack of resources to adequately conduct oversight and enforcement. Many are burdened with licensing systems, which use much of their resources. Others have large backlogs of complaints or are unable to conduct significant number of investigations. Many that started out with adequate funding find their budgets cut a few years later.

Independence is also a problem. In many countries, the agency is under the control of the political arm of the government or part of the Ministry of Justice and lacks the power or will to advance privacy or criticize privacy invasive proposals. In Japan and Thailand, the oversight agency is under the control of the Prime Minister's Office. In Thailand, the director was transferred in 2000 after conflicts with the Prime Minister's Office. In 2001, Slovenia amended its Data Protection Act in order to establish an independent supervisory authority and thereby ensure compliance with the Data Protection Directive. Finally, in some countries that do not have a separate office, the role of investigating and enforcing the laws is done by a human rights ombudsman or by a parliamentary official.

Most data protection laws include restrictions on the transfer of information to third countries unless the information is protected in the destination country. For example, Article 12 of the Council of Europe's 1981 Convention places restrictions on the transborder flows of personal data. Similarly, Article 25 of the European Directive imposes an obligation on member States to ensure that any personal information relating to European citizens is protected by law when it is exported to, and processed in, countries outside Europe. It states:

The Member States shall provide that the transfer to a third country of personal data which are undergoing processing or are intended for processing after transfer may take place only if the third country in question ensures an adequate level of protection.

This requirement has resulted in growing pressure outside Europe for the passage of strong data protection laws. Those countries that refuse to adopt meaningful privacy laws may find themselves unable to conduct certain types of information flows with Europe, particularly if they involve sensitive data. Determination of a third country's system for protecting privacy is made by the European Commission. The overarching principle in this determination process is that the level of protection in the receiving country must be "adequate" rather than "equivalent." Therefore, a reasonably high standard of protection is expected from the third party, although the precise dictates of the Directive need not be followed.

On July 26, 2000, the European Commission ruled that both Switzerland and Hungary provide "adequate" protection for personal information and therefore that all transfers of personal data to these countries could continue. In January 2002, the European Commission recognized that the Canadian Personal Information Protection and Electronic Documents Act (PIPEDA) provides adequate protection for certain personal data transferred from the European Union to Canada. The Commission's decision of adequacy does not cover any personal data held by federal sector or provincial bodies or information held by personal organizations and used for non-commercial purposes, such as data handled by charities or collected in the context of an employment relationship. The Commission is currently looking into the privacy protection schemes in several other non-European Union countries, including New Zealand, Australia, and Hong-Kong.

Another possible way to protect the privacy of information transferred to countries that do not provide "adequate protection" is to rely on a private contract containing standard data protection contractual clauses. This kind of contract would bind the data processor to respect fair information practices such as the right to notice, consent, access and legal remedies. In the case of data transferred from the European Union, the contract would have to meet the standard "adequacy" test, in order to satisfy the Data Protection Directive.

7

Media Literacy

Media literacy is really a necessity in today's world. We live in such a media-saturated environment. We're continually bombarded with messages from newspapers and magazines, movie and television screens, Internet Web sites, chat rooms and listservs. We have to know how to filter out what we don't need or want and how to access and then interpret, analyze and evaluate what's useful. Media literacy is about asking smart questions and making smart choices; it's about using media selectively and reflectively.

Media literate people want to know the source of a message, its purpose and the source's credibility and reliability. They can recognize bias, distortion, stereotyping and sensationalism. They try to get information from multiple sources and to consider any issue from multiple perspectives. Media education develops critical thinking skills. It cuts across all areas of the curriculum and can be integrated into every subject area.

When dealing with print media, we can adjust our reading speed and level of attention to our purpose for reading. We can take time to analyze and reflect on the words, relate them to personal experience and prior knowledge, and decide if we agree or disagree with the statements. Electronic media, on the other hand, bombard us with fast-paced, stimulating sounds and images that have been carefully designed to capture and hold our attention. These sounds and images sort of "wash over us" and leave us with impressions that we don't have time to sort out or consider. That's why understanding how media work and how they affect us is so important. It's so easy to be captivated by television entertainment, electronic games, surfing the Net and popular music. It's important to live intentionally, to consider the trade-offs involved every time we use media (the other worthwhile things we could be doing with our time) and to spend our valuable time only in worthwhile media activities.

Media literacy is an informed, critical understanding of the mass media. It involves an examination of the techniques, technologies and institutions that are involved in media production, the ability to critically analyze media messages, and a recognition of the roles that audiences play in making meaning from those messages.

Media literacy is taught through linked analytic and production activities. As with traditional literacies, "reading" and "writing" are learned together. Although many of us think about television when we consider the media, media literacy takes as its field all media-TV, radio, film, print, rock music, the Internet and even less obvious forms like fashion, children's toys and dolls, or T-shirts.

Today's definition of literacy is more than reading and writing. In order to be functionally literate in our media-saturated world, children and young people-in fact, all of us-have to be able to read the messages that daily inform us, entertain us and sell to us. As the Internet becomes a fact of life, the critical thinking skills that help young people navigate through traditional media are even more important.

Importance of Media Literacy

Media literate people understand that media are constructed to convey ideas, information and news from someone else's perspective. They understand that specific techniques are used to create emotional effects. They can identify those techniques and their intended and actual effects. They are aware that the media benefit some people, but leave others out. They can (pose and sometimes answer) questions about who benefits, who is left out, and why. Media literate people seek alternative sources of information and entertainment. Media literate people use the media for their own advantage and enjoyment. Media literate people know how to act, rather than being acted upon. In this way, media literate people are better citizens.

Television is not the only mass medium that accounts for media saturation. When one considers pop music, radio, newspapers, magazines, computers and video games-in addition to TV-we are exposed to more mass media messages in one day than our grandparents were in a month. The media sell "audience consciousness." They try to predispose people not just to buy certain detergents, cars or aspirin, but to simply buy.

Most governments and businesses have public relations (PR) departments, whose purpose is to get the "good news" about them out into the public consciousness. Many succeed so well that much of what is reported as "news" in fact comes directly from PR departments and press releases.

Democracy and Media Education

Political leaders have discovered the influence of the media. Those who use the media will get their way regardless of public policy or personal integrity.

Visual Communication and Information

For hundreds of years, society has valued literacy-the reading and understanding of texts. In today's society, the visual image is arguably more important than the printed word-yet there has been no corresponding focus on reading the meaning of visual images.

The world economy is fast becoming an information economy, with information a commodity to be bought and sold. A danger exists that new classes of "information-rich" and "information-poor" people may result, with the information-poor unable to afford the information they need to better their lives. Tomorrow's world, in fact, will be increasingly dominated by mass media and communications technologies. Generations of the future will need to understand how the mass media influence society.

Media bring the world into our homes. From them, we learn about war and peace, the environment, new scientific discoveries, and so on. We are dependent upon mass communication for knowing what is going on in our physical, social, economic, and political environments. In other words, almost everything we know about people, places, and events that we cannot visit first-hand comes from the media. We also rely on media for entertainment and pleasure. Television and film have become the storytellers of our generation: these stories tell us about who we are, what we believe, and what we want to be.

Key Concepts of Media Literacy

Media educators base their teaching on key concepts and principles of media literacy. These concepts provide an effective foundation for examining mass media and popular culture.

The following are the eight key concepts for media literacy

1. All media are construction

The media do not present simple reflections of external reality. Rather, they present carefully crafted constructions that reflect many decisions and result from many determining factors. Media Literacy works towards deconstructing these constructions, taking them apart to show how they are made.

2. The media construct reality

The media are responsible for the majority of the observations and experiences from which we build up our personal understandings of the world and how it works. Much of our view of reality is based on media messages that have been pre-constructed and have attitudes, interpretations and conclusions already built in. The media, to a great extent, give us our sense of reality.

3. Audiences negotiate meaning in the media

The media provide us with much of the material upon which we build our picture of reality, and we all "negotiate" meaning according to individual factors: personal needs and anxieties, the pleasures or troubles of the day, racial and sexual attitudes, family and cultural background, and so forth.

4. Media have commercial implications

Media Literacy aims to encourage an awareness of how the media are influenced by commercial considerations, and how these affect content, technique and distribution. Most media production is a business, and must therefore make a profit. Questions of ownership and control are central: a relatively small number of individuals control what we watch, read and hear in the media.

5. Media contain ideological and value messages

All media products are advertising, in some sense, in that they proclaim values and ways of life. Explicitly or implicitly, the mainstream media convey ideological messages about such issues as the nature of the good life, the virtue of consumerism, the role of women, the acceptance of authority, and unquestioning patriotism.

6. Media have social and political implications

The media have great influence on politics and on forming social change. Television can greatly influence the election of a national leader on the basis of image. The media involve us in concerns such as civil rights issues, famines in Africa, and the AIDS epidemic. They give us an intimate sense of national issues and global concerns, so that we become citizens of Marshall McLuhan's "Global Village."

7. Form and content are closely related in the media

As Marshall McLuhan noted, each medium has its own grammar and codifies reality in its own particular way. Different media will report the same event, but create different impressions and messages.

8. Each medium has a unique aesthetic form

Just as we notice the pleasing rhythms of certain pieces of poetry or prose, so we ought to be able to enjoy the pleasing forms and effects of the different media.

Approaches of Media Education

"Media literacy should not be considered as an add-on to the already crowded curriculum. A truly interdisciplinary activity, media literacy should be conceived as a means of facilitating the integration of critical thinking skills, aesthetics, the study of value messages, and the study of the social and political implications of media texts. Media education should permeate many activities in geography and global education, science, and language arts which will be conditioned by the mass media experiences young people bring to the classroom.

Many teachers are now expected to integrate media education into their classrooms, often for the first time. When you consider the scope of media education-from learning hands-on production techniques, to recognizing how the various elements of a specific medium convey meaning, to thinking critically about media issues and media influences-it's easy to see how studying the media lends itself to a number of approaches within a wide variety of subject areas.

The following factors that make media literacy flourish:

— A study of media literacy around the world shows that there are nine factors that appear to be crucial to the successful development of media literacy in secondary schools.

— Media literacy, like other innovative programs, must be a grass-roots movement. Teachers need to take the initiative in lobbying for its inclusion in the curriculum.

— Educational authorities must give clear support to such programs by mandating the teaching of Media Studies within the curriculum; establishing guidelines and resource books; ensuring that curricula are developed; and making certain materials available.

— Faculties of education must hire staff capable of training future teachers in this area. There should also be academic support from tertiary institutions in the writing of curricula and in sustained consultation.

— In-service training at the school district level must be an integral part of program implementation.

— School districts need consultants who have expertise in media literacy, and who will establish communication networks.

— Suitable textbooks and audio-visual materials, which are relevant to the country and/or area, must be available.

— A support organization must be established for the purposes of workshops, conferences, dissemination of newsletters, and developing curriculum units. Such a professional organization must cut across school boards and districts to involve a cross-section of people interested in media literacy.

— There must be appropriate evaluation instruments suitable to the unique attributes of Media Studies.

— Because media literacy involves such a diversity of skills and expertise, there must be collaboration between teachers, parents, researchers and media professionals.

Teaching Strategies and Models

The teacher's attitude to the mass media and to students as avid media consumers is crucial to the success of any media-literacy program. Most students bring to the classroom an enormous amount of information about and experience with the media-in many cases, far more than do their teachers. While it is important for teachers to start where their students are, it is also necessary for them to lead their students to where they are not.

It's important that educators teach inductively, and begin whenever possible using students' direct experiences with the media. The basic method of media studies is that of a "spiral curriculum," a concept developed by educator Jerome Bruner. The fundamental principle of this method is that the key concepts of any discipline can be taught in some form to students at any level. Thus, concepts initially introduced in simple form at the elementary level are, in successive years, explored, developed and extended in increasingly sophisticated ways as the student matures and develops.

To take a relatively simple example, elementary school pupils might begin to explore the concept of the commercial implications of media by talking about the television programs they watch and, with the guidance of a teacher, distinguishing between program material and commercials, identifying the different purposes of each. At a later state they could look at a variety of commercials aimed at children, discussing their reactions to them and perhaps beginning to evaluate their effectiveness. They could also talk about what they would put in commercials for children if they were making them.

Older children could begin to analyze the techniques and appeals of commercials, planning and storyboarding some of their own. They could also explore the relationship between commercials and programming, perhaps examining the link between children's cartoon characters and sales of related products such as dolls or clothing. As they progress through the educational system, they may move on, for example, to more detailed examinations of commercials; studies and techniques; or research into issues such as the effects of ownership and control of media.

Because students are immersed in media, the role of the teacher must be that of a facilitator and a co-learner. The teacher must help students to negotiate meaning, engage in inquiry and research, identify patterns, and create their own media productions. It is important to stress the positive features of the mass media rather than to dwell at length on the negative. It is also essential that students be encouraged to explore the values and the tastes that are relevant to their own immediate cultural context. This fundamental premise of values education implies that the teacher should not be imposing a set of elitist values on the class. It may be difficult to find socially redeeming values in many of the programs that have high audience ratings or in rock videos, but it is these very examples that our students are eager to discuss. Using methods such as the inquiry model and applying the key concepts of media literacy in critical discussion, the teacher can empower students to discover meaning on their own, thus giving them critical autonomy.

By necessity, media teachers will be eclectic. As well, the constantly changing content of the media and of popular culture, along with their many new and evolving forms and technologies, will necessitate the concept of "a movable text" that is made up by the teacher, the class, or both together. Such a text will encompass current newspaper and magazine clippings, new videos, audio tapes, CDs, and resource people from the community. In such an enterprise, it should be evident that media study is ideally suited to the collaborative strength that is gained from team teaching.

To avoid duplicating activities and audio-visual materials each year, teachers, department heads, and principals will have to plan a coherent and, in many cases, a sequential media-studies program. This may prompt the formation of board media-literacy committees, which can organize workshops for teachers and design media curricula especially suited to local needs.

Teachers not familiar with essential equipment such as slide projectors and the video-cassette recorder will need to develop the competency required to make media literacy worthwhile for their students. For example, effective use of the freeze frame or the scanning mechanism on a VCR can enhance the use of video considerably.

Practical media production is an important dimension that complements the application of the key concepts and decoding exercises. Practical activities should never become an end in themselves; otherwise, the critical inquiry that is central to media study may be ignored.

1. Specific Approaches to Media Education

The Inquiry Model

The inquiry model is a structured framework that will help students recognize basic issues and provide strategies for developing subject content. This model helps to stimulate open questioning and encourages students to be intellectually curious about the world; it also demands that they have the proper tools for meaningful research and discussion. Since many of the topics that interest students (such as censorship, bias in news coverage, popular culture trends) need to be focused as soon as possible, this methodology is ideally suited to media study.

The inquiry model is especially suited to the introduction of media-literacy activities in the classroom. For example, one can easily apply the model to a provocative short film, a television documentary, or an excerpt from a feature-film video that reveals a powerful moral dilemma. Through an intense shared experience that raises a whole range of issues, students are enabled to see the value of a structured framework for facilitating focused research and critical thinking.

The inquiry model might be used, for example, to explore the following question: "Why do Canadians seem to prefer American media?" The following alternative solutions might be investigated:

— Media content, from films to television, is predominantly American in origin.

— American programs are generally cheaper to buy; have better production values, which reflect lavish budgets; and have a faster pace than do most Canadian programs.

— Quality Canadian programs may reflect our identity, but most Canadians' indifference about or insecurity in this area compels them to avoid endeavours that hold up the mirror to our society.

— Intense competition in the United States ensures that only the most salable commercial products are seen.

Students might then explore the alternatives by collecting data in the following ways:

— Statistics are available in resources on the Canadian film industry and from the reports of various commissions on broadcasting and the film industry.

— Students could check with Canadian television networks on the comparative costs of buying an American show-especially those in reruns-and of producing a Canadian series.

— Students could watch some typical Canadian shows and compare them with the American product in order to notice differences in themes, characterization and pace.

— Students could check the ratings of one of the better Canadian television series and the box-office take for some of our critically acclaimed films. In addition, by formulating a questionnaire and having a cross-section of people answer it, students could determine whether the results confirm or deny the notion that Canadians are indifferent to or insecure about seeing their identity portrayed.

— Students could write or talk to Canadian media professionals regarding the allegations about the benefits of competition in the United States.

Strategies of Critical-Thinking

The critical-thinking movement in the 1980s has helped to provide some important strategies for teachers of media literacy. According to Robert Ennis, critical thinking refers to a body of intellectual skills and abilities that enable one to decide rationally what to believe or do. It also includes a set of values: the pursuit of truth, fairness or open-mindedness, empathy, autonomy and self-criticism. A "strong sense" critical thinker is one who strives to live in accordance with the values of critical thinking and who is able to think dialogically.

A typical mass-media issue involves a blending of intellectual, affective and moral responses. Many issues carried in the media demand that we move back and forth between opposing points of view. It is here that good dialogical thinking can help us out. Dialogical thinking involves a dialogue or extended exchange between points of view or frames of reference.

Moral Education

The mass media are an ideal resource for the discussion of moral dilemmas, the development of moral reasoning, and the use of techniques such as values clarification. Dialogical reasoning, which has been described as an important part of critical thinking, can play a significant role in discussions of topics such as the pros and cons of the mass media, government control of media, censorship, advertising, and the moral values identified in popular television and films. In relation to media-literacy analysis in a subject context, it is important to stress that teachers need to move beyond conceiving of media simply as audio-visual aids. Ideas that teachers can use to incorporate media literacy into their classes include:

Media Education in English Classroom

Teachers of English have been among the strongest advocates of media literacy in the schools. This is understandable, since the teaching of English contains many components that are prominent in media studies: aesthetics, the use of language, genre study, and the critical analysis of texts. English teachers have incorporated media into their courses through such activities as film-literature comparisons, film and television reviews, examinations of the language of advertising, and script-writing.

Media education in the English classroom, however, has sometimes stressed the negative aspects under the guise of developing a "discriminating response." In such a context, popular culture has not fared very well. Furthermore, what has been examined are primarily literary techniques. What has been left out are all the important ideological, economic, political and historical considerations that inform media texts. Fortunately, many of these interdisciplinary approaches are beginning to spread into English studies and are helping to provide some new dimensions to critical discourse. As secondary school English departments develop optional courses in media, it is to be hoped that these elements will be present.

The following are some ways by which English teachers can incorporate media literacy into their programs:

— Film-literature comparisons, where students assess the reasons for differences between film versions and original texts and their effect on themes, characterization and enjoyment.

— Script-writing, where students are encouraged to try writing film scripts from books and even from poems studied in class. Thinking cinematically often enhances insights into the literary experience. Students should also try to write original scripts, which can be filmed or videotaped.

— Multi-media thematic units, where teachers go beyond simply discussing content and themes, and consider with students the unique ways in which each medium codifies reality.

The methodologies used by history teachers to involve their students in research include having students recognize the standpoint and attitudes of an observer; distinguish among different points of view in the evidence; compare pieces of evidence to see if they confirm one another; and produce a convincing and satisfying account that is as fair as possible to all the sources. It is apparent that there are some important parallels here with many media-literary skills. History teachers can integrate media studies into their classrooms through exploring presentations of historical figures, historical bias and point-of-view, the marketing of politicians, and propaganda.

Media Education in Geography Classroom

Geography is a subject that relies heavily on visual representation. Media images of some well-known places in the world are so strong and fixed that they may interfere with what the teacher may want to convey about the reality of that country. The following are some sample activities that can be used in geography classrooms: comparisons of the images of cities in films and TV, to the socio-economic realities of those cities; deconstruction of travel films; bias in films made by governments or corporations; and depiction of countries as portrayed by governments vs. "structured absences," images that are not included in the official portrayal.

The image of the family in the media frequently contrasts with students' experiences. Popular prime-time sitcoms can be deconstructed in order to see what values are espoused by such shows and the nature of their appeal. The following are other media topics that are ideally suited to family studies: the representation of the family in advertising and film; sexuality and sexual stereotyping in the media; and the culture of violence.

Science and Technology: In addition to their treatment in science fiction, there are numerous references to science and technology in newspapers, films, magazines, and novels. Television, in both news and entertainment programs, constantly packages scientific issues and information. The success of David Suzuki's The Nature of Things (CBC) demonstrates our keen interest in the achievements and issues of science and technology. Some of this material can be integrated into the science curriculum by pointing out connections between the scientific issues raised by the media and the scientific principles underlying them. Students can also explore the strengths and limitations of the presentation of science topics in the media.

Visual Arts: The possibilities for media literacy in the visual arts are enormous. Many of the decisions made in the media are based on aesthetic considerations. The role of art in a mass-media-dominated society is of major concern for aspiring artists. Art teachers need to assess more than just the principles of pleasing form when looking at media; they need to consider all the aspects outlined in the visual arts curriculum.

Music: Students are immersed in rap music and rap videos. While some music teachers use rock as a resource, many consider it inappropriate for their music courses. However, there are many valuable connections that can be made through the comparison of traditional and popular music. The popular-music enables music teachers to help their students investigate the aesthetics, the value messages, and the commercial implications of this pervasive form.

Physical and Health Education

Representation of gender, sexuality, violence, smoking, alcohol, junk food and televised sports in the media are all avenues that can be explored in the classroom.

Media educaiton in Mathematics Classroom

Teachers of mathematics will find that a great deal of research in the mass media depends on statistics. Hence, the skills of compilation and graphing will be important. In the area of television, the methods of rating the most watched prime-time programs depend on the exact use of mathematical information.

Today's resource centres contain not only books, but also a good cross-section of popular periodicals, CDs, and audio and videotapes. In the area of print, many periodicals, such as Time and Maclean's, require not only the traditional reading skills, but also media-literacy decoding skills as well. Resource centre teachers can play a valuable role by helping students and teachers to understand the strengths and limitations of each medium when selecting resource materials.

Interdisciplinary Strategies of Cross-Media Studies

The issues, trends and special events of our time are simultaneously reflected in all or several of the mass media. Hence, whether the topic is the arms race, the promotion of a rock star, an advertising campaign, or sexuality and violence in the media, a cross-media analysis is required. The effective application of the key concepts of media depends on the integration of several media. A discussion of violence in the media, for example, might combine knowledge from history, literature, sociology, psychology, communications theory and linguistics.

As well as being able to "decode" the symbols that dominate their society, students should be able to "encode" them. Just as we must integrate writing with the development of reading skills, we should integrate formal media analysis with media production. Thus, creative or production activities should be an essential component of media studies in the classroom. These creative activities can range from something as short and simple as sequencing a series of photographs to a project as complex as the production of a rock video. Many students will grasp the analytic material only if they have undergone production experiences.

Semiotics

Semiotics, the science of signs, is concerned primarily with how meaning is generated in film, television and other works of art, and how information is encoded in them. Some of the decoding/deconstructing activities in this guide use strategies from semiotics. This approach, which has had considerable influence on European academics and media teachers, is now coming into its own in North America. While it may appear to be intellectually demanding and somewhat abstract, it can yield many rewards for the dedicated media teacher.

Each medium of communication has its own biases and ideology. When we interact with a medium of communication, we are influenced as much by the form of the medium as by its message. To explore this notion further, we should ask the following question about each communication medium: What would life be like without this medium? Finding answers to the following questions might also help us to better understand the effects of our interactions with our media of communication:

— How does the medium work (technically, physiologically)

— When/how was it discovered/invented?

— How did its use develop (socially, economically, politically)?

— Who are its outstanding users? What do they communicate? How?

— What are the medium's present conventions? How did they develop?

— What are its present limitations? How are they best overcome?

— How does the medium affect its users, and how do they affect it?

— How have other media affected this one?

As a counter to the mass media-which are generally conservative, and constitute a major industry in which the profit motive is paramount-teachers can show films and videos that present an alternative vision or a different kind of perception and experience to that of the mainstream media. These should supplement, rather than take the place of, the study of popular models. Many excellent narrative and documentary films by the National Film Board, for example, and by many experimental filmmakers and video artists will challenge students' ways of seeing the world. Of course, good literature and art will do the same. Certainly contemporary culture can be illuminated from many sources: by a small-circulation magazine with a distinctively alternative point of view; by a provocative CBC radio documentary; by a record of a contemporary fusion jazz combo, a small independent rock band, or the work of a performance artist/musician such as Laurie Anderson.

Full-Credit Media Literacy Courses

Media Literacy courses-which are usually offered at the

secondary school level as an optional courses in English or the visual arts-will reflect a great diversity of approaches. The following are examples of areas covered by such courses:

An understanding pop culture would touch on:

— fads and trends
— the coverage of royalty
— the appeal of the current music mega-stars
— pop culture's fascination with rituals
— the nature and power of celebrities
— fashion TV (television programs that cover the world of fashion, showcase the latest trends and profile fashion designers)
— fast-food happiness (the extensive marketing of fast-food restaurants through advertising campaigns that convey the idea that such eateries bring happiness by solving all one's problems)
— the appeal of shopping malls
— pop culture in a foreign country
— the culture of toys
— the appeal of cult film patterns in teen films
— formulas in best sellers
— the appeal of Harlequin romance novels
— the pop culture of the fifties and sixties

The Information Society

The information society can be explored by looking at:

— current theories and research on the impact of the electronic media

— Marshall McLuhan's theories regarding the global village, the nature of perception, and the use of our senses

— the dynamics of third-wave technology (electronic technology and the use of computers)

— the Internet revolution

— the role of new and emergent technology

Course units are often devoted to in-depth study of a specific medium such as film, television or the newspaper. The study of a medium can be subdivided further through the study of specific genres. A unit on genre in films might explore the nature of horror films; in a unit on radio students might explore the suspense drama genre; for television, the evolution of sitcoms might be an interesting topic.

Understanding Television

In order to understand better understand television, students might explore:

— the nature of the television medium

— the dynamics of television production

— script-writing and storyboards

— the use of the portable video camera

— the creation of a mini-documentary and a commercial

— the use of special effects

— applications of the mobile studio

ELEMENTARY MEDIA EDUCATION

As is common with many new areas of study, most of the early development in media literacy has been at the secondary level. In Ontario, media literacy is now well established in secondary schools, where it occupies a mandated portion of the English curriculum, and is supported by a number of good textbooks and other materials. Nonetheless, there is a growing realization on the part of media educators that secondary school, or even the transition years, is far too late to begin a field so central to our culture, so much a part of the lives and development of our children, as media studies.

Many of the issues media literacy naturally addresses-such as gender stereotyping, representation of racial and ethnic minorities, consumerism-need to be dealt with far earlier in students' lives than in early adolescence. If media literacy is worthwhile at the secondary level, it is doubly worthwhile at the elementary. Elementary teachers work hard, attempting to deliver a curriculum that seems to become more complex and overloaded every year.

If media literacy is presented to them as yet another add-on, there will be little hope for its adoption. If, however, media literacy is presented not just as something that meets student needs, but something that will meet teachers' needs to integrate the disparate elements of a broad curriculum, then it stands a good chance of becoming an important feature. In fact, media literacy functions so well as an integrator that it would be worth using even if it were not as intrinsically important as it is.

Curriculum Integration

A class engaged in media study is invariably involved in

language work, both written and oral. But it goes beyond that. If we put the child at the centre of the curriculum, and recognize children as first and foremost makers of meaning, then the centrality of media education is obvious. Children have vast amounts of information thrust upon them-much of it from media sources, much of it verbal or written, much of it visual, much of it manipulative. It is the child's task to make sense of it all, to construct reality from this information. But information is never neutral; and language, oral and written, remains the central tool for the kind of conscious processing of mass media that is essential if children are to think and reflect critically about their media and popular culture experiences.

The goal of media education is critical autonomy. The study of media forms and institutions is also directly connected to social and environmental studies-particularly if we consider the role played by media in current affairs, in leisure, in the transmission of values, in the presentation of historical information, in consumerism, and in a host of other topics. Arts education is also clearly connected to media education, in the creative work that students do in their production activities, as well as the critical work they do in assessing media productions. There are even opportunities to infuse math activities into the media program-conducting surveys of viewing habits and expressing the results, examining the costs of advertising and programming, evaluating the claims in advertising, demographic and sampling concepts, etc.

Teachers concerned about thinking skills can clearly see the benefits of media programs, which are built around critical thinking. Media literacy typically involves both analysis and synthesis, as students move from the examination of media products to the production of their own, and back again. Media literacy also typically moves back and forth between the cognitive and affective domains, as students explore their reactions to a media text and attempt to discover how those reactions were generated. Psychomotor development also takes place during production activities, as students learn to manipulate still and video cameras, as well as other equipment. It also becomes clear, when we look at new concerns teachers are being asked to deal with in the classroom-such as violence, anti-racist education, gender stereotyping and other aspects of popular culture-that these cannot adequately be dealt with without examination of the media.

Media Education in India

Generally speaking, media education in India is still in an experimental stage and the feedback it receives from within the country or continent is very little, as most of the conferences take place in Europe. Another reason for this lack of progress is the fact that the concepts of media education are rather geared to the Western hemisphere.

India is a third-world country and therefore the aims it pursuits in media education are different from those in Europe. For India, the emphasis is rather on development and liberation. Kumar believes that media education should lead to democratic communication, while he refers his concepts of media education to all third-world countries.

In India, there is a clear distinction between the term media education, which describes education aiming at a critical use of media; the term educational technology , which, apart from conveying all teaching techniques, also includes the use of media in school lessons; and the term professional education in the media, which can be regarded as a mixture of a school of journalism and of film.

Keval Kumar's definition of media education could therefore be understood as a teaching method that uses formal, non-formal, and informal approaches to impart a critical understanding of various media in order to lead to greater responsibility, greater participation in the production of media as well as to a greater interest in the sales and reception of media.

According to Kumar, a major aim of media education is making the media more accessible to society (he is thinking less of individuals here), so that they can be used more efficiently for public interest and welfare instead of being simply useful for the producer's profit.

It is regarded as equally important, however, to raise and convey critical awareness, as this enables people to intervene actively in the production process instead of simply passively consuming media.

A further aim is to make this awareness usable in a democratic sense. On the whole, media education in India is aiming at enlightening the masses against despotism as well as it is supporting the liberation from the status of a third-world country. Television and cinema ca be employed for `enlightening´ as it is also accessible for the illiterate. Kumar rightly assumes that uneducated consumers of the media also reflect upon them instead of simply being manipulated by them, as is generally argued.

There is a distinction between media education and educational technology. Media Education is learning about media and educational technology is learning by using media. The latter is integrated into the curriculum of the Indian teacher training institutes (schools of education) to enable teachers to make use of media in their lessons.

Learning about media does not take place within the institute, but is promoted by individual persons or by religious institutions as non-formal activities. These religious, social or political groups that employ media education, do so in order to point to its manipulatory or morally destructivecharacter or even for their own undemocratic (and also democratic) aims. Kumar does not object to this political side, even deems it necessary as long as it helps to improve public welfare, i.e. for social purposes or to remedy any grievances.

Several papers on the subject exist, but there is neither any head organisation nor did any screening of the works take place. Activities in this field partly remain unnoticed. In the south of India, there are some media educationists employed in several church schools, in the Department of Communication as well as in some non-government organisations

Professional groups working in this field include church officials, teachers, university teachers and social workers. Media Education in India is being obstructed by two things: On the one hand, the education system is only brought into line with the exams for which it prepares; on the other hand, there are the curricula which are centrally controlled by the government, so that media education depends on government policy. Kumar identifies another problem in media education itself.It should be taught as a cross-curricular theme, as a subject `media education´ would overvalue the media and separate it from its social context. This over-evaluation would then again lead to a theory of manipulation.

As a separate subject, media education should only be offered in Further Education. Media Education finds no mentioning in the Curricular and it cannot be perceived that it will in the near future. There are classes dealing with the use of media (educational technology) , but none dealing with media education as learning about media. Occasionally, there are seminars and conferences on the topic, but most of the time the media educationist works individually, which is not a surprise in a large country almost as large as a continent

Projects of this kind do take place occasionally amongst media educationalists, but on an entirely private basis. The frequent irrationality of the media, which in India are being controlled almost exclusively by political or commercial interests, nearly call for media education and this is why Keval Kumar ascribes great relevance to it. In India, there is a rise in fundamentalism and nationalism connected with an increasing industrialisation and with only a mall number of people profiting from. Media education is therefore being regarded as a device against despotism.

A Critical Framework for Media Education

To begin with, teachers need a critical framework. The field of media is broad and amorphous, extending not just from traditional media such as newspapers, magazines, television and film, but also now encompassing many areas of popular culture such as fashion, toys and dolls, the nature of celebrity, etc. Anyone attempting to make sense of this area needs a clear conceptual framework that will allow for discussion of a variety of complex and interrelated factors. For elementary teachers, this need is perhaps even greater than for their secondary colleagues because of the more fluid, integrated nature of the elementary class-things tend to just "come up" as the result of student interest or enthusiasm: someone comes in wearing a Bart Simpson Tshirt, or the whole class is swept away by World Series enthusiasm.

A teacher has to be ready to seize "the teachable moment," and a framework that will lead to rational, critical discourse about any text is a must. This is also necessitated by the elementary teacher's need to integrate more, as the same critical concepts have to be applied to a wide variety of different materials as they appear in the curriculum. A number of such frameworks have been developed in various parts of the world in the last few years, as media education has moved forward globally. Most of them express the same things in different ways: it appears that having a framework is what is important, not necessarily having a specific framework.

The central concept of the model is the idea that all communication, all discourse, is a construct of reality. Every description or representation of the world, fictional or otherwise, is an attempt to describe or define reality, and is in some way a construction-a selection and ordering of details to communicate aspects of the creator's view of reality. There are no neutral, value-free descriptions of reality-in print, in word, in visual form. An understanding of this concept is the starting point for a critical relationship to the media.

There are three broad areas within which we can raise questions that will help students to "deconstruct" the media: text, audience and production. A text is any media product we wish to examine, whether it is a television program, a book, a poster, a popular song, the latest fashion, etc. We can discuss with students what the type of text is-cartoon, rock video, fairy tale, police drama, etc.-and how it differs from other types of text. We can identify its denotative meaning and discuss such features as narrative structure, how meanings are communicated, values implicit in the text, and connections with other texts. Anyone who receives a media text, whether it is a book read alone or a film viewed in a theatre, is a member of an audience. It is important for children to be able to identify the audience(s) of a text. Texts are frequently designed to produce audiences, which are then sold to advertisers.

Modern communication theory teaches that audiences "negotiate" meaning. That is to say, each individual reader of a text will draw from its range of possible meanings a particular reading that reflects that individual's gender, race or cultural background, skill in reading, age, etc. Thus the "meaning" of a text is not something determined by critics, teachers or even authors, but is determined in a dynamic and changeable relationship between the reader and the text. The role of the teacher is to assist students in developing skills which will allow them to negotiate active readings-readings which recognize the range of possible meanings in a text, the values and biases implicit in those meanings, and which involve conscious choices rather than the unconscious acceptance of "preferred" readings. Children who can choose meaning are empowered.

Production refers to everything that goes into the making of a media text-the technology, the ownership and economics, the institutions involved, the legal issues, the use of common codes and practices, the roles in the production process. Students are often fascinated by the details and "tricks" of production. It is important that the teacher keep in focus the relationship between the various aspects of production, and the other two broad areas of text and audience. Whenever a media product is discussed, some aspects of construction, text, audience and production should be dealt with. Teachers will quickly find that a discussion moves quite naturally among these broad areas, since all are interrelated and affect each other. It is also important to recognize that an effective media program will involve students in both analysis and production of media products.

In fact, some teachers and support staff are using it as a general model for literacy and critical thinking. North York's elementary media literacy pilot project (on the right sidebar) offers an example of how this may be achieved.

Important Ways of the Media Studying

Unsure where to fit media education into your subject area? Looking at the media in relation to other topics may help.

1. Like history, the media interpret the past to show us what has gone into making us the way we are.
2. Like geography, the media define our place in the world for us.
3. Like civics, the media help us to understand the workings of our world and our individual places in it.
4. Like literature, the media are our major sources of stories and entertainment.
5. Like literature, the media require us to learn and use critical thinking skills.
6. Like business, the media are major industries that are inextricably involved in commerce.
7. Like language, the media help to define how we communicate with each other.
8. Like science and technology, the media always adopt the leading edge of modern technological innovation.

9. Like family studies, the media determine much of the cultural fabric of our lives.
10. Like environmental studies, the media are as large a part of our everyday environment as are trees, mountains, rivers, cities and oceans.
11. Like philosophy, the media interpret our world, and its values and ideas to us.
12. Like psychology, the media help us to understand (or misunderstand) ourselves and others.
13. Like science, the media explain to us how things work.
14. Like industrial arts, the media are carefully planned, designed and constructed products.
15. Like the arts, the media allow us to experience all the arts as no other age has ever been able to.
16. Like politics, the media continually bring us political and ideological messages.
17. Like rhetoric, the media use special codes, conventions and languages that we need to understand.
18. Like drama, the media present life as larger-than-life- and compel us to think of ourselves as an audience.
19. Like Everest, the media are just there.
20. And finally, just as we watch the media, the media go to great lengths to study us!

Future Threats of Media Education

The existence of media education seems to be constantly threatened. There are many reasons for this:

— Media education takes up curriculum time that some people would like to devote to other subjects.

— Media education uses equipment that is expensive to buy and maintain.

— Media education tends to focus on subject material that young people know more about than their teachers.

— Media education examines popular culture, and some people believe that popular culture is not worthy of study.

— Media education tends to reveal commercial and ideological agendas in popular culture that some people would prefer to keep hidden.

— One of the chief outcomes of media education is that students learn to be critical of their information sources, and some people would rather not see that happen.

It is difficult for teachers in many jurisdictions to combat these threats to their subject area. These teachers often work alone, or with only one other colleague on staff-and some of the threats even come from these colleagues.

However, one of the best defenses against criticism of any subject area is the ability to show that your assessment is strong, solid, rigorous and fair-and to show that as a teacher, you are happy to be held accountable for your assessment. Administrators and parents (not to mention the students) are always impressed by teachers and courses with strong assessment-which can forestall many of the day-to-day problems.

A high proportion of encounters between teachers and parents, and between teachers and students, are due to some kind of disagreement over assessment. If the assessment can be developed to the point of being relatively unquestionable, then a course will develop a reputation of making a lot of people happy-including parents and administrators.

Often, in an attempt to make strong assessments, school systems will impose external assessment and evaluation instruments such as tests. In such cases, teachers often have little or no chance to negotiate the assessment before it is imposed. These teachers are often not happy with the situation.

Media educators may get the chance to take the initiative into their own hands. They may be able to make themselves accountable for strong and reliable assessment by establishing it for themselves, and then embracing it voluntarily.

Bibliography

Don Hazen & Julie Winokur, eds. *We the Media: A Citizens' Guide to Fighting for Media Democracy*. New York: The New Press, 1997. Distributed by W.W. Norton.

Ericson, Richard, Patricia Baranek, and Janet Chan. 1989. *Negotiating control: A study of news sources*. Toronto: University of Toronto Press.

Gustein, Donald. *e.con: How the Internet Undermines Democracy*. Stoddart, 1999.

James Curran (ed.) *Media Organisations in Society*. London: Arnold, 2000.

______________ and Michael Gurevitch (eds). *Mass Media and Society*. 3rd edition. London: Arnold, 2001.

______________ et al. (eds), *Bending Reality: The State of the Media*. London: Pluto Press, 1986.

James Winter. *Democracy's Oxygen: How Corporations Control the News*. Montreal: Black Rose, 1997.

Janet Wasko and Vincent Mosco (eds). *Democratic Communications in the Information Age*. Toronto: Garamond Press (co-published with Ablex), 1992).

John Keane. *The Media and Democracy*. Polity Press, 1991.

Kaarle Nordenstreng & Michael Grifffin (eds.) *International Media Monitoring*. Hampton Press, 1999.

Kate Duncan (ed.) *Liberating Alternatives: The Founding Convention of the Cultural Environment Movement*. Hampton Press, 1999.

Marc Raboy and Peter A. Bruck. *Communication for and against Democracy*. Black Rose, 1989.

Oskamp, Stuart. (ed.). 1988. *Television as a social issue*. Newbury Park, CA: Sage Publications.

Peter Phillips, "Building Media Democracy," in Peter Phillips & Project Censored. *Censored 1999: The News that Didn't Make the News*. New York: Seven Stories, 1999, pp. 129-135.

Philip Lee, ed. *The Democratization of Communication*. University of Wales Press, 1995.

Robert A. Hackett and Yuezhi Zhao. *Sustaining Democracy? Journalism and the Politics of Objectivity*. Toronto: Garamond, 1998.

______________, *"News media and civic equality: Watch dogs, mad dogs or lap dogs?"* In Edward Broadbent (ed.), Democratic Equality: What Went Wrong? University of Toronto Press, 2001, pp. 197-212.

Robert W. Mcchesney. *Corporate Media and the Threat to Democracy*. New York: Seven Stories, 1997.

______________. Mcchesney. *Telecommunications, Mass Media, & Democracy: The Battle for the Control of U.S. Broadcasting, 1928-1935*. Oxford University Press, 1993.

Sara U. Douglas. *Labor's New Voice: Unions and the mass media*. Ablex, 1986.

Index